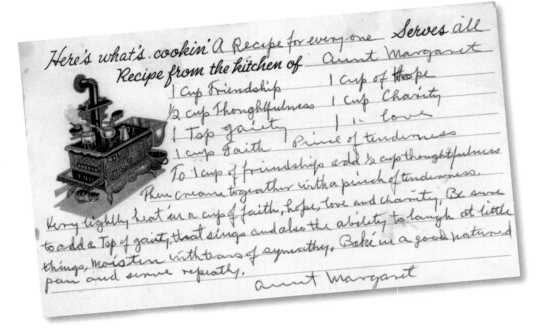

Here's what's cookin' A Recipe for everyone Serves all
Recipe from the kitchen of Aunt Margaret

1 Cup Friendship   1 Cup of hope
1/2 cup Thoughtfulness   1 cup Charity
1 Tsp gaiety   1 love
1 cup Faith   Pinch of tenderness

To 1 cup of friendship add 1/2 cup thoughtfulness.
Then cream together with a pinch of tenderness.
Very lightly beat in a cup of faith, hope, love and charity. Be sure
to add a Tsp of gaiety that sings and also the ability to laugh at little
things, moisten with tears of sympathy. Bake in a good natured
pan and serve repeatly.
                    Aunt Margaret

In memory of Nana, Auntie, and all of the hardworking home cooks
who came before us, and to the future of American home cooking

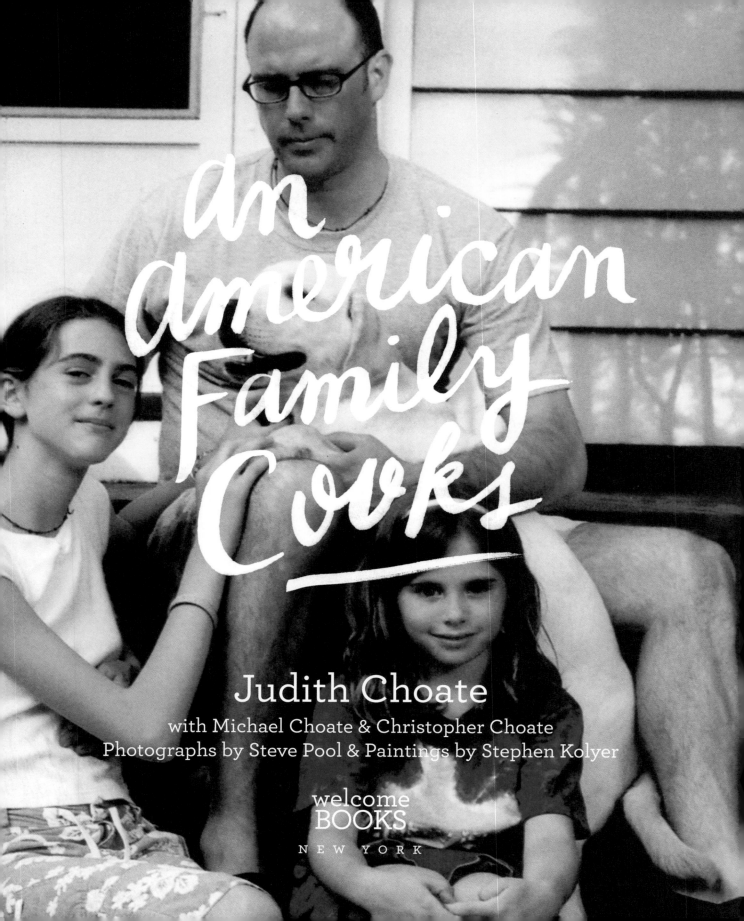

an American Family Cooks

Judith Choate

with Michael Choate & Christopher Choate
Photographs by Steve Pool & Paintings by Stephen Kolyer

welcome
BOOKS

NEW YORK

Contents

Foreword

Michael Choate & Christopher Choate

Michael (Mickey): I like to tease Mom about her cooking being "*la cuisine bonne femme,*" only because my own is so over the top. While my cooking style has, in many ways, vastly diverged from hers, I wouldn't have the passion for food that I do if it weren't for her sharing the joys of the kitchen and family table with me from an early age. Some of my fondest memories are of helping her prepare meat sauce for spaghetti on a Sunday afternoon—a dish I still make to-day, with my own slight changes, of course; or breading veal cutlets for scaloppine—a recipe that I've never been able to reproduce on my own—at least not in a way that reminds me of how much I loved it as a child.

Christmas was always a special time of year because, even though Mom had a full-time job, she'd still spend whatever free time she had making fruitcakes, Christmas cookies, her famous fudge, and our favorite: a gingerbread house. That festive season always culminated in our annual Christmas Eve party, where everyone would leave with a bag filled with homemade treats. Today, I find it hard to imagine how she found the time to do it all. (**Judie:** "I can't remember how I did either.")

I am still amazed that my mom is a self-taught cook. Where did she learn to cook so well? My grand-mother wasn't half the cook she is, although Nana had a way with certain dishes, particularly pies, both savory and sweet. (Writing this conjures up memories of Nana's lemon meringue pie, the tart lemon curd complement-ed by a perfect soft, sweet meringue.) I think my mom's love of food and her passion for cooking is as much about family and friends and the now quaint notion of the shared table as it is the actual dishes she prepares. I believe that it is something that we are in the process of losing in this country, but it has always been, and remains, a vital part of our family life.

My wife and I try, as much as two working parents can in this day and age, to sit down on a regular basis with our children for a family meal. When they were small, my kids ate their share of chicken nuggets at restau-rants, but a glance in our home freezer won't reveal any frozen dinners, processed chicken, or the myriad of (to me) bizarre quick-and-ready meals that fill the vast refrigerator aisles of our local supermarket. And to this day, my chicken "nuggets" are homemade.

Although like us, both of my parents worked, we always sat down for dinner together every night. My father, a dyed-in-the-wool Wasp, could not imagine a life in which a family did not gather for a meal that began with a soup or salad, included a main course consisting of a large hunk of meat with accompanying garnishes and sides, and ended with a homemade sweet. (I can still tick off the meats—standing rib roast, triple-thick rib lamb chops, goose, thin slices of calves' liver, crisp on the outside and meltingly soft in the center—things

Michael, Judith, and Christopher Choate (opposite). Michael and Christopher when they were kids (above).

I can't imagine any mom cooking after a day at work!) But more than the food at the table, there was conversation, connection, and shared experience. I knew what it meant to be part of a whole.

When I walk down the aisles of the supersized chain grocery stores that dot the landscape these days, I wistfully think back to the trips down Eighty-fourth Street with my father on our way to Kircher's Prime Meats on Columbus Avenue—which, by the way, is now a take-out sushi shop. Kircher's was one of those old-fashioned German butchers that one could find all over Manhattan when I was a child. Of course, there wasn't the multitude of cuts and styles of meat that we have today, but you knew that you could purchase the absolute best prime steaks, roasts, chops, and hamburger meat (I can still remember Joe the butcher cleaning the grinder to prepare the crimson beef for my dad's favorite, steak tartare), as well as the tastiest bologna and liverwurst for the sandwiches that were packed into our school lunch boxes. Am I getting old or were those really the days when ground chuck and pork actually had deep, rich flavors?

My dad worked on Broadway, so he would come home in the early afternoon between shows. He would do all of the shopping that my mom had outlined for the evening's meal. Unbelievably, he bought everything fresh, daily, from the butcher or produce market. Mom would arrive home from work and begin cooking immediately in order to have dinner ready by six so that Dad could get back to the theater before the eight o'clock performance. This was our most meaningful time together as a family and I will cherish those memories all my life. I hope this book will convey some of our experiences in a way that will encourage other American families to make the time to share the warmth of the table. Wonderful memories are made there.

Christopher (Chris):

To me, food and family are intrinsically linked. Cooking is nothing more than tradition passed on from one generation to another and, in our family, my mom has just been very good at the passing. For all of us, feeding family and friends is about caring, providing, and nurturing. It is interesting that this emanates from the kitchen, the warmest room in the house, the place where parties begin and, even now, often end.

So many of my early memories are centered on food. I remember eating the same meal on the same night of every week (Monday was chicken, Tuesday was Swedish meatballs, and so forth). This probably wasn't the case (in fact, Mom says it wasn't) but that is how I remember our meals. This feeling of continuity gave me a sense of order and safety—it made me feel cared for. My particular favorite—and my brother Mickey's too—was a very simple roast chicken with steamed rice and fresh peas. I would combine mine with Mom's homemade applesauce to make my own dish. That was, perhaps, my first attempt at cooking.

As a child, I always looked forward to the weekend, when Mom would put a large pot of red sauce with meat to cook on the back burner. She would start it early in the morning and it would simmer all day long. I remember it being bright red, almost alive. Throughout the day, I would snack on a hunk of crusty bread dipped into a cupful of this incredible sauce. I continue this tradition with my daughter, Canada, who is now doing the dipping. And isn't it interesting that both Mickey and I mention Mom's spaghetti sauce as an indelible memory?

Is it the warmth of the sauce cooking, the aroma of the spices, the heartiness of the flavor? What is the indefinable thing that makes it so much a part of our culinary heritage? Particularly since we don't have a drop of Italian blood running through our veins!

Another vivid food memory is the first time that I tried a raw onion. I took one bite and thought it was the strongest, spiciest, most enveloping flavor that had ever assaulted my palate. I ran to the bathroom and washed my mouth out with ice-cold water. I remember sliding my wet fingers over my tongue in an effort to rub the potent onion taste off just like a cartoon character might. Is it this early recollection that has now translated to my adult love of spicy foods?

Mickey and I view Mom's cooking in completely different ways. I think that Mom is a very interesting cook. She seems so in tune with the meals she prepares. She has an almost unbelievable feel in the kitchen. To watch her make bread without using a measuring cup or spoon is truly something special. And it always comes out of the oven in perfect loaves. (**Judie:** "Well, almost always.") It is difficult to ask her cooking questions because it's all so second nature to her. "Mom, how much of this do I use?" "Just enough to get the flavor you want." "Mom, how long does it take?" "Until it is done." She just knows. (**Judie:** "I'm also good at guessing.")

My brother is an unparalleled technical home chef. He is meticulous to a fault. Who do you know who follows classic French technique to *tournée* vegetables for the home table using a fine paring knife and an impeccable turn of the hand? He recreates some of the world's classic dishes with an incredible eye for detail and precision. He is now in charge of our Christmas dinner—always his menu, his way—more classic French than traditional American.

I think that I fall somewhere in between Mom's intuitive method and Mickey's classic style. My house was a popular sleepover spot with my daughter's friends when she was small mostly because I cook great kid food—nachos, chicken fingers, waffles, pancakes, french toast, egg in the middle. The girls all seemed to be as impressed with my cooking as my friends were with Mom's.

I am also considered the "personal chef" to many of my friends. I love to gather people together for multicourse dinner parties complete with menus and wine pairings. I believe that these moments are part of a greater sense of community—of something far more encompassing than just the one table. The conversation, the laughter, the sense of sharing—it all goes out into the ether to make the world a better place.

When I entertain, I often never sit down, even though a place has been set for me, because after so many years in the restaurant business I tend to eat as I cook. (And my cooking is inevitably accompanied by a wound—a burn or a cut—and something usually gets broken—typically an expensive wineglass.) Over the years, like Mom, I've learned to cut corners when I think I can. I used to make all of my pasta from scratch, for instance, but now I frequently buy it freshly made from a local Italian market. I've been told that my meals are much better than those served in many of San Francisco's finest restaurants. Truth to tell, you can't trust hungry people all of the time; however, I gratefully accept the praise, knowing that my passion is part of my heritage and that I am joyfully now passing it on to the next generation.

Introduction

Judith Choate

I didn't plan to write about food; nor, in fact, did I plan to be a cook. It is something that, like Topsy herself, just grew. I have always loved to eat and for as long as I can remember I have loved to cook. Beyond these two comforting pastimes, I also loved to talk about food. I wanted to know the "hows" and "whys," the history and folklore, the sources and the creators. It is the convergence of these passions that has allowed me the pleasure of a wonderfully nourishing career.

In my early childhood, I was on intimate emotional terms with most of the food that we ate. I helped turn the soil and plant the seeds. I watered and watched the plants appear. I knew which bugs were friendly and which were to be squished. I could tell the month by the vegetables the garden produced or by what was taken from the root cellar.

I fed the chickens. I gathered the eggs. I stared, in awe, as Mrs. Lowe, our beloved neighbor, grabbed a fat hen, twisted its neck and then swiftly dispatched its body from its head using her razor-sharp axe against a well-seasoned tree stump. I had a name for each hen and rooster but I knew that they were part and parcel of my food chain.

I climbed the fence into the field behind our house. I sat in the warm earth and ate a melon while it was still on the vine. The juices dried and stuck to my skin, inviting bees and flies to rest and dine on my chubby arms as I helped the farmer, Mr. Yamaguchi, and his sons load the wagon with lusty, nectarous melons for their farm stand at the edge of the highway.

The milk and cream dropped off onto our back porch came from the Yoder family's cows. I knew their names and milking times. Piglets were led around on leashes, dressed in baby bonnets and taught tricks. Farm animals were both friends and feasts.

The early-morning air, breaking sunrise, and a rushing trout stream meant fishing with Uncle Bruce. Speckled trout for breakfast, dipped in cornmeal and fried in bacon grease in a cast-iron skillet over an open fire, was our reward. The turning leaves signaled hunting season and my Aunt Frances's table filled with pheasant, quail, duck, and venison. We didn't have much money but we ate so well!

Even our celebrations, holidays, and family milestones were centered on food. My Christmas stocking held delicacies (my favorites: avocados and tangerines) rather than toys. Celebrations were always eating events—we talked about the table, picnic basket, or covered dish for weeks before the actual date. I anxiously looked forward to the moment, not for the gifts or the significance of the day, but for the foods that I knew we would have.

My mother, the chief cook, always prepared enough to feed a hoard and we always managed to collect one to eat it. In our small town, my mother's cooking and reputation for serving an attractive meal were so well known that invitations to our family table were always eagerly sought. Although she was a widow and held a full-time job, she always seemed delighted to be in the kitchen and her enthusiasm was transmitted to us. My brother, being much older than I, was her most helpful assistant, but I still had to do my share. And when he left for college, I, at five years old, took over his job.

When I was eight, we moved away from the small town and closeness of relatives, friends, and the natural world. Joining my brother, who had moved west, we traveled to San Francisco with all of our culinary traditions and heirloom dishes and left most of everything else behind. How quickly I forgot country life. It was such fun to go to the supermarket and select dinner from a myriad of cellophane-wrapped packets. The meat was trimmed, cut, sliced, and packaged. The vegetables were washed and tied in bunches or placed in cartons or bags. Cans, bottles, and bags replaced the garden, fields, henhouse, dairy, and farmyard.

The most astounding result of our move was the availability of so many new and different ingredients, cuisines, and culinary traditions. San Francisco had a well-known Chinatown, and the city's Italian population and fishing industry also were substantial. Russian River was aptly named. Our neighbors were Lebanese, German, Swedish, and Mexican. So many nationalities, each with special foods and celebrations to share.

When I eventually left home, it was for an even larger city with an even more diverse population. Just as we had done when I was small, I traveled light but carried my family's love of good food with me, to New York City. At seventeen, the ability to share the bounty of the table with newfound friends eased my move into the adult world. I had the beginnings of a kitchen before I had an apartment of my own. Most of my new friends couldn't cook and were amazed that I could. Accustomed to party fare of a jug of California wine and some Ritz crackers, they were astounded by my made-from-scratch entertaining style, which made me an in-demand hostess, much as my mom had once been.

When the peace and love generation of the 1960s beckoned a return to the simpler life, I, along with thousands of others, decided that vegetarianism was the only way to eat. I no longer ate most of the foods of my childhood and I could come up with a solid justification for my every culinary taboo. I forgot about the comfortable food chain of country life. None of my choices dealt with political issues, although there was a blossoming of interest in the methods being used to grow ever larger, more cost-efficient plants and animals. But, as often happens, my culinary passions overtook my desire for a perfect world.

In my early twenties, I married, and a whole new gastronomic world opened up to me. My husband brought a touch of the Victorian table to my kitchen. He had been raised in a staffed household where traditional English-style meals were served three times a day and he thought that this was the only way to dine (for he didn't just "eat.") I found myself making elaborate dishes for breakfast and multicourse meals every evening. It was as though I were getting a course with Mrs. Beeton herself.

With a growing family to feed, I also began to consider myself a serious cook. All the really good "bad" stuff played a big role in my recipe repertoire. Farm-fresh butter, cream, eggs, prime meats, free-range fresh poultry, hearty game, and rich desserts all found a position of honor at our table. I made meat loaves and my fair share of pedestrian meals but, for my children, great food and fine wines were subjects to be learned along with readin', writin', and 'rithmetic.

In my early thirties, I was widowed. Wanting to always be available to my sons, I opened a small bakery called MOM at the end of our city block. My partner in the venture, Stephen Pool (who eventually became my husband), brought his own African-American culinary heritage to both our business and our table. His beloved aunt, Anna Canada, became a loving "Aunty" to my boys and taught me as many of the Southern-folk ways as she could.

At MOM, we made by hand the same chicken and meat potpies that I had grown up on: simple home cooking in a to-go setting. It didn't take me long to find out that being in the food business meant just the

opposite of what I had planned: long, long hours on your feet and little free time to tend your children. The boys helped when they could and knew that no matter the time of day, they would always be well fed. Our success with the pies (which went on to include fruit pies and other desserts—Chris got quite proficient at making our much-requested marble cheesecake) led to the first all-American take-out food store in New York City. We sold our own homemade and canned foods, Amish products, farm-stand produce, and anything else that signified American home cooking. From this evolved catering and consulting. I was able to spend my days and nights doing what I loved most—feeding and talking to people. And the boys grew up just fine!

For many of the years that I found myself preparing meals, I was unaware that my boys, Mickey and Chris, were absorbing much of what was going on in the kitchen. Burgers and dogs, peanut butter and jelly, grilled cheese and Campbell's tomato soup, and those most beloved (and only allowed when Mom was not at home and the sitter had to prepare their meals) frozen TV dinners (Salisbury steak for Mickey and turkey for Chris) could always be found on the menus of their early years. "Mom, do we have to sit at the table until everyone else is finished?" echoed throughout their teens. Yet, when the signs of adulthood appeared and serious dating began, ordering fancy dishes and vintage champagnes in expensive restaurants slipped right off the tongue and into the hearts of impressed young ladies. My pocketbook showed that not much had escaped their notice!

It has been an astonishing experience to find the shoe on the other foot as I observe my two grown-up sons in the kitchen. I have shared with them as much as I could of our American culinary heritage, as well as tried to introduce them to as many types of foods as their palates would accept. Mickey, with his royalist leanings, spends his days with books, as a literary agent. He is a culinary Francophile, a superb cook, and an in-demand recipe tester. He favors all rich foods, mushrooms, anything French, fruit desserts,

Burgundies and Bordeaux, and four-star restaurants. He thinks margarine is an old-fashioned girl's name and granola a Yiddish term for grandmother. When not sending e-mails to his brother dealing with *premier crus* and the latest wine listings or taking inventory of his wine cellar, he can be found at one of the extortionate fancy-food stores or kitchenware galleries scattered throughout New York City or touring the aisles of the large discount grocery stores looking for bargains in prime products.

Chris, ever the surprise, has made a career of wine and food. He began as a runner in a hot New York City restaurant/bar in his teens, went on to manage a three-star Italian restaurant in San Francisco, and was then lured into the wine business. He has an extraordinary palate and tries anything that he finds on his—or anyone else's—plate. As a child, he was particularly taken with any food that could be eaten out of hand between innings, quarters, or at halftime with an ice-cold Coke or, later, a beer. Fine wine and food are now his life. This is from a guy who dunked his peanut-butter-and-jelly sandwich in orange juice.

Our family is now fairly representative of other splintered and extended American families. On those occasions when we can all sit down to dinner together, our immediate clan numbers nine. Mickey and his wife, Laurel, and their children, Alexander and Clara Grace, live in a New York City suburb. Mickey has his office at home and Laurel works in finance in the city. Now seventeen, Alexander is getting more and more adventuresome at the table, even popping into Manhattan for lunch at trend-setting restaurants like Momofuku, while fourteen-year-old Clara is deep into vegetarianism. (**Alexander:** "Pops [Mickey] was the one that really got me to enjoy food. I may have been picky and stubborn at first but over time, due to both his love of cooking and his skill, I have come to enjoy a variety of dishes, particularly those that are meat-based with Pops's sauce on the side.") They both certainly know good food from bad and appreciate their dad's cooking and mom's baking. Mickey and Laurel give wonderful, fun-filled parties for the children; their Halloween celebration (complete with Mickey dressed in some scary outfit and hidden in the basement in a make-believe coffin) is a much-anticipated annual event that includes traditional snacks for the kids and a full buffet for the adults. Their immediate family is extended with "Uncle Kol," Mickey's oldest friend and Clara's godfather, who is not only a skilled chef but also an extraordinary artist whose paintings brighten our lives, our blog, and this book.

Chris, who lives in San Francisco, divorced some years ago and has joint custody of his eighteen-year-old daughter, Canada, who spends every other week and every other holiday with him. He has recently remarried and introduced Heather, a very special woman who seems as though she has always been part of our brood, into our mix. (**Heather:** "It is a joy for me to watch Chris in the kitchen as I take in his passion and gift for putting together culinary flavors, colors, and textures. One of the first things he cooked for me was a roast chicken with carrots and he has wowed me with home-cooked meals ever since.")

Canada, now beginning her first year at Columbia University, loves nothing better than to be in New York City with us, visiting galleries, museums, and every fashion haunt. Tied to San Francisco, Chris and Heather—and Canada when she is at home with them—spend as many weekends as possible exploring the beautiful landscape that surrounds that city. Hiking, camping, and beach walks are very much a part of their urban lives—and, of course, testing every new restaurant that opens along the way. And just as we finished this book, Chris and Heather told us that another Choate is on the way. What joy!

Steve and I divide our time between an apartment in New York City and a farmhouse in central New York State, where we can spend time with friends and farmers and cook about as locally as the seasons

Steve Pool with Christopher and Michael.

allow, and where Steve has room to work on his photography. As much as we love being with our children and grandchildren, we also have a number of friends that we consider to be part of our extended family. First and foremost is my Irish-speakin' almost-daughter, Anne McDonagh (*Aine Nic Dhonnchadha* in Irish) who calls us her American parents. (**Annie:** "Thirty years ago I stood in front of an Upper West Side apartment building, suitcase in hand, right off the boat, as they say. I met Judie and Steve as I walked in the front door. They immediately welcomed me into their family, where I happily remain to this day. Judie is the mom I always wished I had, as well as the best girlfriend, matron of honor, party organizer, and dispenser of invaluable advice that anyone could ever ask for. Leaving Ireland at a young age was traumatic, but I feel blessed every day that Judie and Steve came into my life and eased the transition. How gray things would be without their glorious friendship, love, and of course food.") Annie lives in Virginia with her not-so-Irish-speakin' husband, Henry, but we see her as often as time and distance allow; it is never enough. We spend as much time as we can in Upstate New York, cooking, grilling (at our very own "Galaxy Restaurant" on the top of a glorious hill that takes in the Adirondacks and the Catskills), and toasting with Lynn and Doug with whom we also vacation every fall on Cape Cod and sometimes elsewhere, too; Joel, affectionately known as the "Art Director," dines with us at least once a week; Mary and Tim live around the corner and have shared moments with us since they first walked into MOM more than thirty years ago; Greg and Ellen pop in from St. Paul to their pied-à-terre in Manhattan as frequently as they can for coffee every morning and dinner as often as possible; Aris (a great dinner companion along with his partner, John) can always be counted on to create beautiful flower and basket arrangements for every holiday and celebration; there are just so many friends, young and old, who enrich our lives. Mickey tends to call them our "cronies" and Chris just shakes his head at the number and variety of people who continue to gather at our table.

We are known as Grammy and Ackies to Alexander and Clara Grace, and MooMoo and PopPop to Canada. We are now the standard-bearers for our culinary heritage. One of our great joys is the time we spend in the kitchen with our grandchildren, who all love to help, particularly in the summer when canning and processing garden-fresh foods are the focus. They all love a party but no one more so than Clara Grace, who I am counting on to be the hostess with the mostest in the next generation of Choate cooks. (**Clara:** "I would have to say the best of our family memories occur in the kitchen and around the table. Whenever we all get together it always consists of having a large and often extravagant meal that almost every family member participates in creating some aspect of. I know this sounds cheesy, but I think our family really bonds a lot when we're cooking. Even though I'm now a vegetarian, there is always something delicious for me to eat. And of course there is also dessert, which is my favorite!")

We all gather together every other Christmas and, whenever possible, vacation together at some point during the year. The joys of the table are reviewed as we filch tidbits from one another's plates.

Laurel is a terrific baker. Alexander is becoming the image of his dad at the table and disdains Clara's move into the vegetarian life. They love both their mom's homemade oatmeal scones (page 224) and sitting at the table of a three- or four-star restaurant with their dad as he orders his favorite plates. Mickey has spoiled his family, cooking each their preferred dishes for almost every meal—a practice that would drive me mad! (**Laurel:** "One thing I found interesting reading through this book as Grammy, Mickey, and Chris were working on it is that I never realized how much a person puts into a recipe and makes it their own. Once I started sharing recipes with people it became obvious that I don't just read the recipe and do everything it says. There are always little adjustments that I make to improve it for my taste. I just never really realized that!")

Canada, on the other hand, has spent so much time with her dad making the San Francisco restaurant rounds that for years she would eat almost anything. Her favorite food was—and I think still is—caviar, and she could discern the differences among all of the various styles. She too has changed her eating habits, and now considers herself a pescatarian. Canada has become an extraordinarily gifted and artistic baker, creating spectacular cakes for all occasions. She remains a great dining companion and a terrific help in the kitchen. (**Canada:** "If there is one specific thing that I really love about being in a family of cooks, it's that I have learned how to find pleasure in the necessary. Although we all have to eat, I know that it doesn't have to be a chore; eating can be like art or music, and cooking what you eat gives you control over your experience.")

In their own lives, the men plan and execute four-star meals. Yet, from time to time, I will receive a last-minute call asking for advice. The constancy of the calls seemed to signal that the time had come for us, together, to create a journal of the foods that we so love to cook.

The new American home cooking that we practice in our family has evolved in a manner much as it does for a traditional French culinary apprentice. The main difference is, of course, that we did not begin in a restaurant setting but in a home kitchen. The fundamentals of conventional home cooking—stocks, stews, soups, pastries and cakes, canning and preserving—were passed on to me and I have passed them

Clara, Canada, and Alexander Choate in 2003 (left) and 2012.

on to my sons, who, in turn, are passing them along to their children. Because cooking has interested us, we have eagerly learned from every cook with whom we have come in contact. In the process, we have been able to grasp the classical French techniques upon which much of Western cuisine is based, as well as the procedures and techniques necessary to produce all varieties of "ethnic" meals. And, I think, because we all enjoy cooking so much, we are able to do so with ease.

As a cookbook writer it has been fairly effortless for me to broaden my understanding of "foreign" cuisines. Over the years I've come to appreciate how current American cooking incorporates the best of so many of them. At home, we now stir-fry, wrap an enchilada, bake a pizza, or use phyllo dough as easily and frequently as we grill a steak or bake a pie. Health concerns have inched their way into classic recipes as well as hybrid ones, so that we create many of our favorites with an eye to saving calories, fat, and cholesterol, as well as time. The kitchen has become the true melting pot of our nation.

Since I began cooking almost seventy years ago, I have seen so many changes in the American kitchen and marketplace. I have an easy remembrance of the good old days when the refrigerator truly was the ice box, when bottled milk was left, undisturbed, on the doorstep (even in New York City), when basement shelves were lined with home-canned goods and most moms were housewives and prepared dinner at midday, supper in the evening, and the whole family gathered for a formal, midafternoon Sunday meal after church. Professionally, I have had the excitement of meeting the often fractious but fashionable demands of catering meals for multitudes and the joy of working, either as a cook or a writer, alongside some of America's most accomplished chefs. The adventuresome palates of my children and our love of sharing great meals has been the icing on the cake.

All during my years of cooking, I have found that, for me, it is most rewarding when there is a crowd to feed. I love holidays and celebrations and like nothing better than turning an ordinary weekday meal into an event by welcoming new people to our table. My friendships continue to be glued together by a love of eating and the warmth of the family table. Throughout this book, recipes will often reflect the enthusiastic sharing of tastes and adventures that so many wonderful friends have experienced with us.

As you turn these pages, you will find that each one of us cooks in a very defined way. Mickey is disciplined and rigorously follows French tradition. As he has gotten older, he experiments and trusts his own instincts more, but no matter how relaxed, that veal chop will be sauced with the richest reduction you can imagine. Chris, on the other hand (and, perhaps because he lives in California, where pristine products are always available), is more straightforward in his approach, with the grill and simply cooked meats and vegetables playing a great role in his meals. And his Italian restaurant influence is strongly sensed in many of his dishes. As I get older, I value nature's bounty more than ever. I try to buy organically grown products and purchase my raw ingredients from local farmers as much as possible. I cook simply, with an eye to good health. But I still like to finish the meal with a luscious dessert.

While I continue to cook with "a little of this" and "a little of that," my sons keep asking me "How much?" and "What for?" I have written many, many cookbooks that answer some of these questions, but nowhere have I been able to share the joy of cooking that we feel when working together in the kitchen. It seemed to me that it was time to combine our love of cooking and eating with my ability to write it all down. Our irreverence and sense of adventure when it comes to food add to the process a great deal of pleasure and fun, which are always to be found at our table and, we hope, at yours.

Judith with grandchildren Alexander, Canada, and Clara.

Some Thoughts About How We Cook

When I thought about organizing this book, I focused on the traditional cookbook divisions—appetizers, soups, salads, etc. Early on, I had hundreds of recipes and struggled over which to eliminate; rather like my children, I loved many of them equally but knew that some would eventually have to find a life outside of mine. In a fit of stewing, I finally realized that this is not the way I cook. We are a family that cooks by meals—some fancy, some not so fancy, and some just plain everyday that result in nothing more than getting a nourishing meal on the table. But often those everyday meals will have something absolutely yummy that will find its way into a fancy, we-gotta-impress dinner. So, I decided, that is how I would put this book together. You'll find all kinds of meals and single dishes on the following pages. Of course you can, just as we do, mix and match recipes—hijack one from Christmas and put it in the middle of summer if that's what you feel like eating. We won't mind one bit.

SHOPPING, INGREDIENTS, SUPPLIES, AND TECHNIQUES

When I was young everyone thought I would be the one with sand in my shoes and travel the world, but I've fooled the seers and have lived in the same New York City apartment for over fifty years. As you would imagine, I know my neighborhood very well and, over time, have often been saddened by many of its changes. But one thing has remained steadfast: my favorite market, Zingone Brothers, has been on Columbus Avenue longer than I've been alive.

As markets go, Zingone's is not very modern—the floor is worn wood, the fridges are often being worked on, the shelves are stocked with only the items that customers use daily, but in this old-fashioned Italian-family-owned grocery, I've been continuously well fed for what seems like forever—from my early svelte modeling days through beginning-to-gray middle-age to the expanding midsection of my grandmother years. Zingone Brothers—now owned by the widowed Mrs. Zingone, her children Dominic and Mary, Uncle Nick, his sons Richie and Nicky, and Uncle Angelo—has been my culinary bedrock. The younger generation has gone from calling me "mom" from my days owning a bakery of the same name to the more familiar "hey, Jude" or even "J." I've watched them grow up and have families of their own right along with my boys. Uncle Nick and Uncle Angelo always show courtly respect but love to banter with me. Uncle Nick knows I'm a sucker for a bargain and will whisper conspiratorially, "What are we cooking today?" and then offer whatever veg or fruit might be showing

a little wear, which he knows I'll be willing to turn into something tasty. Uncle Angelo will often show me how his wife cooks whatever seasonal vegetable is on the stand in front of the store. He can wax poetic about his crates of baby artichokes or cranberry beans and I am immediately wrapped in his deep love of the land and his visceral connection to the country of his birth.

Although it is no longer possible to shop the way I once did when the butcher, the fishmonger, Zingone's, and the bakery were all within two blocks of my apartment, I still do a pretty good job of shopping throughout the week for our meals. I also keep a fairly well-stocked freezer—but it is essentially only used for emergencies. We have a neighborhood farmers market on Sundays and, if I choose, a quick subway ride takes me to the much-acclaimed Union Square Greenmarket on Wednesdays, Fridays, and Saturdays, where I can shop the stands of fresh and local fish, meat, game, flowers, mushrooms, potatoes, veggies, and salad greens—both known and exotic. Just a short walk from my front door I find Whole Foods, Zabar's, and Fairway, all well-known emporiums of great food and kitchen supplies. Wine stores abound with bargains to be had that nightly allow a glass to toast our good fortune. Shopping for food and supplies is as much pleasure to me as cooking. Even in the bigger, more-impersonal meccas, if you frequent often enough you get to know the employees and they will then turn your shopping experience into a visit with old friends.

If you are like me, it is extremely difficult to put together and maintain a food budget. When shopping I am often lured by the products at hand or a moment's inspiration. "I can't pass up those beautiful tomatoes." "The wild salmon is in and it's so much better than the farmed." "I know we don't need another dessert but I'm in the mood to bake today." All that said, it does help to think ahead and stick fairly close to your plans.

Over the years I've come up with some rules that put ease into ingredient shopping and home cooking:

1. Cook ahead. For working cooks, meals made in advance are simply the most economical and efficient way to feed the family and minimize kitchen time. They require purchasing in bulk and creating a number of meals out of one main ingredient. This is an especially great tactic when the main ingredient is purchased on sale or discounted at a big-box store. A whole pork loin is always in my plans for make-ahead meals (page 90).

2. Buy what's local and in season. Almost all produce is less expensive when purchased in season, particularly at local markets or farm stands. As well, many chain supermarkets now feature homegrown products as a way to support community farmers, cheese makers, bakers, and so forth. Many meat products are also less expensive during a particular time of year—i.e., lamb in the spring or turkey during the fall and winter holidays.

3. Think outside the normal dinner box. You don't have to have the traditional protein, starch, and veggie on every plate every night. A great frittata, a mixed-up salad, unusual grains tossed with legumes or vegetables—all make great complete meals. And, what about breakfast for dinner? Like Multigrain Waffles with Sautéed Mushrooms (page 190) instead of sweet waffles with maple syrup. (Although when I was a child, sweet waffles were my special dinner treat and there's no reason why they can't still be!)

4. Use less animal protein, even if you have a family of meat eaters. To begin, at least serve smaller portions. Introduce ethnic dishes that use less meat with wonderfully tasty results. I'm not a great lover of tofu, but since Steve and our granddaughters are, I have learned to like it well enough to use it frequently in place of traditional proteins. There is a multitude of ways to heighten flavor and satisfy the palate without piling on the meat.

5. Never throw food away! As soon as your meal is over, prepare any leftovers for use in another meal—as in Impromptu Soups (page 164)—even if it is just a few vegetables that can be tossed into tomorrow's salad or a bit of meat that can be chopped up to make a sandwich. It takes just a moment to do—the same amount of time it takes to scrape the plate into the garbage.

6. A well-stocked pantry is key to saving time and money without sacrificing quality. It eliminates last-minute, impulse shopping as well as gives you the ingredients to make the most with what you have on hand. (**Mickey:** "I would say that stocks, at least chicken, should be a pantry staple. The left-over carcass from a roast chicken can be easily turned into a quick, flavorful stock. Accumulate bones and scraps in your freezer until you have enough to make a big batch.") Always having stock available lends itself to quickly putting together countless go-to recipes: soups, risotto, sauces, and so forth.

7. Prepare foods you enjoy, but don't hesitate to try new things. Sneaking interesting and cost-effective ingredients into your normal repertoire is a great way to expand your creativity as a cook and save money at the same time.

Frequently, particularly when I am teaching novice cooks, I get asked about organic versus nonorganic products. I try not to proselytize (even though I love the meats from Gaia's Breath Farm, see Sources), and instead hand them my cheat sheet, which covers the definition of conventional and organic as well as the most commonly used definitions for commercially packed, USDA-sanctioned meat. So here it is.

The simplest description of the difference between organically and conventionally grown produce is that organic produce is grown using only natural fertilizers and natural methods of pest and weed control, such as hand weeding and crop rotation, while conventionally grown is brought to maturity with the use of chemical fertilizers with herbicides and insecticides, which control weeds and insect infestations. Neither method addresses the cost, both economically and environmentally, of bringing the product to market.

For meat, the following definitions are currently in use:

Organic (USDA): Meat from animals raised from birth without the use of growth hormones or antibiotics (vitamin and mineral supplements allowed) and fed 100 percent organic grass or grain. The animals should have open access to pasture and the meat may not be irradiated.

Natural: Minimal processing of and no artificial additives administered to the meat. Many producers use their own definition, which, in some cases, indicates that from birth onward, neither antibiotics nor growth hormones were used on the animals or in their feed. If prepackaged, the label will so designate.

Raised Without Antibiotics: Simply that—the animals have not received any antibiotics. This does not indicate any of the other conditions of production.

No Hormones Administered: Simply that—the animals have not received any growth hormones, either through injection or in the feed. This does not indicate any of the other conditions of production.

100 Percent Grass Fed and Pastured: This simply indicates that the animals fed solely on pasture and grass. This does not indicate any of the other conditions of production, including the circumstances of their feeding.

Drinks and Nibbles

Chris Talks About Wine

To me, there is nothing more overwhelming than being asked to choose the appropri-ate bottle of wine. I rely on Chris to share his wine knowledge, often calling from the wine shop pleading for help with the selection. I never ask Mickey, although he has a terrific palate, as his wine choices are usually a bit out of my price range. No $6.99 bottle for his table!

Chris: If you saw my family enjoying an elaborate home-cooked meal or dining in a restaurant, you would think that I came out of the womb with a corkscrew in hand, but that is far from the truth. I got into wine almost by accident. At my first restaurant job, when I was nineteen, the "extensive" wine list had screw-top red and screw-top white. I was hired to work the door; a gangly six feet one, I didn't make a very intimidating figure. I quickly migrated to the bar, where I prepared blue vodka drinks with twelve-inch plastic whales hanging off the sides. After doing almost every job in the joint I finally ran the place for a while, before moving to California.

Once in San Francisco I was hired as a waiter for a respected restaurant company that had multiple outlets in the city. After a few months, I had the opportunity to go to another property and become the bar manager, which I jumped at. I knew how to run a bar based on my NYC experience, but I still knew nothing about wine.

Although I was in charge of the bar at the new spot, the general manager handled the wine buying. A couple of months after I started, he abruptly left the restaurant and the purchasing was suddenly dumped into my lap. I was terrified! I'll never forget my early wine appointments. I sat stone faced, not saying a word, because if I didn't speak I couldn't be wrong or stupid. After three months of being talked at and told what I was tasting, a few things finally started to sink in.

I spent the next few months paying much more attention, remembering what I was tasting and trying to identify the flavors in the wines for myself rather than being told. I think the one thing that engaged me early on is that wine is a living, ever-changing thing. It is alive. The same grape can taste so different because of where it was grown or how the wine was made.

Many in the wine industry and most wine enthusiasts will tell you that they have had one moment when the light went on. This was mine: Some friends from New York came to visit at the end of my first six months as a "wine buyer." The Fog City Diner was all the rage then, and wanting to impress my visitors, I took them there for dinner. I excitedly grabbed the wine list, as the wine bug had already started to take hold. On the list was a 1990 Kistler chardonnay. One of the single vineyards. I want to say Hudson, but I'm not entirely sure. At this early stage in my wine career I had heard of Kistler, but I'd never got close to a bottle. I think it was $60 on the list, which was a small fortune to me at the time—but I had to try it. After the server poured me a taste, I had an epiphany. I understood fruit, oak, acid, balance, complexity, finish, quality—all in a single smell and taste.

From that point on I was obsessed. I'm not a great reader, but I even started reading about wine. I smelled everything before I ate it to train my nose and to become really familiar with defining aromas. After a couple of years, I got the opportunity to run a bigger wine and bar program. This opportunity allowed me to become deeply immersed in the California wine scene, where I have happily spent the last twenty years.

I had one other important experience that enormously expanded my understanding and appreciation of wine. This simple exercise allowed me to understand wine for what it is—a delicious beverage. Wilfred Wong, who is one of the head buyers for Beverages & More in California, used to run the wine department in the Ashbury Market in San Francisco's Haight Ashbury district. He had the coolest wine set in town. One day I was checking out the store and Wilfred and I got talking. He invited me up to his tiny office to taste two wines. After I tried them, he asked which one I preferred. I pointed to one of the glasses and he said, "Now you're a connoisseur." I understood at that moment that wine was something to be enjoyed, and if you could say you liked one more than another, then you were already on your way to becoming a wine enthusiast. I owe Wilfred a debt of gratitude and I still thank him every time I see him. He allowed me to relax and enjoy wine and he showed me that it wasn't as complicated as I had previously thought.

Wine is now a profound part of my life. My job, my passion, my hobby—you name it. I have very vivid wine memories where I can still taste the wine, even feel it on my palate. The 1990 Kistler is one, as is my first Chateau D'Yquem at Masa's, which Mickey and I were lucky enough to try both the 1976 and 1977 side by side with foie gras. Another was the moment Burgundy made sense to me at Boulevard with my dear friend Dan Dargan, who got the Burgundy bug years before I did; 1995 Dujac, Nuits-Saint-Georges did it to me.

Now that I sell wine for a living my palate is very different from what it was when I bought wine. I used to get very excited about those big, buttery California chardonnays that I cut my teeth on; now I hardly ever drink them. Today I think more about whether I can sell it or who would buy it. I used to completely break the wine down, meticulously analyze its quality and take lengthy notes. I still have a fair palate, but it used to be much sharper. I enjoy mostly European wines, especially the wines of Italy. I drink Burgundy and Champagne whenever I can. I love a chilled rosé. I would say I prefer high-acid whites with little to no oak and I prefer lighter reds, again with little or very well integrated oak—if anybody cares. I have made wonderful friends through wine. I have gotten to hang out with some of the brightest people in the industry. I have had the great pleasure of being both yelled at and complimented by the icon Robert Mondavi. It has been a fantastically wonderful experience.

One of my only regrets is that my family hasn't been able to reap the benefits of my life in wine. We are the only Choates who live on the West Coast. In fact, my family refers to Canada, Heather and I as the "West Coast Choates" and my brother's family as the "East Coast Choates." Mickey, the wine snob in the family, would have really enjoyed having so much access to wineries, tastings, and special events. Despite the distance between us, I have become the family sommelier. I often get consultation calls from Mickey while he is out shopping for wine. I know it kills Mickey to walk past the grand cru Burgundy and shop for a

$15-and-under everyday wine. He created a special wine memory when he shared a 1990 Chateau Montrose with Pop and I at Pop's sixtieth birthday at Gramercy Tavern. The wine received 100 points from Robert Parker, the wine critic, which doesn't really matter to me, but held great importance for Mickey. That said, the wine was absolutely magnificent and yes, I can still taste it. Canada enjoys a glass of Champagne, which isn't surprising given she has expensive tastes in all facets of life. I also get calls from Mom when she is entertaining and needs a wine pairing or when she needs some wine advice for her writing. We have managed a few trips to the wineries and a few overnights in the wine country when they've come to visit, but their exposure to the wine community here has been limited. I know all their personal tastes: Mom and Laurel—pinot noir (and also for Laurel, Kistler chardonnay on special occasions); Pop—rosé and almost anything red; Mickey—EXPENSIVE!; Heather—Nebbiolo (that's why I married her). So I can always order something that's sure to please.

I will offer some wine suggestions throughout the book, and while they may not be perfect for everyone, they work for me, and that is one of the most wonderful things about wine—there is no right or wrong. The best wines are simply the wines that make you happiest.

Making Hootch

Some years ago, when Anne, my almost-daughter, returned to the United States from living in the South of France, she came toting her homemade *coing* liqueur. Unfortunately my high-school French did not include *coing*, so I hadn't a clue what the flavor might be until she began proclaiming the fecundity of the quince tree on the hill behind their house in Draguignon. I couldn't much discern the normal astringency of the dry, tart fruit in the ambrosial liqueur that Anne had produced. It was, in fact, so wonderfully aromatic and nectarous that I became a devoteé of homemade liqueurs.

I searched high and low for the *alcohol pour fruits* that is readily available to the home brewer in France, but had no success. So, I turned to the 151 proof alcohol that had recently been reintroduced to liquor stores in Upstate New York. When Anne came to visit, we went at the moonshine full force! At first, we tried quince as she had done abroad, but the quince were just too dry and flavorless, so we threw out the bathtub gin that we produced.

We moved on to peaches, pears, and even rhubarb. The first small batch of *pêche liqueur* ('cause I was getting to be seriously French) was so strong that it almost killed us—it was true rotgut. So we changed our main ingredient to the far milder vodka and the results were much better. You can use 151 *if* you dilute it with an equal amount of water. However, I still prefer the smoothness of vodka. I try to make liqueur every summer and/or fall, usually with my best buddy, Lynn. I particularly love pear liqueur—or as I now call it *"poire Judith eau de vie,"* but we have made blackberry and elderberry, both from wild fruit, as well as limoncello. We all love to give our homemade hootch as gifts so we always bottle them in attractive containers that make a statement.

You can make liqueurs out of almost any fruit or berry. A good proportion is 1¼ pounds of chopped fruit (I don't peel it) or berries to about 3 cups of vodka (or 1½ cups 151 and 1½ cups water). To this you add 1 to 1¼ cups of sugar—depending on the sweetness of the fruit—or more if you really like a syrupy liqueur. You then mix it all together and pour it into a nonreactive container with a cover. Place the covered container in a cool, dark spot for at least one month, stirring about once a week. For a stronger fruit flavor, store for up to three months. Then strain the liquid through cheesecloth into one large or a few small glass containers with covers. Keep the containers in a cool, dark spot. The longer the liqueur stands, the mellower the flavor. However, over a very extended period of storage, the sweetness will often decrease. If the end result is not as sweet as you like, you can always add just a bit of heavy sugar syrup.

Cocktail Treats

Isn't it amazing that not so long ago (well, maybe long ago to some readers) we had a small piece of Melba toast with maybe a squeeze of pimento cheese as a cocktail tidbit with a "7 & 7" or "bourbon and branch." Now we are served or serve an array of wonderfully diverse hors d'oeuvres with ever more complex mixed drinks or fine wines. After years as a caterer when I made thousands of small plates, I no longer have such a wide repertoire of bite-size treats; I tend to rely on my pastry swirls, e.g., Olive Swirls (page 40), hummus (page 42), a bowl of nuts, or perhaps some olives, marinated veggies (such as artichokes or peppers) and bread sticks. But if I have a bowl of stunningly sweet and delicious Sun Gold cherry tomatoes and/or little red cherry tomatoes I chop them up with a bit of extra virgin olive oil and sea salt and heap them on some slices of stale baguette that I've toasted and rubbed with garlic. If I happen to have some fresh basil, oregano, parsley, or chives on hand, a tablespoon or two will also go in. These simple improvised bruschetta are the perfect accompaniment to a chilled rosé or sparkling Prosecco cocktail in the summertime.

Another favorite cocktail snack is a pretty bowl or basket heaped with fava beans, which we eat raw with shavings from a big block of Parmesan or ricotta salata cheese to accompany a lovely crisp white wine. I must admit favas are a pain to prepare—even raw, you have to carefully pull off the outer skin once you've shelled them. It does keep you occupied, however, and slows down your consumption of wine a bit. Otherwise, you have to blanch the raw beans for a few seconds to loosen their outer skin and then peel them before eating. Just remember that the green, grassy flavor is worth the work.

Mickey: As far as I am concerned, it's essential to start a dinner party with hors d'oeuvres and Champagne. This combo stimulates the appetite and if you are a good cook it prepares your guests for the meal ahead. To me, the perfect get-the-party-going hors d'oeuvres are oysters or other raw or lightly cooked seafood dishes, like a ceviche (page 50), or tuna tartare, because they're not too heavy or filling—which is particularly important when your dinner

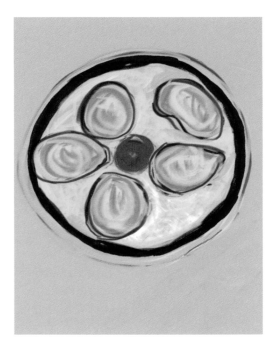

party consists of multiple courses (**Judie:** "Just like Mickey's always do!"). These light dishes match perfectly with Champagne as well. For less formal occasions, I like to make little crostini because they are so easy: I toast up sliced ficelle (a very thin baguette), and coat each slice with arugula pesto, which I then layer with a piece of roasted mushroom or a mound of eggplant caviar (diced peeled eggplant sautéed with onion and garlic until very soft and fragrant, and seasoned with mild curry powder), and top it off with roasted red and yellow pepper strips. Whether to rub the toasts with garlic first is up to the cook. Mini-pizzas—just a round of toasted baguette topped with either a touch of marinara and mozzarella and a basil leaf or a white-bean puree with a parsley leaf—are other favorites. When we have big gatherings, my best buddy Steve Kolyer, aka Uncle Kol, generally does the hors d'oeuvres (page 277). And no matter what the occasion, don't forget *Gougères* (page 149)! French they may be, but our American family devours them.

Chris: I let the occasion dictate what I am going to do for treats to serve with drinks. My annual Super Bowl party always gets Buffalo chicken wings and roasted-onion dip for the chips with super-cold beer (PBR if I get my say). When I'm feeling fancy I love to do caviar service with boiled quail eggs cut in half to form the perfect little caviar vessels, which I serve with Champagne or Moscato d'Asti. I also like all kinds of crostini, which I always offer with a crisp white wine. I often make a large crostini on grilled country bread rubbed with garlic and topped with either Sweet 100 tomatoes and basil or Mushroom Ragout (page 191). My favorite cocktail is the margarita, so chips, salsa (of all types), and guacamole (page 49) are always an excellent accompaniment. And never forget the ultimate Americano cocktail treat—the deviled egg. Whenever I make them they are always quick to disappear.

Cocktail Hour

We do, from time to time, slip in a cocktail or two—particularly during the summer months. Two of our favorites are perfect summer refreshments, but that doesn't mean you can't have them on a cold winter's eve.

Mickey's Hemingway Daiquiri

Mickey: The Hemingway daiquiri, otherwise known as the Papa Doble or Floridita, is my favorite cocktail. The story is well told that it was Ernest Hemingway's preferred drink at the El Floradita bar in Havana. Hemingway had an aversion to sugar, so the original cocktail was made without simple syrup, making it a difficult libation for today's palate. The amount of simple syrup can be altered to suit your taste. I think it is the epitome of a great cocktail—the slightly exotic flavor comes from the maraschino liqueur. Try and find a nice ruby grapefruit so the color of the garnish is more on the pink side. I use a candied grapefruit peel that I make myself, but a grapefruit twist will suffice.

> 2⅓ ounces white rum
> 1⅓ ounces simple syrup (1 cup sugar and 1 cup water brought to a boil and then cooled)
> 1⅓ ounces fresh lime juice
> ⅓ ounce maraschino liqueur
> Ruby red grapefruit twist (for garnish)

Fill a cocktail shaker with ice. Add the rum, syrup, juice, and liqueur and shake and shake until your hand is freezing. Strain into a chilled large martini glass, garnish with a grapefruit twist and serve.

Chris's Margarita

Chris: Even though I started my career in a surfer-themed bar with really, really good Tex-Mex food, it wasn't until I moved west and experienced the true margarita, as it was originally made in the 1940s, that I became a margarita fan. There are only three high-quality ingredients used in equal parts. This is an unadulterated recipe that has nothing to do with the chain-restaurant frozen drink. Simple, delish, and well-balanced.

> Salt, to coat the rim of the glass
> ¼ cup Herradura Silver tequila
> ¼ cup Cointreau
> ¼ cup fresh lime juice

Wet the edge of a large martini glass and then dip it into salt. The salt should just lightly coat about ½ of the rim. Fill a cocktail shaker with ice. Add the tequila, liqueur, and juice; shake and shake until your hand is freezing, and then shake a little longer. Taste for balance, and if it is too tart, add a tiny amount of superfine sugar and shake again. Strain into the prepared glass and serve.

Grilled Red-Devil Quail

SERVES 6

I grew up eating wild birds; they were easily hunted and cheap to bring to the table. But I never much liked them. (A long time ago I was at a dinner party where tiny little birds were served whole and I have never recuperated from seeing that tiny corpse on my plate; this is one of my very few food no-nos.) Mickey, Chris, and Steve all love quail, however, so they are often on our menu, particularly in the summer, when they are eaten hot off the grill, out-of-hand with cocktails.

Although once only attainable by stomping through the woods with your bird dog, quail is now readily available at most butcher shops and specialty food stores, fully dressed and often boneless. I've even seen them in the supermarket. Mickey likes his quail marinated in olive oil, rosemary, and garlic; Chris cuts the back out, flattens the birds and pan sears them (sometimes serving them atop a scoop of Barolo risotto), while I like to put an Indonesian spin on mine. This is probably because the spices entice me more than the meat. Although we usually opt for the grill, quail can also be quickly cooked on the stovetop. Whichever you choose, you don't want to overcook them, as they will very quickly toughen.

You can use my marinade or the boys' simple one to grill quail, or any type of poultry, game, lamb, or pork.

 CHRIS'S SUGGESTED WINE PAIRING
AN EARTHY FRENCH PINOT NOIR, SUCH AS A VILLAGE BURGUNDY

6 whole quails, cleaned and split in half lengthwise
Juice of 1 lemon
1 tablespoon tamarind dissolved in 2 tablespoons warm water
2 fresh red or green hot chilies (or more or less as desired), stemmed and seeded
1 cup unsweetened coconut milk
¼ cup minced onion
1 tablespoon minced garlic
Salt

1. Preheat and oil a grill.

2. Generously rub the quails with lemon juice. Grill each side for 2 minutes. Remove from the grill and set aside. Do not turn off the grill or let the fire die.

3. Strain the tamarind though a fine mesh sieve, pressing on the solids to extract all liquid. Combine the liquid with the chilies, coconut milk, onion, and garlic, and process in a food processor until smooth. Season with salt.

4. Using the flat side of a cleaver or a heavy-bottomed frying pan, pound each halved quail to flatten slightly.

5. Place the quail, skin side down, in a large frying pan. Pour the tamarind mixture over the quail and place the pan over medium heat. Bring to a simmer and then lower the heat and keep at a low simmer for 6 minutes.

6. Immediately remove the quail from the sauce and return to the hot grill, skin side down. Grill for 2 minutes or until crisp. Remove and serve immediately.

Olive Swirls

MAKES AS MANY AS YOU LIKE

When my mom made pie pastry, she always used the left-over dough to make what she called cinnamon swirls. She created these by simply rolling out the remaining dough into a freeform sort of rectangle and sprinkling it with cinnamon sugar. She then rolled it up into a log, which she cut, crosswise, into slices about a quarter inch or so thick. She placed these on a cookie sheet and baked them for about 15 minutes in a 375°F oven, turning out sweet little swirled cookies that went perfectly with a cup of tea. They were a childhood favorite and something I introduced to my boys when I made pastry.

Today, when I make pie pastry (page 70) and have some left over, I use it to make a savory hors d'oeuvre rather than the cinnamon-scented cookie that I had always loved. I use my mom's technique and translate it to a filling of olive paste, or pesto, or grated Parmesan cheese and smoked paprika. Like Mom did, I roll out the dough, but then I coat it lightly with olive paste (or whatever filling I happen to have on hand). The little savory swirls are so popular that I often make up a whole batch of pastry dough just for them. When I do, I store the extra unbaked swirls, frozen and labeled, for a quick cocktail tidbit. Bake them frozen, at 375°F, for about 20 minutes.

Here is my recipe for olive paste—aka tapenade—but don't hesitate to purchase jarred olive paste from your favorite specialty food store—most that I've tried are pretty good. This makes quite a bit, but it will keep for about a month, covered and refrigerated.

TIP: In addition to being used as a filling for olive swirls, olive paste can be used as a condiment for meat, poultry, or fish; as a dip for crudités; as a topping for croutons, baguette slices, or sliced, cooked potatoes; or as a spread on your favorite sandwich.

Olive Paste or Tapenade

MAKES ABOUT 4 CUPS

¾ cup olive oil

¼ cup finely chopped red onion

2 tablespoons minced garlic

1 cup finely chopped red bell pepper

1 cup finely chopped yellow bell pepper

1 cup finely chopped green bell pepper

2 cups chopped black olives, such as kalamata, niçoise, Gaeta, or other deeply flavored black olives

1½ cups chopped toasted walnuts

⅓ cup chopped flat-leaf parsley

2 tablespoon finely chopped basil

½ cup red wine vinegar

Coarse salt and freshly ground pepper

1. Heat the olive oil in a large, heavy-bottomed saucepan over medium heat. Add the onion and garlic and sauté for 5 minutes or just until they begin to color. Stir in all of the bell peppers and sauté for 10 minutes or just until the peppers are softened. Stir in the olives, walnuts, parsley, and basil. When well combined, stir in the vinegar. Taste and season with salt and pepper. Bring to a simmer and cook for 5 minutes.

2. Remove from the heat and transfer to the bowl of a food processor fitted with the metal blade. Process, using quick on and off turns, until slightly chunky but not pureed. Scrape into a nonreactive container and allow to cool before using or storing. If storing for a long period of time, cover the top with a thin layer of extra virgin olive oil.

Gold-Standard Hummus

MAKES ABOUT 4 CUPS

Of all the recipes in my world, why do I want to talk about hummus? Mainly because it has been a constant on my table for so long. I first tasted it at about ten years old when a friend invited me to dinner. Everything on her Syrian family's menu was new to me, but hummus and kibbeh were the two dishes that struck a chord, probably because, in 1950, the flavors were so different from anything I had ever tasted before. Kibbeh fell by the wayside, but beginning with my foray into vegetarianism in the sixties, I have continually made some version of hummus, and even now I almost always have a batch in the fridge. I use it for sandwich fillings, as a dip, thinned down as a sauce for grilled veggies, or as a salad dressing, and Steve dips it straight from the container as an afternoon filler-upper. My various mixtures differ tremendously—some stray so far from the original that they don't really have the right to be called hummus any longer, but we still call them so. This version (which makes a substantial amount intended for gift-giving or sharing) appeared in my first cookbook, in 1970 (*The Gift Giver's Cookbook*, written with my great friend Jane Green), and it remains our standard. Many variations have been developed along the way, sometimes with a view to reducing calories or fat and sometimes just to excite our taste buds with a jolt of heat or spice.

Hummus has long been a mainstay on the menus of vegetarian restaurants, and more recently has started popping up as a spread (in place of butter or olive oil) to accompany bread in many bistro-style restaurants. I also see it served with greater and greater frequency in starred restaurants as a component of a complex presentation.

Mickey: At large gatherings I always serve a bowl of the traditional-style hummus along with freshly made crisp pita chips (simply cut pita into small triangles, brush with olive oil, season with sea or garlic salt, and bake at 350°F until lightly browned and crisp). Some of Mom's versions seem a little iffy to me, being a traditionalist, but her friends seem to egg her on to make mixes that are even more exotic.

3 (15.5-ounce) cans garbanzo beans (chickpeas), well-drained with juice reserved

8 cloves garlic (or more or less as desired)

¾ cup tahini (sesame seed paste)

Juice of 5 lemons (or more or less: we like ours lemony!)

Extra virgin olive oil (optional)

Coarse salt

1. Combine the drained garbanzos, garlic, and tahini in the bowl of a food processor fitted with the metal blade. Begin processing and, with the motor running, add the lemon juice along with just enough of the reserved garbanzo juice to make a smooth, thick puree. Add the lemon juice a bit at a time until you get the amount of acidity that you like. Here I like to add some extra virgin olive oil to smooth out the paste and add a bit of fruitiness to the mix; however, it isn't at all traditional or necessary. Season with salt and process to incorporate.

2. Scrape into a nonreactive container, cover, and refrigerate for up to 1 week.

3. Serve at room temperature with crisp chips or raw vegetables.

TIP: If you want to add an elegant touch, sprinkle the top of the hummus with fresh pomegranate seeds or a mix of black and toasted sesame seeds when serving.

Variations to the Gold-Standard Hummus

1. To the Gold Standard, add the zest of 1 orange, 3 tablespoons chopped fresh flat-leaf parsley or cilantro, hot chili pepper (serrano, jalapeño, bird, etc.), or hot sauce to taste.

2. Replace the garbanzos with any other type of cooked, canned bean that appeals to you. I use cannellini and black beans most frequently.

3. For a reduced-fat version, eliminate the tahini and add about ¾ cup nonfat yogurt, (preferably thick, Greek-style yogurt) and use the juice of only 3 lemons (or if you want a sweeter version, replace the lemon juice with fresh orange juice and zest) and then season with a hit of sesame oil. With this lower-fat version, I like to add 3 tablespoons or so of chopped fresh cilantro, flat-leaf parsley, or watercress.

4. For an Italian take on the original, use 3 (15.5-ounce) cans of cannellini beans, drained well, ¼ cup fresh flat-leaf parsley leaves, 3 tablespoons roasted garlic puree, and the juice and zest of 2 lemons (preferably Meyer lemons). Process as above, adding about ½ cup of extra virgin olive oil to make a smooth, thick puree. Season with coarse salt and freshly ground pepper.

5. For a strongly flavored Middle Eastern version, use the Gold Standard recipe, replacing the garbanzos with cooked dried fava beans or lentils. Season with toasted ground cumin, cinnamon, and Aleppo pepper, and then fold in about ¼ cup chopped fresh mint.

6. For a particularly unusual but quite delicious flavor, replace the beans with a head of cooked cauliflower. Eliminate the lemon juice and add about ½ cup of fresh orange juice and a hint of cumin to balance the cauliflower flavor.

7. To thin the hummus down for use as a sauce or salad dressing, use the reserved bean juice, water, olive oil, orange or lemon juice, or vinegar. Thin slowly, tasting as you go, until you reach the desired consistency and flavor. If the desired flavor is reached before the consistency is thin enough, use cool water, a teaspoon at a time, to continue thinning.

Marinated Yogurt Cheese

MAKES ABOUT 2 CUPS

Once upon a cookbook-writing career, I penned a book called *Cooking with Yogurt,* **in** which I tried to reinvent recipes using yogurt in place of higher-fat ingredients. I was so into yogurt that I had 3 or 4 yogurt makers and was determined to make the best home-made yogurt to be found—this was long before the now ubiquitous Greek yogurt was introduced to supermarket shelves. Although I rarely make yogurt from scratch anymore, from time to time I do make yogurt cheese, which isn't really cheese at all. It is simply yogurt that has been drained of most of its liquid, resulting in a soft, spreadable hybrid not unlike cream cheese. If you use Greek-style yogurt, the draining time will be shortened and the yield will be a bit more, due to its thickness. One cup of yogurt produces approximately ⅓ cup of yogurt cheese. And guess what—if you don't want to make yogurt cheese, you can use this same marinade with bocconcini or a goat cheese log, cut into slices.

6 cups plain fine-quality yogurt
¾ cup extra virgin olive oil
2 tablespoons sliced garlic
1 tablespoon minced shallot
2 tablespoons chopped fresh basil leaves
1 tablespoon fresh rosemary needles
1 tablespoon chopped fresh thyme
1 tablespoon chopped fresh sage
1 teaspoon freshly grated lemon zest
Sea salt
Cracked black pepper or dried red pepper flakes
Olives for garnish (optional)

1. Line a large sieve or colander (or two small ones) with a piece of damp muslin, a triple layer of damp cheesecloth, or any other clean, moist, white cotton cloth. Pour the yogurt into the prepared sieve or colander and place it over a bowl large enough to hold it without the bottom of the sieve touching the bottom of the bowl. Cover lightly with plastic film. Set aside to drain for 8 hours for a soft cheese or 12 hours for a very firm cheese.

2. When the yogurt has firmed, remove it from the sieve and form it into a log shape. Wrap in plastic film and refrigerate for at least 3 hours or up to 24 hours.

3. Remove the yogurt cheese from the refrigerator and unwrap. At this point, you can eat it just as it is, rather like a soft goat cheese. But, to marinate for this recipe, cut crosswise into disks and place the disks in a shallow baking dish.

4. Combine the olive oil with the garlic and shallot in a small bowl. Add the basil, rosemary, thyme, sage, and lemon zest, and season with salt and pepper flakes, stirring to blend. When well blended, pour the mixture over the cheese disks. Cover with plastic film and refrigerate for 12 hours.

5. When ready to serve, remove the cheese from the fridge and allow to come to room temperature. Add some olives if desired, and serve with toast, croutons, crackers, or baguette slices.

6. If not using immediately, pack the cheese disks into a shallow container. Pour in the marinating oil, cover, and refrigerate until ready to use. Will keep, covered and refrigerated, for up to 1 week.

Spicy Bean Dip

MAKES ABOUT 8 CUPS

For as long as I can remember, this dip has been a staple in our house. When my mom made it, the cooking fat of choice was bacon or lard and the beans were mashed with butter. No matter the mix-ins, it is the go-to dip (with homemade tortilla or pita chips) for television watching (for the guys, this usually means sports), game or cardplaying, or even for a late-night easy-to-put-together burrito, taco, or tostada. My mom had a wonderful electric bean crock that she served it in to keep the dip warm and gooey.

Whenever we are in San Francisco, I always visit the Rancho Gordo stand (see Sources) at the Ferry Plaza Farmers Market to stock up on their various heirloom beans. For this dish, I like to use Santa Maria pinquito beans. Rancho Gordo calls them "the classic pink bean for California tri-tip barbecues." I find that they make a deeply flavored dip.

Although a lot of professional chefs now seem to forgo the traditional presoak for beans, I stick to my old-fashioned ways. I have bitten into one too many more-than-al-dente beans in restaurants to give up presoaking. I have found, however, that adding salt and/or acidic ingredients, such as tomatoes, early in the cooking cycle does not seem to affect the end result as I had originally been taught. And, although my mom used an electric mixer—which was the absolute wonder of her kitchen—you can quite easily use a food processor fitted with the metal blade to mash the beans—just don't overprocess to a really smooth puree.

1 pound (2 cups) dried pinto beans, rinsed and picked clean

1 jalapeño or other hot chili (or more or less as desired), seeded and minced

1 cup chopped onions

1 tablespoon minced garlic

2½ tablespoons chili powder

1 teaspoon ground cumin (or more or less as desired)

½ cup olive oil

¾ cup cheddar cheese

⅓ cup sour cream

Tabasco or other hot sauce

Coarse salt

1. Place the beans in cold water to cover by 1 inch and set aside to soak for 8 hours or overnight.

2. Drain the beans and transfer to a large, heavy-bottomed saucepan or Dutch oven. Add water to cover by 2 inches, along with the jalapeño, onions, and garlic. Stir in the chili powder and cumin. Place over medium-high heat, stir in the olive oil and bring to a boil. Lower the heat and simmer, stirring frequently and adding additional boiling water as needed to keep the beans moist, for about 2 hours or until the beans are very, very soft and almost all of the liquid has been absorbed. Remove from the heat and stir in the cheese, sour cream, and Tabasco. Taste and season with salt.

3. Transfer the mixture to the bowl of a heavy-duty mixer with the paddle attachment and beat until the cheese has melted into the beans and the mixture is almost smooth. Taste and, if necessary, season with additional Tabasco and salt. Scrape into a bowl and serve or set aside to cool.

4. When cool, transfer to a container with a tight-fitting lid and refrigerate for up to 5 days or freeze for up to 6 months. If frozen, thaw and reheat before using.

Holy Guacamole

SERVES 6 TO 8

It wouldn't be a Choate family cookbook without guacamole. Avocados are right high on our list of favorite foods. The story goes that when I was a wee one, my mom would mash an avocado and put a bit of the mash on a saltine cracker for me. I would quickly lick off the avocado and hand back the saltine for a refill. I would keep this up until the saltine was too soggy to hold. She didn't make the now ubiquitous guacamole; just plain old avocado with a little salt was fine for us. I often still eat an avocado for lunch with just a touch of salt and a squeeze of lime juice, but every now and then I mix up a bowl of guacamole to serve with drinks or to finish off our favorite burrito dinner. Since I don't want to get caught double dipping, I now eat my chip along with the dip!

4 large ripe avocados

1 serrano chili (or more or less as desired), stemmed, seeded, and minced

1 clove garlic, minced

1 cup cored, peeled, seeded, and diced ripe tomatoes

½ cup finely diced red onion

2 tablespoons minced fresh cilantro leaves

2 tablespoons fresh lime juice (or more or less as desired)

Salt

1. Peel the avocados. Place in a large shallow bowl and chop into small pieces. Stir in the chili, garlic, tomatoes, red onion, and cilantro. Season with the lime juice and salt.

2. Serve with tortilla chips, pita chips, crackers, or as a side with burritos or tacos.

Scallop Ceviche

SERVES 4 TO 6

Every fall we head to the outer Cape—specifically to Provincetown, the last enclave on the tip of Cape Cod. Our friends Eddie and Richard very graciously loan us their house, a charming two-story within easy walking distance (through the cemetery shortcut) of busy Commercial Street in the heart of "P-town." We are usually joined by our very close friends Lynn and Doug, who are as enthusiastic as we are for what has become the annual seafood run. We usually load the car with vittles so we don't have to shop much, other than our daily run to Mac's Seafood (see Sources) in Truro Center. Dinners are over the top, yet simple, with the daily "catch" always being the star, and lunches are usually created from the remains of the previous night's dinner.

Every dinner begins with oysters—at least six per person. Sometimes I'll also make a gravlax or ceviche as an extra appetizer to accompany the Champagne, Prosecco, or some new white that Doug and Steve have picked up at the wine shop conveniently located around the bend in the road.

The scallops are always day-boat and pristine. Although they can be eaten just "as is" (which I often do as I cook), this ceviche is one of our favorite ways to down the sweet morsels. It is not really a defined recipe, but I will give you an idea of how to duplicate it.

For four to six people, you will need one pound of very fresh scallops. If large, cut them crosswise into thin slices; if delicate little gems, leave them whole. Place the scallop slices or whole scallops in a nonreactive bowl—glass is great. Cover with Moscato vinegar (this is important, no other vinegar seems to create the same slightly sweet taste that complements the ethereal flesh of the scallops). Grate the zest from about half of a large organic orange into the bowl. Then, to your taste, add finely diced jalapeño and chives. Stir, cover, and refrigerate for about twenty minutes, but no more than an hour. If you marinate them too long, they will "cook" completely and turn to mush, which you definitely don't want to happen. When ready to serve, fan the slices out on individual plates, drizzle the marinating liquid over the top, and sprinkle on a bit of sea salt.

 CHRIS'S SUGGESTED WINE PAIRING
AN UNOAKED CHARDONNAY

Just Everyday Meals

🍷 Chris's Wine Advice

Everyday meals call for everyday wine. Don't overthink your choices or your budget. There are plenty of under $10 wines in the market that are well made and pleasant to drink. I also find that value imports tend to offer more authenticity and less winemaking manipulation.

Tomato Salads

I discovered my favorite way to eat a tomato when I was just about eighteen months old. I was sitting in the corner of the garden watching tomatoes being picked for canning. Imitating the women, I pulled a ripe one from its stem and put its warmth up against my nose to both feel and smell its pungency—it is a moment indelibly implanted in my mind. My mom pulled the tomato in half for me and sprinkled it with salt. "Taste," she said. The juice was at once warm and cool, acidic and sweet, with the almost acrid smell of the greenery as the perfect accent. I still think that there is no experience to compare with sitting outdoors eating a ripe tomato bursting with the sun's warmth, emitting the still green smell of the plant, with the flavor heightened by a sprinkling of salt. Coming in at a close second is that warm tomato placed on a thick slice of homemade white bread slathered with creamery butter and sprinkled with sea salt.

Here are two salads that highlight summer's best. One is a contemporary take on my childhood favorite. It can only be made in the summer when tomatoes are perfection. And that's okay. We are too spoiled anyway, so a little waiting for something wonderful does us good. The whole family makes this salad basically in the same way— though Chris and I always include garlic, and Mickey tends to highlight the tomatoes. In the second recipe, the slightly tart, fruity flavor of the Middle Eastern spice sumac helps accentuate the sweet acidity of the tomatoes, while the ricotta salata adds the necessary salt.

If you cube the tomatoes and eliminate the bread for either salad, the mixture can be used as a topping for bruschetta. We generally use balsamic vinegar but other sweet vinegars work well also and we all like a slightly spicy extra virgin olive oil.

What Are Heirloom Tomatoes?

For the most part, they are tomatoes raised from seeds saved from those days when tomatoes could just be tomatoes, not perfect, uniformly red and round, firm-fleshed, shippable globes. There are many, many different varieties, colors, shapes, and flavors. They might be red, yellow, multicolored with stripes and speckles, purple, green, or pink. Heirlooms are generally misshapen or, at best, oddly shaped, but, oh, what flavor. Even supermarkets offer them occasionally along with very sweet and deeply flavorful small cherry or pear-shaped tomatoes. But they really stand out at summer's farm stands and farmers markets.

Heirloom Tomato-Basil Salad

SERVES 6

2½ pounds organic heirloom tomatoes, preferably a mixture of colors

4 cloves garlic, minced (optional)

Sea salt and freshly ground pepper

¾ cup extra virgin olive oil

¼ cup balsamic vinegar

½ cup fresh basil chiffonade

4 thick slices rustic bread, well toasted

1. Wash the tomatoes well. Core and cut into cubes or into any style slice you like. Place in a nonreactive bowl. Add the garlic and season with salt and pepper. Set aside to marinate at room temperature for 30 minutes.

2. Add the olive oil and balsamic vinegar, tossing to coat. Toss in the basil and then the bread. Let stand for 5 minutes before serving with extra toast to dunk in the salad juices.

Cherry Tomato-Ricotta Salata Salad

SERVES 6

2½ pounds cherry or pear tomatoes, cored and cut in half lengthwise, OR plum tomatoes, cored, seeded, and diced

1 medium red onion, finely diced

¼ bunch flat-leaf parsley, leaves only, chopped

½ teaspoon ground sumac

6 tablespoons fruity extra virgin olive oil

¼ pound ricotta salata, crumbled

Coarse salt and cracked black pepper

Combine the tomatoes, onions, parsley, and sumac in a large container. Add the olive oil, tossing to coat well. Toss in the cheese and let stand 5 minutes. Taste and season with salt and cracked black pepper. Serve immediately or store, covered and refrigerated, for up to 8 hours.

Every-Night Salad

Once we moved to California in the late 1940s we had salad with our dinner every night, usually following the main course. This happened even if the main course was a sandwich or a bowl of soup. It is a good and healthy habit that I have enjoyed almost every day since. To me, the perfect simple salad is a subtle blend of sweet and bitter greens tossed with balsamic or other home-made vinaigrette, although my mom always added lots of other raw veggies such as tomatoes, cucumbers, carrots, and mush-rooms. This might have been because she did not have the broad selection of greens that are now available—red and green leaf lettuces, Bibb, Boston, romaine, arugula, endive, radicchio, spin-ach, kale, chicory, mâche, and escarole, to name just a few. My favorites are the leaf lettuces, except when I make Caesar salad, which demands a crisp romaine—this doesn't happen often, as Steve likes neither romaine nor Caesar dressing. Occasionally, I'll sneak in a wedge of iceberg drizzled with Thousand Island or blue cheese dressing. I'll let you choose your greens, but I'll share my balsamic vinaigrette recipe; a squirt bottle of which is always on my kitchen shelf. This recipe yields enough dressing for a few salads, and having it on hand makes pulling a nightly salad together very easy.

Balsamic Vinaigrette

MAKES ABOUT 2½ CUPS

½ cup balsamic vinegar
1 teaspoon red wine vinegar
2 teaspoons Dijon mustard
2 cups olive oil
Salt and pepper

Combine the vinegars with the mustard in a large glass jar with a lid, shaking to blend. Add the oil, season with salt and pepper, and shake, shake, shake. The dressing should emulsify and stay that way for the duration of its life. If not, shake, shake, shake each time you use it. Store in a cool spot, but not in the fridge.

TIP: Nobody believes me, but I swear by this method for keeping lettuce fresh. When you buy lettuce, trim it, and cut into pieces. Place the lettuce pieces in a sink full of ice-cold water and splash around to wash off the grit and refresh the leaves. If your tap water is not icy cold or if the lettuce looks particularly wilted and tired, add lots of ice cubes to the water. Then, dry the lettuce thoroughly in a salad spinner (in batches) and store, airtight, in resealable plastic bags in the fridge. It will stay fresh for days. This same trick works beautifully for fresh herbs as well.

Octopus Salad

I love my stovetop grill pan almost as much as I love
grilling outdoors. It is the perfect tool to bring one of
my favorite dishes, grilled octopus, to the table year-
round. I buy fresh, cleaned baby octopus that only
requires a good rinse before cooking. Then I toss the
octopus with olive oil, salt, and pepper and put it in
the very hot grill pan. It curls and dances as I tong it
around the pan and in just a few minutes it is cooked
to perfection—tender, moist, and slightly charred
around the edges. If you grill it too long, it toughens
and you will have to cook and cook and cook to tenderize it. So quickly remove it from the grill, cut it into

bite-size pieces, and add to any type of salad. I often make a base of greens, such as spinach or arugula, then add some sliced radishes and scallions, and a nice citrus-garlicky
dressing. Just follow my lead and grill up some octopus, make your choice of salad, and
drizzle on a citrus dressing—if you didn't think you liked octopus, you will now.

I always make a full batch of this dressing, but you can easily halve the ingredients
if you prefer. Just remember that, although the recipe makes quite a bit, it keeps for a
couple of weeks if covered and refrigerated, and makes a lovely sauce for any grilled
fish, shellfish, or poultry.

 CHRIS'S SUGGESTED WINE PAIRING
A CRISP WHITE—PERHAPS A SANCERRE, FROM THE LOIRE

Citrus-Herb Dressing

MAKES ABOUT 1 PINT

5½ ounces fresh grapefruit juice

1⅓ ounces fresh orange juice

1½ tablespoons fresh lemon juice

2 tablespoons roasted garlic (see Sidebar, page 155)

1 to 2 tablespoons honey, plus more if needed

Chopped fresh thyme, parsley, or tarragon—
 I use about 2 teaspoons

6 ounces olive oil

3 ounces green, spicy extra virgin olive oil

Coarse salt and freshly cracked pepper

Combine the grapefruit, orange, and lemon juices
with the garlic and honey in a blender and process
to blend. With the motor running, slowly add the oils
and process to emulsify. Season with salt and pepper. Taste and add honey if needed. Remove from the
blender and whisk in the herbs. Store, covered and
refrigerated, for up to 2 weeks. Allow to come to room
temperature before using.

Braised Radicchio

SERVES 4 TO 6

I am crazy about radicchio—not only because it is so assertive and pungent but also because it is so beautiful. In the summer we generally simply grill it, just as the Italians do, and serve it warm with a drizzle of extra virgin olive oil. But in the winter I like to do a bit more. This is one of my favorite side dishes—a quick braise to serve with grilled pork chops or chicken breasts. It is so delicious, and now that I think of it, the mix would also make a great toss with some pasta and a good amount of extra virgin olive oil.

TIP: I use prosciutto in this recipe but you could substitute almost any type of ham or cured meat.

1 tablespoon olive oil

1 cup prosciutto slivers

1 teaspoon minced garlic

2 heads radicchio, washed well and cut into thick ribbons

¼ cup chicken stock or nonfat low-sodium chicken broth

½ teaspoon frozen orange-juice concentrate

½ teaspoon freshly grated orange zest

Salt and pepper

1 tablespoon balsamic vinegar (preferably white)

Heat the olive oil in a large sauté pan over medium heat. Add the prosciutto and garlic and cook, stirring frequently, for 4 minutes or so, or just until starting to color. Add the radicchio and toss to combine. Continue to cook, stirring frequently, for about 3 minutes or until the radicchio begins to color. Add the broth, orange-juice concentrate, and orange zest, stirring to blend well. Season with salt and pepper. Lower the heat, cover, and cook for about 15 minutes or until the radicchio is very soft and the mixture is well flavored. Remove from the heat and drizzle with the balsamic vinegar.

Braised Baby Artichokes

MAKES AS MANY AS YOU LIKE

Along with the forsythia tumbling over the transverse walls in Central Park, arti-chokes are my signal that spring has arrived in New York City. The park offers that longed-for burst of energy from the vernal equinox, and Zingone Brothers grocery presents crates of baby artichokes that satisfy my hunger for culinary renewal. My mom used to buy gunny sacks of artichokes for one slim dollar from roadside stands in California and we feasted on them for days, dipping pulled-off leaves of steamed giant-size artichokes into melted butter with a hint of lemon juice. Now, I prefer a quick mix of extra virgin olive oil and aged balsamic as I scrape off the bit of flesh each leaf yields to make a comforting meal. But there are so many things to do with fresh artichokes, particularly when they are the tiny type. This recipe couldn't be simpler and the result can be served as a light lunch, an appetizer, a side dish, or an hors d'oeuvre.

CHRIS'S SUGGESTED WINE PAIRING
FROM MY POINT OF VIEW, NOTHING PAIRS WELL WITH ARTICHOKES, SO YOU ARE ON YOUR OWN!

2 pounds of fresh baby artichokes, washed well
1 lemon
Olive oil, for cooking
2 shallots, minced
2 cloves garlic, minced
Zest and juice of 1 orange, preferably organic
½ cup dry white wine
Coarse salt and freshly ground black pepper

1. Fill a large bowl with cold water. Cut the lemon in half and squeeze the juice into the water. Then add the squeezed halves.

2. Working with one artichoke at a time, neatly cut the top prickly tip off (this is best done by laying the artichoke on its side and making one swift slice with a sharp knife). If the artichokes have stems, peel off the tough outer skin with a vegetable peeler and trim the bottom. Pull off any damaged outer leaves and then cut each artichoke in half lengthwise. Immediately place the cut artichoke into the lemon water to keep it from discoloring. Continue trimming until all of the artichokes are halved.

3. Cover the bottom of a large sauté pan with a nice layer of good olive oil. Place over medium heat. Add the shallots and garlic and cook, stirring frequently, for about 2 minutes or just until the aromatics have softened slightly. Add the artichokes, cut side down.

Add the orange zest, orange juice, and white wine, and season with salt and pepper. Cover and bring to a simmer. Lower the heat and keep at a low simmer for about 20 minutes or until the artichokes are very tender.

4. Remove from the heat and drizzle with extra virgin olive oil. Taste and, if necessary, season with additional salt and pepper. Serve warm or at room temperature, or cool and store, covered and refrigerated, for up to 1 week. Allow to come to room temperature before serving.

Beets and Their Greens

Beets are one of our favorite veggies and, I think, among the few that every member of the family loves. In the summer I pickle and can beets and in the winter I roast them, often with orange zest and extra virgin olive oil. When they are tiny and sweet, I shave them raw over all kinds of salads. The big fat ones can be pushed through the mandoline and then baked into crisp chips. The greens either get tossed with garlic and oil and mixed into pasta or are put to work as a simple side dish. Along with their goodness, beets are beautiful, as they're now available in multiple colors—red, white, pink, candy-striped, yellow—a veritable rainbow. The versatility of beets just can't be beat—pun intended!

To use the greens for a pasta dinner, I remove all of the tougher stems and then cut the larger leaves into pieces (otherwise they clump together once cooked). I heat some olive oil, warm some minced or sliced garlic in it, and add the greens with either a little water or chicken broth and red chili flakes and salt. A quick sauté is all that is needed to season and wilt the greens. If you like, you can add some diced roasted red pepper, chopped grilled mushrooms, or, in fact, anything you like. I often add some beans once the greens have wilted—well-drained canned cannellini beans work well. This combo, with a good measure of grated Parmesan, will give you a filling, delicious, and economical peasant-style meal. Or just toss the sautéed greens on their own with cooked pasta—I usually use spaghetti with a liberal dose of freshly grated Parmesan over the top.

🍷 CHRIS'S SUGGESTED WINE PAIRING
EXPLORE THE ALTO ADIGE (ITALY)—MAYBE A KERNER, ONE OF MY FAVORITES

Bok Choy, Shiitakes, and Tofu

SERVES 4 TO 6

Even with its wide availability, bok choy seems to find a home only in Asian dishes. Either mature or baby, this mild, slightly sweet veg always has its delicate flavor covered up with garlic, ginger, or Asian sauces, including too much soy. Even when I go the Asian route, I try to treat it with respect and let it shine. I love the easily found white bok choy, but can never resist the not so easily found flowery purple variety.

3 heads bok choy

1 cup homemade vegetable or chicken stock or canned vegetable or chicken broth

1 tablespoon cornstarch

½ cup light soy sauce

1 tablespoon light brown sugar

1 (1-inch) piece ginger, peeled and minced

2 tablespoons olive oil

2 pounds extra-firm tofu, well-drained and cut into ¾-inch cubes

1 tablespoon sesame oil

1⅓ pounds shiitake mushrooms, cleaned, stems removed, and cut into quarters

3 small hot chilies (or more or less as desired), stemmed, seeded, and minced

3 cloves garlic, minced

1. Wash and dry the bok choy. Using a sharp knife, cut the root end from each head. If the leaves are wider than 2 inches, cut them in half. Set aside.

2. Combine ½ cup of the stock with the cornstarch in a small bowl, stirring to dissolve. Set aside.

3. Combine the remaining stock with the soy sauce and brown sugar in a large saucepan over medium heat. Stir in the ginger and bring to a boil. Immediately whisk in the reserved cornstarch mixture and cook, stirring constantly, for about 3 minutes or until thick. Remove from the heat and set aside.

4. Heat the olive oil in a large sauté pan over medium-high heat. Add the tofu and fry, turning about every 30 seconds, for about 4 minutes or until golden on all sides. Using a slotted spatula, transfer the tofu to a double layer of paper towels to drain.

5. With the sauté pan still on medium-high heat, add the sesame oil. When hot, add the mushrooms and sauté for 2 minutes. Add the bok choy, chilies, and garlic, and sauté for 1 minute. Stir in the reserved tofu along with the soy-ginger sauce and cook for about 1 minute or just until blended and hot. Remove from the heat and spoon equal portions into each of six large, shallow soup bowls. Serve immediately.

Champp

We love nothing more than to tease our almost-daughter, Anne McDonagh, about her Irish heritage. When she first came to America, Mickey and Chris were just into their teens and ribbed her constantly, testing her naiveté about American expressions. She still cringes at the mention of "cooties," "high-waters," and other unmentionable (in this book anyway) terms. She took plenty of heat about potatoes, too, but that did not keep her from introducing us to colcannon and champ, two traditional side dishes dear to her Irish-speakin' heart. They are both nothing more than mashed potatoes with, in the case of colcannon, chopped cabbage, and in the case of champ, chopped scallions. I tend to make the potatoes richer in cream and butter than the traditional recipe calls for, and my abandon makes Annie crazy. If she watched Mickey make his mashies, she would faint as he follows the Joël Robuchon recipe, adding a good portion of milk and a cup of butter. Her version is, of course, much healthier than mine (and Mick's), but I still like mine better, so that is what I'm sharing!

TIP: Russet potatoes are drier and lighter than Yukon gold while the Yukons are richer and creamier in taste and texture. Either potato variety is a good choice for making champ, depending on your taste.

TIP: There are three tricks to making great mashed potatoes:
1. Cut the potatoes into uniform pieces so that they cook evenly.
2. Once cooked and drained, dry them out a bit before combining with the milk and butter.
3. Always use hot milk (or cream) into which the butter has been melted.

2 pounds Yukon gold or russet potatoes,
   peeled and cubed

Salt

¾ cup milk

½ cup unsalted butter, room temperature,
   cut into cubes

2 bunches scallions (white and green parts),
   washed, trimmed, dried, and chopped

Freshly ground pepper

1. Place the potatoes in a saucepan with cold water to cover by about 1 inch. Season with salt and place over high heat. Bring to a boil, then lower the heat and simmer for about 20 minutes or until the point of a small knife can be easily inserted into the potatoes.

2. While the potatoes are cooking, combine the milk and butter in a small saucepan over low heat. Heat until the milk is very hot and the butter has melted. Remove from the heat, but keep very warm.

3. Remove the potatoes from the heat and drain well. Return the potatoes to the cooking pan and place over low heat. Cook, stirring lightly, for a minute or two just to remove any excess moisture.

4. Push the potatoes through a food mill or ricer into a warm bowl. Slowly add the hot milk mixture, beating with a wooden spoon to blend and lighten. Add the scallions, stirring to incorporate. Season with salt and pepper and serve.

TIP: Left-over champ makes great potato pancakes. When chilled, it will form into cakes very easily. Fry in clarified butter (or olive oil or—best of all—bacon fat) for a few minutes or until heated through and nicely browned around the edges.

The Chicken Potpie That Nana Made and We All Still Make

SERVES 6 TO 8

Chris: Longing for home on a chilly, foggy San Francisco afternoon, I decided to make a chicken potpie. I was feeling a bit challenged as I wasn't sure that I could live up to my potpie heritage. Nana, Mom's mom, made the flakiest piecrust you have ever tasted and I had spent my teenage years living off of the acclaimed chicken pies that my mom made at her bakery. I called Mom and got the basic recipe, did my shopping, and announced to Canada that we were going to have a MooMoo dinner. I was worried that I had overestimated my skills but forged ahead. I was aiming for Nana's light, buttery crust and a pie that could be cut into nice even pieces with just a modest oozing of gravy. But although the finished pie looked terrific, the crust wasn't as flaky as I had hoped and the filling ran all over the place once I cut into it. Didn't matter—Canada loved it and so did I.

Determined to master the craft, we added chicken pie to our favorite menu list. After a few tries, I'd like to think that mine is now equal to Nana's. I always use organic vegetables, but conventional can easily be substituted.

🍷 CHRIS'S SUGGESTED WINE PAIRING
A FRUITY CALIFORNIA PINOT NOIR

Canada: I love making chicken pie with my dad—it's a family affair. My favorite job is peeling the potatoes. Then when it goes in the oven the clock just seems to move in slow motion. But it is worth the wait because when we sit down to eat, I feel immediately warm and cozy and it fills me up fast. Eating the leftovers in my lunch the next day is great, too.

My mother made extraordinary pastry, as did my father's sister, Mary Frances. Their skill intimidated me, and until I decided to make potpies commercially, I never made my own pastry; I would always ask Mom to make it for me. So, when business called, I had to spend many, many hours carefully watching her make her famous pie dough. Torturing us with her skill and our ineptitude, she worked with me and my dear friend, Hu Pope, who would be making the pastry daily in the bakery. Of course, the fact that she never measured anything and kept telling us that it was all in the feel didn't help either. We eventually got it, but I still believe that it was mainly the use of a big Hobart mixer and a commercial pie-shell press—which kept our hot hands from touching the dough—that gave our acclaimed pastry the same flaky texture of her homemade dough. Years in the bakery eventually eliminated all intimidation and now I fearlessly tackle pastry making. I usually do a fine job but I still miss my mom's touch. Since I made chicken pies every day for ten years, today I generally leave their preparation to the kids, except for those chilly days when I most miss my mom.

When I was a child, chicken pie was often made from left-over roast chicken and gravy. It is one of those homey dishes that can be made in almost any way—it can be chicken or turkey, it can be dark and white meat, or all white meat, chopped, shredded, or cubed; the vegetables can be diced, sliced (Chris's method), or chunked; mushrooms, fennel, squash, or other ingredients can be added. You get the picture. This is the basic recipe—it's up to you to make it your own.

1 (4-pound) chicken, rinsed and cut into pieces (or 2 pounds boneless, skinless chicken breasts cooked in about 3 cups canned, nonfat low-sodium chicken broth)

Coarse salt and freshly ground pepper

Nana's Flaky Piecrust (recipe follows)

4 organic carrots, washed well, trimmed, and cubed

3 medium organic potatoes, washed well and cubed

1 organic onion, diced

1 cup frozen petit peas, thawed

2½ tablespoons chicken fat or butter

2½ tablespoons sifted all-purpose flour

1. Place the chicken in a heavy soup pot, cover with cold water, and season with salt and pepper. Place over high heat and bring to a boil. Lower the heat to a simmer, cover, and cook for about 1 hour or until the chicken is cooked through.

2. While the chicken is cooking, make and roll out the pastry (recipe follows). Fit one piece into a 10-inch pie plate. Set aside.

3. Remove the chicken from the heat and strain the liquid through a fine sieve, separately reserving the chicken and cooking liquid. Set aside to cool.

4. When cool, remove and discard the chicken skin. Pull the meat from the bones and, if necessary, cut it into bite-size pieces. Place the meat in a heatproof bowl and discard the bones. Set the meat aside.

5. Preheat the oven to 450°F.

6. Pour 3 cups of the reserved cooking liquid into a large saucepan. Place over medium-high heat and bring to a boil. Add the carrots, potatoes, and onion and again bring to a boil. Season with salt and pepper, lower the heat, and simmer for about 12 minutes, or just until the vegetables are barely cooked. Remove from the heat and stir in the peas. Drain the vegetables, reserving the liquid.

7. Place the chicken fat or butter in a saucepan over medium heat. When melted, stir in the flour. When blended, whisk in 2 cups of the hot broth, cooking for about 5 minutes or until the broth has thickened. Pour the thickened gravy over the chicken meat. Add the cooked vegetables along with the thawed peas, gently folding the mixture together. If the mixture seems too thick, fold in some of the remaining unthickened cooking liquid.

8. Pour the mixture into the prepared pie plate. Fold the top crust in half over the rolling pin, lift, and place over the filling. Unfold to cover the filling and attach to the bottom crust by pressing the excess dough from the edge of the top and bottom crust together with your fingertips. Fold the pressed dough edge up and inward, making a rim around the edge of the pie. Starting at the edge opposite you, pinch the dough between your thumb and index finger around the edge of the pie at about ¾-inch intervals, forming a fluted design. (The pie may be made up to this point and stored frozen, well wrapped, for up to 3 months).

9. Place the pie on a baking sheet in the preheated oven and bake for 15 minutes. Lower the heat to 350°F for an additional 20 minutes or until the crust is golden and the filling is almost bubbling out.

Nana's Flaky Pie Pastry

ENOUGH DOUGH FOR ONE DOUBLE-CRUST 10-INCH PIE

2½ cups all-purpose flour, sifted

¼ teaspoon salt

Pinch of sugar

¾ cup plus 1 tablespoon vegetable shortening, chilled

½ cup unsalted butter, cut into cubes and chilled

½ cup ice water

1. Combine the flour, salt, and sugar in the bowl of a food processor fitted with the metal blade. Process to aerate and blend.

2. Add the shortening and butter, and using quick on-and-off turns, process just until crumbly. With the motor running, add the water and process just until the dough begins to form a ball. Scrape the dough from the processor bowl and divide it into two equal pieces. Wrap each piece in plastic film and refrigerate for about 30 minutes to chill before rolling. The dough may also be frozen; thaw before using.

TIP: If you can find excellent quality lard and you aren't concerned about fat in your diet, use it in place of the vegetable shortening and butter when making a savory pie. It adds a wonderful meaty flavor.

Making Perfect Pastry Dough

My mother never used a food processor to make her dough but I think it turns out great pastry, particularly because the processor allows you to make quick and easy work of the job without handling the dough too much. However, if you overprocess, the heat created from the machine's motor will toughen the dough.

Some pastry recipes give an approximate measurement for the water, but approximations are, I think, a bit scary. How do you tell when enough is enough if you're not a seasoned cook? Most approximations are based on flavor so it really becomes a matter of taste, but with pastry making it is all up to the kitchen witch. Rainy days, humid days, hot days, warm kitchen, glutinous flour—all of these play a role in how much water will suffice to create a dough that just holds together and does not toughen. I've found that a half cup of water is nearly always the correct amount. Add the water slowly and watch carefully. The incorporation moves much more quickly with the food processor than it does when making dough by hand.

If you have never made pastry before, the rolling out is usually the most daunting step. Wondra flour is terrific for flouring the work surface and the rolling pin as it only adds a fine coating of flour to the dough. Then, don't panic; use a light hand, pushing the dough out from the center, sprinkling it and the rolling pin with more Wondra if it starts to stick. Lift the pin gently as you near the edge of the pastry to prevent breakage. When the desired size is reached, lift the pastry by carefully folding it in half over the rolling pin and slip it, still folded, into the pie plate. Slowly unfold it to cover the bottom of the plate and remove the rolling pin. Do not stretch the dough or it will shrink when baked. If the pastry tears, not to worry—just gently pinch it back together. Smooth the pastry down into the plate with quick pressing movements.

Pepper Steak

SERVES 6

Pepper steak—you say, what? And no, I'm not talking about steak au poivre! Although I had a recipe for it in my favorite cookbook, *Meat and Potatoes*, until recently I had long forgotten about this childhood favorite. Once the made-at-home replica of take-out Chinese food, as well as a mom-and-pop diner specialty, pepper steak probably hasn't been seen on a restaurant menu for decades. A couple of years ago, a big bag of bargain bell peppers brought up some nostalgia for my mom's cooking and what popped to mind but pepper steak. Once I got it going in the pan, I knew why it had been popular—thrifty, aromatic, vaguely Chinese, and quite delicious! We loved it and it has made a return to our everyday meals. Traditionally, pepper steak always has celery; however, I'm not a fan of cooked celery so I eliminate it. Feel free to add a cup of bias-sliced stalks if you are looking for the authentic 1950s taste.

1½ pounds lean top-round steak, cut about 1½ inches thick

Approximately ¼ cup Wondra flour

Salt and pepper

3 tablespoons canola oil

½ cup nonfat low-sodium beef broth

¼ cup light soy sauce (or more or less as desired)

1 teaspoon minced garlic

1 teaspoon minced ginger

6 large button mushrooms, cleaned and sliced

1 large onion, thinly sliced lengthwise

1 large red bell pepper, cored, trimmed, seeded, and cut lengthwise into thin strips

1 large green bell pepper, cored, trimmed, seeded, and cut lengthwise into thin strips

2 cups cherry or grape tomatoes, halved, or 3 medium tomatoes, cored and cut lengthwise into sixths

1 tablespoon cornstarch dissolved in 1 tablespoon cold water

½ cup sliced scallions, including some green part

Cooked white rice for 6

1. Using a chef's knife, slice the steak crosswise into strips about 3 inches long and ¼ inch thick. Sprinkle the strips with the flour and season with salt and pepper.

2. Heat the oil in a large frying pan (or wok) over medium-high heat. Add the beef, without crowding the pan, and fry, lifting and turning frequently (tongs help), for about 5 minutes or until nicely browned. Remove from the pan and place on a double layer of paper towels to drain.

3. Using paper towels, carefully wipe the excess oil from the pan, leaving any browned bits on the bottom. Return the pan to medium heat and add the broth, soy sauce, garlic, and ginger and bring to a simmer. Return the meat to the pan, cover, and simmer for about 15 minutes or until the meat is tender.

4. Add the mushrooms, tomatoes, onion, and bell peppers. Stir in the cornstarch mixture and bring to a simmer. Simmer, tossing and stirring, for about 1 minute or until the sauce has thickened. Stir in the scallions and remove from the heat.

5. Serve, spooned over rice.

Beef Stew

SERVES 6 TO 8

Although we don't eat a lot of beef, I have kept a good, hearty stew in our menu rota-tion throughout the years. It is so easy to put together and gets better the longer you let the flavors meld, making it a terrific do-ahead recipe to store in the fridge (or freezer) for a busy winter day. The red wine adds some oomph, but it isn't a necessity, and can be replaced with beef stock or even water. But no matter what you do, a good stew has to have carrots and potatoes.

 CHRIS'S SUGGESTED WINE PAIRING
USE A BETTER VERSION OF WHATEVER YOU USED TO MAKE THE STEW

2 pounds boneless, lean beef stew meat, cut into 1½-inch cubes

1 cup all-purpose flour

Salt and pepper

3 tablespoons canola oil

3 cloves garlic, minced

1 cup diced onion

1 tablespoon tomato paste

1 bay leaf

2 cups beef stock or nonfat low-sodium beef broth

1 cup dry red wine (optional)

1 pound carrots, peeled and cut into large pieces

1 pound Yukon gold potatoes, peeled and cut into large pieces

1 (10-ounce) package frozen petit peas, thawed

1. Place the beef on a cutting board and sprinkle with the flour and salt and pepper. Using your hands, toss until each piece of meat is generously coated.

2. Heat the oil in a large Dutch oven or other heavy-bottomed pot over medium-high heat. When hot, lower the heat slightly, and add the seasoned beef, a few pieces at a time, and sear, turning occasionally, until all sides are nicely browned. Using a slotted spoon, lift the browned meat to a plate and continue searing until all the meat has been browned. If the pan gets too dry, add a bit more oil, but you do want to keep all of those little browned bits in the bottom.

3. Add the garlic and onions to the hot pan and cook, stirring frequently, for about 4 minutes or just until the aromatics start to soften. Stir in the tomato paste and bay leaf and cook, stirring, for a minute or so.

4. Return the meat (along with any accumulated juices) to the pan. Add the stock (or broth) along with the wine. Add just enough water to allow the liquid to cover the meat by 1½ inches. Bring to a boil and then lower the heat and simmer for about 30 minutes, or until the meat is just about cooked.

5. Add the carrots and potatoes, raise the heat, and bring to a simmer. Taste, and if necessary, add salt and pepper. Lower the heat and cook at a low simmer for about 20 minutes or until the meat and vegetables are tender.

6. If the cooking liquid seems too thin or watery, work 1 tablespoon of butter into 1 tablespoon of all-purpose flour, and when totally incorporated, stir the mixture, a bit at a time, into the stew until the gravy is as thick as you like. Let it cook for a couple of minutes to remove the raw flour taste.

7. Stir in the peas and cook to just heat through.

8. Remove the bay leaf and serve family style in a large tureen or bowl at the table, or in individual portions in large, shallow soup bowls.

Stuffed Cabbage

SERVES 6

When a chill is in the air, I'm drawn to making substantial meals, and stuffed cabbage is surely one of those. A perennial favorite throughout Eastern Europe, Scandinavia, Russia, and the Middle East, it won't be found on American menus—unless you are dining in a mom-and-pop restaurant in the heartland. There seem to be a million fillings—meat, vegetable, or starch based, while the sauce ranges from tomato to sour cream. I have always made a tomato sauce. I use either regular cabbage or Savoy—never red, but only because it looks yucky in the tomato base. You can adapt the recipe to your taste by incorporating favorite herbs—dill is one of mine—and differing mixtures of ground meats and grains. This recipe is a family original using ground sirloin and long-grain rice. I add mushrooms to the sauce because we all like them, but they are definitely optional. And, by the by, the filling and sauce are perfectly companionable to stuffed bell peppers, eggplant, or squash.

12 large green cabbage leaves

1 pound ground sirloin (or ground chicken or turkey)

1 cup cooked long-grain rice

3 cups canned diced tomatoes in puree

1 cup beef (or chicken) stock or nonfat low-sodium beef (or chicken) broth

3 tablespoons light brown sugar

2 tablespoons (or more) red wine vinegar

1½ cups minced onion

1 large egg

2 tablespoons finely chopped fresh parsley leaves

1 tablespoon minced garlic

1 tablespoon tomato paste

Coarse salt and freshly ground pepper

1. Set a large bowl of ice water aside.

2. Bring a large pot of water to a boil over high heat. Working with one at a time, place the cabbage leaves in the boiling water for about 1 minute or until just barely softened. Immediately dip each softened leaf into the ice water to stop the cooking. Drain well and pat dry.

3. When all of the leaves have been blanched and dried, set them aside. (If the main vein at the core end of the leaf is very thick, you can pare it down slightly with a paring knife. Don't get overzealous, as the leaf has to be sturdy enough to hold the filling.)

4. Preheat the oven to 375°F.

5. Combine the tomatoes, stock, light brown sugar, and vinegar in a large Dutch oven. Stir in 1 cup of the onions, place over medium heat, and bring to a low simmer. (Here you can add sliced fresh mushrooms or rehydrated dried mushrooms if you like.)

6. While the sauce is coming to a simmer, combine the meat and rice with the remaining ½ cup of the onions in a mixing bowl. Add the egg, parsley, garlic, and tomato paste, and season with salt and pepper. Using your hands, gently squish the mixture together until well combined without mashing the rice.

7. Working with one leaf at a time, place a portion of the filling near the core end. Fold in each side of the leaf to almost cover the filling. Fold the stem end over

and continue to roll to completely enclose the filling. Using a toothpick, close the roll together at the end by weaving the toothpick in and out to hold the leaf tightly around the filling.

8. Carefully place all of the cabbage rolls into the simmering sauce, cover, and transfer to the preheated oven. Bake for about 45 minutes, or until the filling is done and the leaves are very tender. Serve immediately, or cool and store, covered and refrigerated, for up to 3 days. May also be frozen.

Chris's Paella

SERVES 6 TO 10

Chris: A few Christmases ago, friends gave me a wonderful gift—a paella pan, Spanish olive oil, saffron, and Spanish sweet pimenton. I wasted no time in taking it all for a test drive, making my first paella to celebrate New Year's Eve with my daughter, Canada. I love one-pot cooking, so my love affair with paella began instantly. Unfortunately, I failed to get a good, golden crust on the bottom (the mark of a truly excellent paella) on my first attempt, but I made it again within a few weeks and nailed it. Paella has become a go-to recipe for me and as long as I am familiar with the heat source, I can now almost always get a great crust without burning the bottom layer of rice. The most traditional heat source would be an open outdoor fire, but I haven't tried that one yet. I did have to purchase a heat diffuser for my stove to help distribute the heat evenly over the bottom of the pan, which I highly recommend. You can add almost any seafood, meat, sausage, or veggie you like. Whatever you do, you will eat well!

 CHRIS'S SUGGESTED WINE PAIRING
STAY IN SPAIN, PERHAPS AN UNOAKED TEMPRANILLO

8 threads saffron per serving

½ cup dry white wine

¼ cup Spanish olive oil

1 chicken leg or thigh per serving

¼ cup diced onion per serving

1 clove garlic, minced, per serving

1 red bell pepper, stemmed, seeded, and diced

1 green bell pepper, stemmed, seeded, and diced

As much chorizo as you like, cut into chunks

½ cup uncooked Valencia rice per serving

½ teaspoon pimenton per serving

1 cup hot chicken, fish, or vegetable stock (or broth) per ½ cup rice, plus a little extra in case the rice eats up the liquid too fast

2 prawns per serving

2 clams per serving

1 artichoke heart (or more) per serving

1. Place the saffron threads in a small pan over medium heat and toast, stirring occasionally, for about 1 minute or until fragrant. Add the wine and bring to a simmer. Immediately remove from the heat and set aside.

2. Heat the oil in the paella pan. When hot, add the chicken and fry, turning frequently, for about 15 minutes or until just barely cooked through. Move the chicken to the outer edge of the pan.

3. Add the onion and sauté for 5 minutes. Then, stir in the garlic and sauté for another minute. Stir in the red and green pepper and sauté for about 4 minutes or just until it begins to soften. Add the chorizo and cook, stirring, to brown slightly.

4. When the chorizo is nicely colored, add the rice and cook, stirring, for about 2 minutes or until the rice is glistening with oil and the pan juices. Stir in the pimenton and then the saffron-infused wine.

5. Add the hot stock and bring to a boil. When boiling, scrape the bottom of the pan. Immediately lower the heat to a bare simmer. Do not stir again, as you want the crust to form in the first 10 minutes. Place the prawns, clams, and artichoke hearts on top of the rice; the rising steam will cook them. (I tend to push the clams slightly into the rice to ensure that they get enough heat to cook and open.) Cook for another 15 minutes and then check the rice for doneness. It should be just a tiny bit toothy.

6. Remove from the heat and serve directly from the pan. You can garnish with lemon wedges and chopped parsley if you want to fancy it up, but we usually just dive right in.

Judie's Paella

When our friends Lynn and Doug joined us in San Francisco one year, Chris served his much-loved paella, a dish he continues to improve upon, always aiming for the perfect crunchy, just-below-burnt rice bottom. Once home, Lynn insisted that I replicate Chris's dinner, so I followed his recipe and took a stab at the perfect paella. Mine was nowhere near as good as his—to which Chris said, "You've got better chops than that"—but it was still pretty darn good. Unfortunately I made enough for twelve instead of the six I was aiming for, so being inundated with leftovers meant that paella didn't pop back up on the everyday menu for quite a while.

Roasting Chicken Three Ways

Every cook I know—doesn't matter whether they're a home cook or a seasoned chef— thinks that they have the perfect method to roast a chicken. And I can tell you that any cook worth his salt does in fact; each one may be different, but I've found, no matter the style, the roast is usually delicious. I've had my share of roast chicken prepared by great chefs as well as ordinary cooks and only occasionally have I had a bad one. When people talk about tasteless, dry, stringy meat, I just don't get it! I don't know if I'm worth my salt but my method is pretty straightforward and has fed many mouths over the years. In the old days, I didn't (nor did anyone I knew) brine my bird, but now I always do.

To brine, mix equal parts sugar and salt (about 3 tablespoons each) with whatever herbs you have on hand in a resealable plastic bag. Fill it about half full with cold water, seal, and shake and shake to dissolve the salt and sugar. Wash and clean up the chicken and place it into the bag, reseal, and refrigerate for a couple of hours. Then remove the chicken from the fridge and drain it. Rinse the chicken under cold running water and pat dry. Set aside for about 20 minutes to come to room temperature.

Preheat the oven to 450°F. Cut a lemon in half and rub the skin with the cut side, making sure that the juice really coats the skin. Season both the skin and the cavity with salt and pepper. If you like, stuff an onion, a lemon, an apple, or a bunch of herbs into the cavity—do remember that whatever you put in will flavor the meat. Place the chicken on a rack in a roasting pan and transfer to the hot oven. Roast for about an hour or until the skin is golden brown and crisp and an instant-read thermometer inserted into the thickest part reads 160°F. I know, the USDA says 175°F, but I find that if you roast to 160°F and then let the chicken rest for a bit before carving, the internal temperate still rises and the meat is thoroughly cooked without being overcooked.

🍷 CHRIS'S SUGGESTED WINE PAIRING
AN EARTHY OREGON PINOT NOIR

Chris: I kinda steal from the Zuni Café (a highly acclaimed San Francisco restaurant whose chef, Judy Rodgers, is known for her roast chicken with bread salad among other deliciousness), giving my roasters a 48-hour dry brine. I wash and dry the bird (one no bigger than 3½ pounds) and then generously pat with coarse salt. (**Judie:** "I think Zuni uses a salt and pepper mix for their dry brine.") If I have them on hand, I place some herbs—parsley, sage, thyme, or rosemary, or a combo—under the skin. Don't overdo the herbs—you just want a hint of their flavor in the meat.

I lay the seasoned chicken in a small roasting pan and place it in the fridge for 48 hours—this means I have to decide that I'm going to have roast chicken for dinner 2 days hence, so I generally plan it for a Sunday supper. About an hour before I am ready to roast, I preheat the oven to 450°F and remove the chicken from the fridge to bring it to room temperature. About a half hour before I am ready to roast, I put the pan in the oven to get it good and hot. I pat the skin dry and pop the chicken into the very hot pan and even hotter oven and roast for 1 hour. Moist and fragrant meat and extra crispy skin is the result. I know my method cannot be challenged!

Mickey: Unlike my usual obsessive behavior, I do different things when roasting a chicken. Sometimes I brine the chicken and sometimes I just cook the whole breast with a salt-and-butter rub in a hot oven. I've recently tried a *Cooks Illustrated* method of putting the salted, whole chicken in a preheated, hot pan in the oven and cooking it for about 25 minutes. Then, the oven is turned off and the chicken sits in the hot oven for another 25 minutes until it is done. In typical crazy Mickey fashion, I usually prepare a reduced chicken *jus* using my veal *jus* technique. I cook the *jus* down until it's nice and viscous and glossy. I then sauce the sliced breast and legs and mashed potatoes (which I almost always serve with roast chicken).

Fake Tandoori Chicken

SERVES 4 TO 6

If you want to try a completely different take on roasting chicken, give my tandoori chicken a go. In case you are unfamiliar with this dish, a tandoor is a traditional Indian (and other Southeast Asian) clay oven that uses wood or charcoal as its heat source. Temperatures in the oven are maintained at 450°F to 500°F. I have an old stove that seems to hit and hold that temperature well, and during the summer months, we heat up our charcoal-fired grill as high as the thermometer on the lid says it can go and tandoor our chicken in the hot smoky heat. It turns out an absolutely delicious roasted chicken. It may not look quite as glorious as a tandoor-burnished traditional Indian one, but it sure tastes great. Just a hint of the spices permeates the extremely tender, moist meat. I do recommend that you try it—I believe that my fake tandoori chicken will become your go-to dinner-party dish.

You can either leave the chicken whole or cut it into pieces. When I use cut-up chicken I make the classic slits in the skin to absorb the marinade. For the whole bird, I simply marinate it in the yogurt-spice mixture for 24 hours. A longer marinade might turn the chicken mushy but this amount of time seems perfect. If you want the chicken to be really orange-brown, you can brush it with orange food coloring before putting it in the marinade—though I personally prefer a more natural hue.

2½ cups plain whole yogurt

2 tablespoons fresh lime juice

½ to 1 hot red chili, seeded and chopped

¾ cup chopped onion

1 tablespoon minced fresh ginger

1 teaspoon minced fresh garlic

1 tablespoon paprika

2 teaspoons garam masala

1 teaspoon turmeric

1 (3½- to 4-pound) roasting chicken, preferably free-range and antibiotic free

1. Combine the yogurt and lime juice in the bowl of a food processor fitted with the metal blade and process to just combine. Add the chili, onion, ginger, and garlic and process to blend. Add the paprika, garam masala, and turmeric and process until almost smooth.

2. Place the chicken in a large resealable plastic bag. Add the yogurt mixture, seal, and toss to cover well. Place in the refrigerator and allow to marinate for 24 hours, turning the bag from time to time to insure that the marinade tenderizes all of the chicken.

3. About 30 minutes before you are ready to roast, preheat your oven to 500°F or make a very hot large charcoal fire on one side of a covered grill—you will want the temperature to reach 500°F before you add the chicken.

4. Remove the chicken from the plastic bag and turn it so that excess marinade drips out of the cavity. Place the chicken on a rack in a roasting pan or on the grill rack on the far opposite side of the grill fire. Cover and begin roasting, turning the chicken occasionally to insure that it is cooking evenly. Add charcoal as necessary to maintain the hot fire. If preparing in the oven, cooking should take no more than 40 minutes; on the grill, it can take about 2 hours for the chicken to be perfectly cooked throughout.

5. Remove from the oven or grill and let rest for about 15 minutes before cutting into pieces.

Chicken Meets Lemon

To me, lemon and chicken are the perfect mates. Even a grilled half chicken seasoned with a touch of lemon juice and zest and salt and pepper makes an easy, quietly elegant meal. One of my favorite chicken-lemon duos is also one of my go-to dishes when we gather friends for a Saturday-night supper. Here's what you do: place chicken pieces, skin side down, in a single layer in a baking dish (a decorative one can come straight to the table). Mix 1 cup of lemon juice with ½ cup each of olive oil and chicken stock, 2 tablespoons of minced garlic, and 1 tablespoon of lemon zest. Pour it over the chicken and season with a good amount of salt and pepper. Place in a preheated 400°F oven and bake for about 45 minutes or until the chicken is cooked through and golden brown. Remove from the oven and sprinkle with lots of chopped parsley. Serve with garlic bread, a tossed salad, and a crisp white wine. You'll never get your guests to leave the table.

Another chicken-lemon match came a while back, when I got it in my head to try to find what used to be normal-size chickens—about 2 to 2½ pounds. An impossibility! You can find a chicken breast half that weighs almost that much but no delicate small birds are to be sourced anywhere, unless you buy those fattened little creatures called Cornish game hens (yes, I know they are just little chickens, but somehow they don't

say that to me) or are lucky enough to have a butcher that carries real *poussin* (chickens under 1 month old that weigh under 2 pounds). So, my best buddy Lynn cornered Chrissy Chiacchia from Gaia's Breath Farm (see Sources) at the Cooperstown Farmers Market and got her to agree to raise some small chickens for me to try.

When the chickens came home to roost I had forgotten exactly what I had planned to do with them, but it didn't take long to come up with a dish that would do them proud, of course using lemons. I thought about doing a braise on the grill. I had a container of Kalamata olives and a small jar of three preserved lemons on hand, which I felt might be the perfect flavor combo to give a pungent punch to the little guys. The mix of the smoke from the grill and the wonderful farm-fresh flavor of the tender chicken, wedded to the lemons and salty olives, made for a very memorable and oft-repeated meal.

Grilled Chicken with Kalamata Olives, Potatoes, and Preserved Lemons

SERVES 4 TO 6

TIP: This recipe should serve six people unless you are used to giant pieces of chicken— it would then feed four amply. And, if you don't have a grill handy, it will work just fine in the oven.

3 (2- to 2½-pound) chickens, rinsed and patted dry

3 small fresh spring onions or very small sweet onions

1 cup white wine

⅓ cup extra virgin olive oil

3 preserved lemons with their preserving liquid

1 cup Kalamata olives

About 2 to 3 tablespoons torn fresh mint leaves

About 1 tablespoon fresh thyme leaves

About 1 tablespoon torn fresh sage leaves

About 1 tablespoon torn fresh basil leaves

Whatever chicken giblets that came with the chickens except the livers

About 2 pounds small new potatoes, halved

Freshly ground pepper

1. Preheat the grill or oven to 400°F. If using charcoal, as we do, build a hot fire on one side of the grill and place the grill racks on. I don't have any real experience with gas grills but would imagine you could heat one side of a gas grill as well.

2. Place an onion in the cavity of each chicken.

3. Place the chickens in a large baking dish—I use my largest cast-iron skillet. Pour in the wine and olive oil.

4. Slice the lemons crosswise, and randomly place the slices around the chickens and into the liquid. Add the olives and herbs to the pan along with the giblets. Nestle the potatoes around the chickens. Pour whatever preserved lemon liquid that remains in the container over the chickens and then liberally sprinkle pepper over all.

5. Place the pan on the grill away from the fire. Cover and roast, adding coals to keep the fire at about 400°F for the first hour. Continue to roast for about another 30 minutes or until the chickens are golden brown and cooked through. The fire can be less hot for the final 30 minutes. This seems like a long time and it may take less, depending how hot and reliable your grill is. If cooking in the oven, the chickens should be done in about 40 minutes.

6. Remove from the grill or oven and let rest for a few minutes. Cut each chicken in half and serve with the potatoes, lemon slices, and olives, and any pan juices.

OVERLEAF: *Grilled Chicken with Kalamata Olives, Potatoes, and Preserved Lemons*

Favorite Chicken

I had my first inkling that Mickey was going to turn into a bon vivant/gourmand after he went to college. His credit-card charges at the refined, really-for-parents-alumni-and-visitors dining room gave the first indication; then, when he moved into a townhouse, the calls for kitchen advice and wine suggestions began to come fast and furious. And finally, one evening late in his university years, we met for dinner at a country inn and he ordered "scotch, neat" and I knew I was in for trouble. As Frenchified as his taste became, what eventually came to be known simply as Favorite Chicken was the first dish I heard his friends request he make. It is a simple recipe, but it always manages to be the diner's favorite. Although I have tried to make it for Alexander and Clara, they always say, "It doesn't taste like Dad's."

Mickey: Favorite Chicken was the first dish I really cooked extensively and made my own. It wasn't a dish that Mom prepared regularly for us when we were growing up, but I think it evolved out of her breaded veal cutlets, which she did often make. I first attempted it during my senior year in college, when I lived with roommates in an on-campus townhouse. Then, when I graduated from college, I sometimes made Favorite Chicken for Uncle Kol. I'd serve it with some cheap Mouton Cadet red wine and we'd sit and eat together like grown-ups at the beat-up old table in the TV room in the apartment I had grown up in. I'm sure I made it for my first dinner party and I know I made it for Laurel when we first began dating. (**Laurel:** "I remember very clearly when Mickey made me Favorite Chicken for the first time [then called Chicken Mickey—it only came to be known as Favorite Chicken once the kids came along]. He was very proud of it as a meal, not just a main course. I thought it was delicious then and still do today. It is the combination of the balsamic vinaigrette, salad, rice, and chicken cutlets that makes this Favorite Chicken. Perhaps the fact that Mickey could make even chicken cutlets special should have been my first clue that I was getting involved with someone who has extraordinary cooking skills!")

Favorite Chicken is not just a breaded boneless chicken breast fried in vegetable oil, it's also what accompanies it. Originally white rice but now brown, and a simple green salad (always with cucumber, and I like endive and tomatoes, although the rest of my family doesn't) tossed with balsamic vinaigrette. Fresh lemon is squeezed on the chicken but the vinaigrette is what ties everything together because you sort of mix everything up on the plate and eat it just like my brother used to do with roast chicken, rice, peas, and applesauce when we were kids. A further note: the chicken must be breaded with Progresso Italian Style bread crumbs, and I actually prefer to slice and pound the chicken breasts very thin, myself. We still eat this dish several times a month.

Here's how you make it: pull off the tenderloins from boneless chicken breasts. Holding the knife horizontally, slice the breasts in half by laying your palm on top of each breast half and carefully cutting through the breast to make two thin pieces. If the pieces are too thick, pound them with the side of a large knife or cleaver to flatten slightly. Dip the thin cutlets and tenderloins first in flour, then in beaten eggs, and finally in Italian-style bread crumbs. Heat a nice slick of vegetable oil in a large frying pan over medium-high heat. When hot, add the breaded chicken and fry, turning once, until both sides are light golden brown. This should take about ten minutes, but if very thin it will take less. Serve with lemon slices, steamed brown rice, and green salad (mesclun, cucumbers, sliced endive and sliced tomatoes) with balsamic vinaigrette. For the balsamic vinaigrette I use 2 parts olive oil, 1 part balsamic vinegar, 1 tablespoon Dijon mustard, plus celery salt, black pepper, and if you have them on hand, onion powder and garlic powder.

CHRIS'S SUGGESTED WINE PAIRING
EITHER A CHARDONNAY OR A VERY LIGHT RED WINE

Chicken Under a Brick

Some years ago—perhaps with the advance of "up-scale"—that is, not "red sauce"—Italian restaurants, everyone was grilling chicken under a brick (or *pollo al mattone* as Tuscans call it). It became so popular that it was no longer actually cooked under a brick, but under a heavy cast-iron implement made specifically for the job. Traditionally, the chicken is not split into 2 pieces; it is simply opened up by cutting out the backbone. But I prefer to cut it in half for quicker and easier cooking. (**Chris:** "I still use a brick wrapped in aluminum foil and, of course, keep the chicken in one piece in the correct Italian way.")

I use Cornish game hens and cut out the backbone and split the birds in half along the breast; then, I marinate the meat for about 30 minutes in some olive oil, lemon zest, herbs (usually rosemary and oregano, but you can use whatever you have on hand), and just a little lemon juice. I put my grill pan on high heat, and when it is glowing, I quickly season the birds with a good dose of salt and pepper and pop them in skin side down, cover with my cast-iron "brick," and wait a few minutes until they get golden brown and crusty. Then I give the birds a turn, cover again, and in another few minutes we sit down to devour some deliciously moist and lemony chicken with crisp, salty skin.

🍷 CHRIS'S SUGGESTED WINE PAIRING
AN IGT TUSCAN SANGIOVESE

Talking About Pork

We're all big fans of pork—which is a great bargain meat. I buy a whole loin on the bone, even when it's just for the two of us. I cut the hunk into pieces—usually one half and two quarters. The half I may or may not bone-out, and then I use it when friends are joining us for a weeknight dinner, and the quarters I use to make cutlets, stir-fries, medallions, or loaves. The bones that I remove are frozen for later use, either to be grilled with some zesty spices or added to beans or greens for additional flavor.

Pork tenderloins are my go-to for all kinds of meals—everyday and fancy. I love to give them a quick grill (wrapped in prosciutto to add a little seasoning and fat) to feature at a picnic or later on sandwiches. An easy fix is a quick sear on top of the stove and a 15-minute or so roast in a very hot oven. The meat is delicate, virtually fat-free, low in calories, and quite sweet. Shingled out over some couscous or polenta and drizzled with a little citrus vinaigrette (page 59)—it makes for a perfect quick-and-easy elegant meal.

Commercially available pork—that is pork found in supermarkets and most butcher shops—is so lean that its flavor is almost nonexistent and it can be very tough and near tasteless when grilled or roasted. So, we brine it before we cook it—whether on the grill, in braises, or in the oven—to add a subtle hint of herby saltiness and to tenderize. I generally do about ½ cup each of salt and sugar along with whatever herbs complement the finished dish—or if I am just roasting or grilling, whatever herbs I have on hand in addition to a bay leaf or two.

One of my favorite grills is a bone-in pork loin (brined) coated with olive oil, lemon zest, and salt and pepper, with herbs tucked in between the bones, and wrapped in garlic scapes. By the time the roast is ready, the scapes have disintegrated but permeated the meat with a definite sweet garlic flavor.

On more ambitious cooking nights, I will stuff a boneless pork loin. Because its flavor is relatively mild, you can use almost any stuffing for pork—fruit and nut is an old favorite, but an herbaceous bread stuffing would work, as would an aromatic rice or mushroom mixture. You can also wrap the pork with bacon, pancetta, prosciutto, or very thin slices of smoky ham. Mickey makes a version of this particular recipe—always for his annual Christmas tree-trimming party—and Chris is famed for his Tuscan Pork in Milk (page 93).

Garlic Scapes

If you aren't familiar with garlic scapes, they are simply "flower stalks" of hardneck garlic plants. Scapes are generally cut off of the growing plant early in the growing season as they pull energy from the developing bulb. Until recently, the scapes went into the garbage heap or the compost, even though they are edible and quite delicious. Both farmer and consumer awareness has brought them to the market—although usually only to farmers markets or roadside stands.

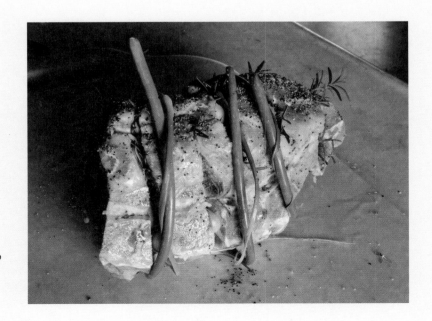

Stuffed Pork Loin

SERVES 8 TO 10

2 cups chopped dried apricots

½ cup raisins or chopped dried plums
   (or "prumes" as Mickey used to call them)

½ cup chopped walnuts, pecans, or whole pine nuts

1½ cups Calvados or other apple brandy or apple cider

1½ cups dry white wine

1 (5-pound) boneless pork loin

3 tablespoons unsalted butter

1¼ cups finely diced onion

About 2 cups dried bread crumbs or cubes
   (made in-house, as chefs say)

Coarse salt and pepper

About 2 tablespoons canola oil

1. Combine the apricots, raisins, and nuts in a bowl. Add the Calvados and ½ cup of the wine and set aside to marinate for at least 1 hour. (If you prefer an alcohol-free stuffing, use the cider.)

2. Using a sharp knife, carefully cut the pork open to make a neat, flat, solid piece of meat. This is best done by cutting from one side into the center (without cutting through to the edge) and then carefully folding the cut flap out. Then, cut from the interior out through the thicker piece to open another flap. Then gently push down to flatten the entire piece out. Cover with plastic film and let it come to room temperature.

3. When ready to stuff, place the butter in a frying pan over medium heat. Add the onion and garlic and sauté for about 4 minutes, or until softened. Scrape the warm onion mixture into the marinating fruit and nuts, stirring to blend well. Add the bread cubes, a bit at a time, to make a firm but wet stuffing. Season with salt and pepper.

4. Preheat the oven to 450°F.

5. Uncover the pork and carefully cover with an even layer of the stuffing, leaving about a 1-inch border

around the edges. Roll, cigar fashion, from the bottom up to make a neat log. Using butcher's twine, neatly tie the roll closed. Rub the exterior with oil and again season with salt and pepper.

6. Place the stuffed loin in a roasting pan along with the remaining white wine. Roast in the preheated oven for 30 minutes or until nicely colored. Lower the heat to 375°F and roast for an additional hour or until an instant-read thermometer inserted into the thickest part reads 160°F.

7. Remove from the oven and let rest for 15 minutes. Untie and cut, crosswise, into thin slices. Drizzle any pan juices over the sliced meat and serve.

Tuscan Pork in Milk

SERVES 6 TO 8

I really love this traditional Tuscan dish that Chris introduced to our table. Easy to prepare, it is a bit surprising to lovers of "red sauce" Italian food. It is Chris's go-to when entertaining friends for a Sunday supper, but I use a smaller piece of pork loin for an easy "just us" dinner. Chris is a more casual cook than Mickey and this has just the right amount of ease while still clearly saying, "I love to cook."

 CHRIS'S SUGGESTED WINE PAIRING
A BARBERA FROM THE PIEDMONT REGION

2 tablespoons olive oil

1 (5-pound) boneless pork shoulder, tied, or 4-pound boneless pork loin

Salt and pepper

4 cloves garlic, smashed

5 cups whole milk

½ lemon

1. Preheat the oven to 275°F.

2. Over medium-high setting, heat the oil in a heavy-bottomed pan or Dutch oven with a cover large enough to hold the pork tightly.

3. Generously season the pork with salt and pepper and place it in the hot pan. Sear, turning occasionally, for about 12 minutes, or until nicely browned on all sides.

4. Remove the pork from the pan and lower the heat. Add the garlic and cook, stirring, just until colored, about 1 minute.

5. Raise the heat and add the milk. It will bubble up for a few moments. Once the milk has settled, return the pork to the pan along with any accumulated juices. Cover and transfer to the preheated oven. Braise for 45 minutes and then uncover and flip the pork.

6. Again, cover the pan and return it to the oven. Braise for an additional 40 minutes or until a meat

thermometer inserted into the center reads 155°F. Remove from the oven and transfer the pork to a warm platter. Tent lightly to keep warm.

7. Place the pan over medium-high heat and bring to a boil. Lower the heat and simmer for about 5 minutes, or until reduced slightly. Using an immersion blender, process the sauce until smooth. Season with salt and pepper and add a squirt of lemon juice to brighten the flavor.

8. Cut the meat crosswise into generous slices and serve along with the sauce and a big mound of polenta.

Pork Scaloppine with Arugula Salad

SERVES 6

This is a favorite recipe that I make using the small cutlets that I cut from the loin (see page 90) and then pound to the requisite thinness. The finished dish rather mimics the classic and expensive veal scaloppine; in fact, I think it is better. You can also purchase thick boneless pork chops and cut them in half, crosswise. I generally allow two pieces per person. This recipe can be used with boneless chicken breasts instead. If you prefer the bone-in, just pound the meat around the bone; the bone will give you a handle to gnaw away on.

🍷 CHRIS'S SUGGESTED WINE PAIRING
A CHIANTI CLASSICO

  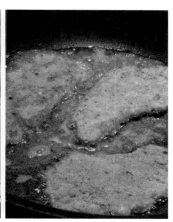

12 small pieces pork loin, trimmed of all fat and
sinew, about ³⁄₈ inch thick

2 large eggs

¼ cup milk

2 cups bread crumbs (plain or seasoned)

½ cup Wondra flour

Coarse salt and freshly ground pepper

¼ cup olive oil, plus more for dressing

6 large handfuls baby arugula (or other small
salad greens), washed well and dried

Juice of ½ lemon

Lemon quarters for drizzling

1. Preheat the oven to 200°F.

2. Line a baking sheet with parchment paper and
set aside.

3. Place each piece of pork between 2 sheets of waxed
or parchment paper. Working with one piece at a
time and using a small, heavy frying pan, pound the
meat out to about ⅛-inch thickness.

4. Combine the eggs and milk in a shallow dish,
whisking to blend well.

5. Combine the bread crumbs and flour in another
shallow dish. Season with salt and pepper and stir
to blend.

6. Working with one cutlet at a time, dip the meat
into the egg mixture, allowing excess to drip off.
Then, dip it into the bread-crumb mixture. If you prefer a heavy coating, again dip it into the egg, and then
the bread-crumb mixture. Place the coated cutlets
within easy reach of the stove.

7. Heat ¼ cup of the olive oil in a large frying pan
over medium-high heat. When very hot but not smoking, begin adding the cutlets, without crowding the
pan. Fry, turning once, for about 3 to 4 minutes, or until crisp and golden brown. Transfer to a double layer
of paper towels to drain. Then, carefully transfer to
the parchment-lined pan and place in the preheated
oven to keep warm while you continue frying the remaining cutlets. If the oil gets too dark and filled with
bits of the cooked coating, pour it out, wipe the pan
clean with paper towels, and start again with fresh oil.

8. When all of the cutlets are cooked, place 2 on each
of 6 warm dinner plates. Place the arugula in a mixing bowl and drizzle with olive oil and the juice of ½
lemon. Season with salt and pepper and mound equal
portions on top of the cutlets on the plates. Serve
with a lemon quarter for drizzling on the meat.

Making Mole

I got to be a self-proclaimed expert at Mexican cooking when I was doing a lot of consulting—advising large companies on how to introduce "ethnic" products into an ever-expanding marketplace. I will admit that I'm a bit lazy these days and don't use the mortar and pestle like I should, so mole making is not quite as time-consuming as it once was. Since Steve loves nothing better than the time he spends in Oaxaca, Mexico, an area known for its great moles, I have continued to make some version of this wonderfully rich, satisfying sauce for our "authentic" Mexican meals. I generally keep the sauce on hand to make chicken in mole sauce, which I serve with pinto beans, rice, and guacamole. It also gives us an excuse to serve *cerveza preparada* (a tomato juice, beer, and hot-sauce mix) or margaritas, toasting the many wonderful cooks south of our border.

The following is the sauce I make for mole *negro Oaxaqueño*. It is the base for chicken in mole sauce, Oaxaca-style. Tradition says to cook the chicken first to get a good, rich stock, and then proceed with the recipe, but I always have plenty of chicken stock in the freezer, so I use that to prepare the sauce and then introduce the chicken. Once I have the sauce made, I sear the chicken pieces (if cooking for a crowd I use all of

the sauce and cut up two whole chickens, but you could use any parts you like), add them to the sauce, and cook for about twenty-five minutes just before serving. When it's just me and Steve, I use about two cups of the sauce for a boneless, skin-on chicken breast half and a couple of legs. You can garnish with toasted sesame seeds or chopped cilantro if you like. Tradition also says to "use lard" but I opt for the healthier olive oil instead.

2 ounces guajillo chilies, seeded and stemmed

4 pasilla chilies, seeded and stemmed

4 ancho chilies, seeded and stemmed

5 tablespoons olive oil

Two ½-inch-thick slices French or Italian bread

1½ cups canned diced fire-roasted tomatoes with green chilies with juice

1 cup chopped onion

¼ cup diced dried apricots

¼ cup black raisins

¼ cup unsalted peanuts

¼ cup slivered almonds

¼ cup cilantro leaves

2 tablespoons minced garlic

1 tablespoon sesame seeds

1 teaspoon cracked black pepper

1 teaspoon dried thyme

1 teaspoon dried oregano

¼ teaspoon ground cloves

¼ teaspoon ground cinnamon

3 cups chicken stock or canned nonfat low-sodium chicken broth

2 bay leaves

2½ ounces unsweetened chocolate

Salt

1. Break the chilies into pieces and place in a small heatproof bowl. Cover with very hot water and set aside to soak for 1 hour or until very soft.

2. Heat 1 tablespoon of the olive oil in a frying pan over medium heat. Add the bread and fry for about 4 minutes, or until the bread is turning brown and the olive oil has been absorbed. Remove from the heat and set aside.

3. Drain the chilies, separately reserving the soaking water.

4. Combine the chilies with the tomatoes, onion, apricots, raisins, peanuts, almonds, cilantro, garlic, sesame seeds, pepper, thyme, oregano, cloves, and cinnamon in a large mixing bowl. Add the reserved bread pieces and toss to blend.

5. Working in batches, puree the mixture in a high-speed blender or food processor fitted with the metal blade, adding the reserved soaking water as needed to make a very thick pastelike puree.

6. Heat the remaining ¼ cup of olive oil in a large frying pan over medium heat. Add the paste and fry, stirring frequently, for about 7 minutes, or until the paste has taken on some color.

7. Scrape the paste into a large saucepan. Add the chicken stock and bay leaves and place over medium heat. Bring to a simmer, stirring frequently. Add the chocolate and continue to stir until the chocolate has melted into the sauce.

8. Season with salt, lower the heat, and cook, stirring occasionally, for about 25 minutes or until the flavors have blended nicely. (You can make the sauce up to this point; then cool, place in a nonreactive container, cover, and refrigerate for a few days or freeze for up to 3 months.)

9. If using the sauce immediately, sear the chicken as suggested, add to the sauce, and cook as directed in the introduction to the recipe.

Fancy Dining

Chris's Wine Advice

Fancy dining doesn't always mean fancy wine, but it sure is a great excuse to splurge. Champagne, with its high acid, cleanses the palate between bites and is an incredibly versatile food wine. It is particularly pleasing with salty foods or anything fried. I've even paired a beautiful rosé Champagne with red meat. Fancy dining is THE time to break out that special bottle that you have been holding on to for a festive occasion, a great time for the classic combos—a big Napa Valley cabernet and steak, Syrah with grilled lamb, or white Burgundy with lobster.

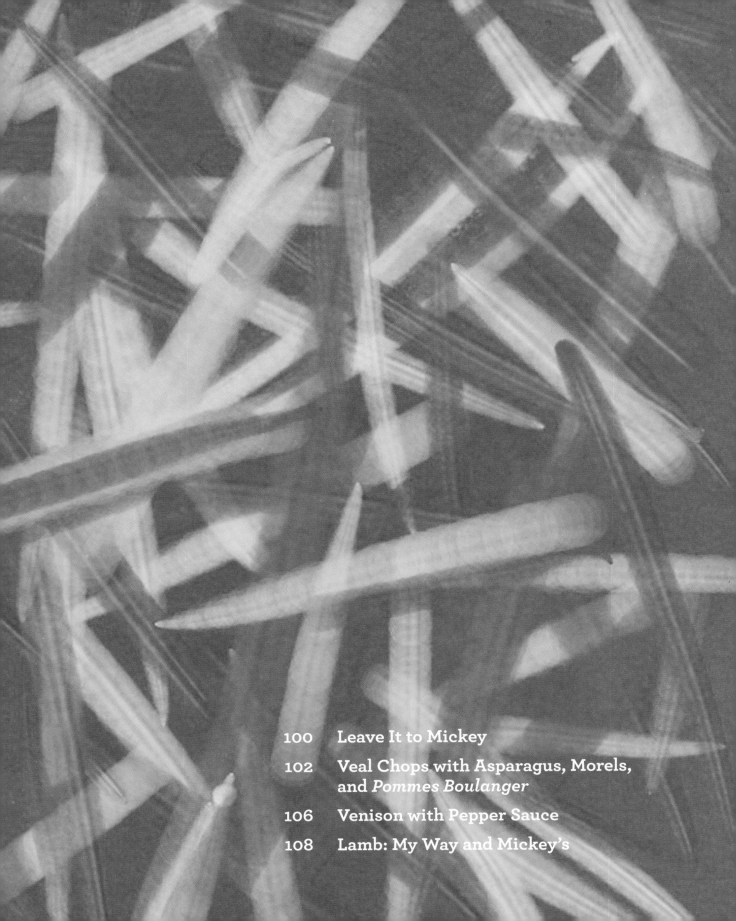

Leave It to Mickey

When fancy dining is in order, Mickey is the cook to go to in our family. In my younger days, a dinner party sent me straight to the French pantry, but I now can't even fathom myself making *boeuf en gelée* with tiny carved vegetables nestled into the aspic in the middle of a blistering New York summer. That era is long past and now my entertaining menus are not much different from most of my everyday meals. This is, in part, because in recent years I've found that since most of our friends so regularly frequent restaurants, they tend to enjoy simpler, homier dishes when they dine in. And so do we. Mickey, on the other hand, truly cooks the kind of food that he loves to eat—guests or no guests—and that's usually off-the-chart luxurious, multicourse meals that are time-consuming to prepare. We wouldn't have a collection of recipes that our American family cooks without Mickey adding his take on fancy, French-inspired dining.

Veal Chops with Asparagus, Morels, and *Pommes Boulanger*

SERVES 6

We've talked about Mickey's cooking being over the top, and this is a classic example. He once told me that he could only sleep well when he had veal, chicken, fish, and lobster stock in his freezer. I remember getting an excited call from him one morning, announcing that he had cooked his stock all night, getting up every two hours to check on it, and it was perfection. I shake my head in wonderment.

To make this dish, you do have to start with great, rich veal stock (page 152) or throw caution to the wind and purchase some ready-made veal demi-glace. (**Mickey:** "To me, this would be unacceptable. There is no way you can convince me that ready-made can compare to homemade. And it really isn't difficult to make a great reduction at home—all it takes is time on the stove. You can do other things while it cooks.") For those of you without Mickey's French leanings, a demi-glace is (to quote him) "just a classic *sauce espagnol* with the addition of some wine that has been reduced by half."

Mickey:
Because veal and lamb are costly, home cooks tend to abstain from cooking these meats except on special occasions. Since I particularly enjoy both and cook them often, I have been delighted to discover that Costco sells reasonably priced, excellent veal chops

and racks, rack of lamb, strip steaks, and whole beef filets. I go early to avoid the usual long lines and people loading up on frozen chicken fingers, pizzas, and other unappealing processed foods—that kind of shopping drives me over the edge.

Veal is, in addition, avoided because of commercial raising and processing methods. Mom only buys farm-raised veal, which, frankly, costs substantially more than what I buy at Costco. Farm-raised veal is almost unrecognizable as it is a much deeper pink that the pale, almost white industrial supermarket veal. Certainly, I support any attempt to raise animals more humanely and do buy from local farms as often as I can, but I still shop for value also.

I have to say that I think that you need more than one pair of hands to bring this meal to the table, but Mick seems to manage all alone. Of course, he always has his *mise en place* done and his stock and *jus* at hand. Lessons we should all learn.

🍷 CHRIS'S SUGGESTED WINE PAIRING
GO BIG! PREMIER CRU RED BURGUNDY

6 veal chops, frenched and tied

Coarse salt and pepper

1 tablespoon canola oil

5 tablespoons unsalted butter, room temperature

2 tablespoons olive oil

1 pound asparagus, trimmed, with stalks peeled

1 pound morel mushrooms, rinsed to eliminate grit and
  insects (if you can't find morels, use porcini, which
  I often do, or other deeply flavored wild mushrooms)

3 cloves garlic, crushed

2 sprigs fresh thyme

1 cup Veal *Jus* (page 153)

Pommes Boulanger (recipe follows)

1. Season the veal with salt and pepper.

2. Heat 2 tablespoons of the oil in a large sauté pan over medium-high heat. Add the chops and sear both sides to make a nice brown glaze. Cook, turning occasionally, for about 15 minutes, or until just about cooked to medium. Add the butter, and as it melts, begin basting the chops with the butter and pan juices.

Continue basting for another 3 minutes, or until the meat is well glazed and medium. Remove from the heat and let rest a minute or two.

3. While the meat is cooking, place two additional sauté pans on the fire. Put 1 tablespoon each of olive oil and butter into each pan. When just hot and blended, add the asparagus to one pan and the mushrooms, garlic, and thyme to the other. Season both with salt and pepper and cook, turning occasionally: the asparagus for about 6 minutes, or until crisp-tender and starting to color; and the morels for about 10 minutes, or until just softened. Remove and discard the thyme sprigs.

4. Lay equal portions of the asparagus across six warmed dinner plates. Place a veal chop on top of each and nestle equal portions of the potatoes against the veal. Spoon morels over each chop and around the plate. Drizzle the veal *jus* over all and serve.

Pommes Boulanger

¼ pound slab bacon, diced
1 large onion, thinly sliced crosswise
2 pounds fingerling potatoes, peeled, halved lengthwise
2 sprigs fresh thyme
Approximately 2 cups chicken stock
Salt and pepper
1 teaspoon fresh thyme leaves

1. Fry the bacon in a large sauté pan over medium heat, stirring occasionally, for about 12 minutes, or until golden brown and crisp. Using a slotted spoon, transfer the bacon to a double layer of paper towels to drain, leaving the pan on the fire.

2. Add the onion to the hot pan and fry, stirring frequently, for about 6 minutes, or just until the onion begins to color. Add the potatoes and fry, stirring occasionally, for about 5 minutes, or just until the potatoes begin to color a bit. Add the drained bacon and thyme sprigs, stirring to blend.

3. Pour in the stock—it should just barely cover the potatoes. The amount you need will depend on the size of your pan. Raise the heat and bring to a simmer. Season with salt and pepper as needed, remembering that the bacon has already added salt to the mix. Cook, stirring occasionally, for about 15 minutes, or until the stock has reduced and the potatoes are tender and beautifully glazed. You may need to add more stock if it reduces before the potatoes are cooked.

4. Remove the thyme sprigs and add the thyme leaves. Taste and, if necessary, season with additional salt and/or pepper.

Venison with Pepper Sauce

SERVES 6

Mickey: I don't know why Americans—except seasoned hunters—don't eat more venison; it is so tender, plus it's exceptionally lean and healthy. I suppose the vision of Bambi is a bit of a deterrent, along with the fact that farm-raised venison meat is prohibitively expensive for most of us. Even if you're a hunter, you can't bag enough deer to make this meal. Depending on its size, 1 tenderloin usually serves a hearty eater, so you need at least 6 tenderloins for this dish.

To create the pepper sauce, you will have to make a venison *jus* using the trimmings from the tenderloins (cut off the narrow tips, which will cook unevenly) cooked in veal stock

with an added *mirepoix* following my instructions for making Veal *Jus* (page 153). You will need approximately 1½ cups of the *jus* to use as a base for the sauce which gets slightly sweetened with the addition of dried currants. If you want to make a classic French *sauce grand veneur*, you can finish the pepper sauce with the addition of about 2 tablespoons of red currant jelly.

You have to take care not to overcook venison; it should be served medium-rare at the very most. Although you can serve this dish with almost any fall starch and vegetable, my choice would be a sweet-potato or butternut-squash puree, bitter greens or brussels sprouts, and some wild mushrooms. (**Judie:** "Always those wild mushrooms!")

CHRIS'S SUGGESTED WINE PAIRING
CÔTE RÔTIE (AN EXPENSIVE SYRAH FROM FRANCE)

6 venison tenderloins, trimmed of all fat and
   silverskin, narrow tips removed
Salt and pepper
1 tablespoon canola oil
Pepper Sauce (recipe follows)

1. Preheat the oven to 375°F.

2. Season the tenderloins with salt and pepper.

3. Heat the oil in a heavy ovenproof frying pan over high heat. Add the seasoned tenderloins and sear, turning occasionally, until nicely colored on all sides.

Transfer to the oven and roast for about 10 minutes, or until a meat thermometer registers 135°F (for rare). Remove from the oven and allow to rest for a few minutes before slicing.

4. Cut crosswise on the diagonal into thin slices. Place 1 tenderloin on each of 6 dinner plates, slightly fanning the slices. Drizzle with the pepper sauce and garnish the plate with whatever starch and/or vegetable you choose.

Pepper Sauce

1 tablespoon canola oil

2 shallots, peeled and minced

2 cloves garlic, peeled and chopped

3 sprigs fresh thyme

1 bay leaf

1 tablespoon juniper berries

1 cup red wine

¼ cup red wine vinegar

2 cups venison *jus*

1 tablespoon freshly cracked black pepper

¼ cup dried currants

1. Heat the oil in a large saucepan over medium heat. Add the shallots and garlic along with the thyme, bay leaf, and juniper berries and sauté until the aromatics have softened, about 4 minutes. Add the red wine and red wine vinegar and bring to a simmer. Simmer for about 15 minutes, or until the pan is almost dry. Add the venison *jus* and season with salt. Cook, stirring occasionally, for about 10 minutes or until reduced to a saucelike consistency. Add the cracked pepper and set aside to infuse for 5 minutes. (If the pepper has been freshly ground it can be quite potent, so allow it to infuse accordingly).

2. Pour the sauce through a fine-mesh strainer into a clean small saucepan. Place over low heat and stir in the currants. Cook, stirring, to just reheat and soften the currants slightly. Taste and, if necessary, adjust the seasoning. Use immediately or cool in an ice bath and freeze, tightly covered, for later use.

Lamb: My Way and Mickey's

Many years ago, during a time of mourning, my dear friend Jane Green provided din-ners to our grieving family. The first meal she delivered was centered around a perfectly cooked leg of lamb and I have forever since thought of lamb as providing a meal filled with generosity and kindness. As such, I consider it the perfect "welcome to our table" meal when guests are expected.

I think everyone has a favorite way of roasting a leg of lamb—mine is quite simple. Make any number of slits in the flesh and fill each one with a peeled clove of garlic. Generously sprinkle with salt and pepper and coat with a thin layer of celery seed. Roast in a very hot oven—about 450°F—for an hour or so and then turn it down to 350°F and roast until a meat thermometer registers 135°F for rare. You can also throw some potatoes, carrots, turnips, parsnips, or onions into the roasting pan if you want. I like to serve a little mix-up of grated horseradish and chopped fresh mint along with it.

This is a long introduction for Mickey's take on lamb, which is entirely different from mine. It is far more refined and takes you a step further into the art of elegant entertaining, at which Mickey is a connoisseur.

Mickey: You now know that I love veal, but I love lamb equally. This wasn't always the case. Mom often made a whole bone-in leg of lamb for Sunday dinner (**Judie:** "And I still do if company is coming!") and always for Easter. My dad adored that traditional meal, but it was never my favorite. It was too gamey for my young palate. Laurel and Chris don't enjoy lamb at all and Steve eats it only to please us, but Mom and Alexander share my love of it.

I first began to really appreciate lamb when Mom was working on Chef Charlie Palmer's first book and I helped her test the recipes for the home cook. Charlie always had lamb on the menu and I had begun to enjoy eating it at his restaurant. Eventually, I learned how to make it by observing the cooks in his kitchen.

My favorite preparation is a whole boneless loin of lamb. If you want to try this dish, you will need to find a butcher who will sell you a whole half-lamb saddle and either ask him to debone it for you, or better yet, bone it out yourself. (I like to save the bones in my freezer for lamb stock.) Here's my tactic: I wait until I see loin chops on sale at my local family-owned supermarket; then, I head right to the butcher and ask for the half saddle. He usually sees me coming—I know he thinks I'm nuts, but that doesn't bother me in the least. I would do anything necessary to make friends with my butcher—even let him think I'm a raving lunatic if it makes him happy. Anyway, find a butcher friend and convince him to sell you the whole loin. Then, teach yourself to bone it—it's truly not hard and Internet sites can easily take you through the steps.

If all else fails, use a rack of lamb. It's more expensive per pound than the loin but will do in a pinch. Most price clubs sell frenched rack of lamb, but it is often Australian, which is much cheaper and, I think, not anywhere as near as good as American.

I basically cook lamb loin exactly as I cook venison or pork tenderloins. I preheat the oven to 400°F. I season the meat very well and then sear it in a hot ovenproof pan until nicely colored on all sides. Then I add a good chunk of unsalted butter, a couple of smashed garlic cloves, and a bit each of fresh rosemary and thyme to the pan, and transfer it to the preheated oven. I roast the meat, frequently basting with the herby butter, for 10 to 15 minutes, or until an instant-read thermometer reads 135°F (for rare). This method of cooking meat is one I absorbed while working with Mom on various chefs' books. Serve it with a lovely *jus* and *Pommes Boulanger* (page 104).

 ## CHRIS'S SUGGESTED WINE PAIRING
A NAPA VALLEY CABERNET FOR MOM AND BORDEAUX FOR MICKEY

Friday Still Means Fish

🍷 Chris's Wine Advice

I say again that you should really just drink what you like—there is no right or wrong when it comes to wine. However, I do love to drink a crisp white with no oak when I have fish. With seafood dishes particularly, I like a wine pairing from the same region: for instance, an Albariño with a coastal Spanish dish like paella. If you do decide to go to a red, I suggest it be something on the lighter side—grilled salmon and pinot noir is one of the great combinations.

Steve's Every-Night Shrimp Creole

SERVES 6

One winter family vacation in the Caribbean, my wonderful husband, Steve, went on a shrimp-Creole binge, ordering it for dinner every night. I knew that he was doing it to annoy my mother and that if she would just quit snarking, "Why are you ordering that again?" he would move on. But like all old mother-in-law jokes, she kept asking and he kept ordering. Thereafter he never ate it again—until laughing memories of that holiday propelled him to binge once more. In memory of Nana, Steve asked me to devise a recipe. Having a freezer full of frozen peppers presented the perfect opportunity to do so. Here is what I came up with and what will forever be known as Steve's Every-Night Shrimp Creole. You can serve it over rice or, as I do, over grits.

 CHRIS'S SUGGESTED WINE PAIRING
OFF-DRY GERMAN RIESLING—KABINETT LEVEL

2 tablespoons olive oil

½ cup diced onions

1 cup finely diced red bell pepper

1 cup finely diced green bell pepper

½ cup sliced button mushrooms

1 tablespoon minced garlic

1 bay leaf

½ teaspoon red pepper flakes

½ teaspoon dried thyme

½ teaspoon dried basil

1 tablespoon tomato paste

2 cups chopped canned tomatoes

1 cup bottled clam juice

1 to 1½ pounds shrimp, shelled and deveined

Salt and pepper

1 tablespoon chopped fresh parsley

1. Heat the oil in a large frying pan over medium heat. Add the onions, bell peppers, and garlic, and sauté for about 5 minutes, or until the aromatics are beginning to soften. Stir in the bay leaf, red pepper flakes, thyme, and basil, and continue to sauté until the vegetables begin to color, about another 5 minutes. Stir in the tomato paste and cook for a minute or so. Add the tomatoes and clam juice and bring to a simmer. Simmer for about 15 minutes, or until the flavors are well blended.

2. Add the shrimp and return to the simmer. Continue simmering for about 4 minutes, until the shrimp is cooked through. Remove from the heat, stir in the parsley, and serve over rice or grits.

Dungeness Crab at Home

I love, love, love Dungeness crab. When growing up in San Francisco, my brother would go down to Fisherman's Wharf—this was when it really was a fisherman's wharf—and buy a bucketload of live crabs for a couple of dollars. Sometimes he would have them steamed, but usually my mom would boil them at home. We always did this on a Friday night—we spread newspapers out on the floor and put sliced lemons and a big green salad in the center. Sourdough bread was warmed, sliced, and wrapped in a towel. Each of us—we usually had a crowd—got their own crab, crackers, and pick. I don't remember clearly (probably because I was too young to drink), but I think a big jug of Gallo wine was likely the beverage of choice. The feasting lasted for hours.

I try to replicate that childhood dinner every time we go to San Francisco, and of course if friends have traveled with us, it is the first meal I want to share with them. Chris and I take a trip to the Ferry Plaza to pick up fresh crab—and, I assure you, not

for just a couple of bucks anymore—and some sourdough bread from Acme Bakery. Chris boils up the crabs in a big vat of beer-flavored water and I toss a great green salad (page 58). Chris chooses some wonderful white wine from his cache and the feast begins. I admit it's not a pretty sight. Chris never has enough of the proper tools and I imagine we must look like participants in a Jane Goodall documentary as we crack the shells with a mallet and pick out the crabmeat with bamboo skewers—the intensity and focus are probably not too far removed from Ms. Goodall's hungry apes.

 CHRIS'S SUGGESTED BEER PAIRING
ANCHOR STEAM

Soft-Shell Crabs

The grocers and commercial vendors have cleaned up our food so much that I'd guess soft-shell crab must be about as adventurous an eat as anyone can have today. I can't wait for their early spring arrival (along with that other harbinger, shad roe) and once they hit the market, we have them at least once a week—marveling at the remarkable fluctuation in price every time we shop the seafood counters at New York's Citarella or Wild Edibles.

They are also part of the spring family get-together cook-a-thon at Mickey and Laurel's. Laurel and the kids are squeamish about soft-shell crabs and not only refuse to eat them but leave the kitchen when I prepare them. The rest of us wrap them in soft white bread and spoon on left-over salsa, warm butter, and lemon juice, or whatever vinaigrette is hanging around. Yummy!

You don't really need a recipe to cook soft-shell crabs—the simpler they are prepared and served, the better. For each person, you need 2 (if large) or 3 (if small) cleaned, rinsed crabs. Pat them very dry before cooking. For stovetop cooking you need a very hot pan and a slick of clarified butter or nonthreatening oil like grapeseed oil (depending on

whether you want the taste of butter or prefer no additional flavor detracting from the sweet meat). Lightly coat both sides of each crab with Wondra flour and season with salt and pepper. A word of warning: when placing the crab into the hot pan, lay them in from front to back (that is, holding a crab in your fingertips place the side nearest you into the pan first) and gently lower the crab into the oil; otherwise the residual moisture in the crab will splatter back at you when it hits the hot pan and can cause a nasty burn. Using this method, it will still splatter but usually away from you. Cook for 3 minutes; then, turn and cook the remaining side for 2 minutes. Transfer to a double layer of paper towels to drain. If desired, you can add about ¼ cup of unsalted butter to the pan and place over high heat. When the butter begins to foam, begin shaking the pan back and forth, allowing the butter to turn a lovely brown without burning. Stir in ¼ cup of fresh lemon juice, a teaspoon of lemon zest, and a tablespoon of minced parsley. Season with salt and pepper. Place the crabs on a serving platter and spoon the lemon butter over the top.

If you are grilling them, you need to do nothing more than rinse and pat dry. Place directly over a hot fire and grill for the same amount of time required for stovetop cooking. I like to place lemon halves on the grill with the crab and then squeeze the hot lemon juice over the crab once cooked. And since it's spring, you might as well throw some fresh asparagus on the grill to make the meal a true welcome to that wonderful season.

🍷 CHRIS'S SUGGESTED WINE PAIRING
PINOT GRIS FROM ALSACE

Scallops with Roe and Fiddlehead Ferns

I'll admit that this is a recipe that can rarely be made—and only in the springtime.
But like all good things, it is worth the wait. For years I was a little iffy about fiddle-heads—the tightly curled, unopened frond of the ostrich fern that pops up in the moist earth in early spring—as I found them too astringent and slightly bitter for my palate. Plus, I kept remembering a warning about them carrying toxins some years ago (which turned out to be false) and that scared me a bit.

However, time and tides change as does my taste, and I have become a devotee. As much as we now all love them, we only have them but once or twice a season because we don't want to come up empty in the years to come. You can cut only 3 of the 7 scrolls in the very early spring, when the plant is still near to the ground and completely unfurled; more, and you will kill it. Much as with ramps, overharvesting of the ferns is taking its toll throughout the Northeast. I usu-ally pick them with my best friends—Lynn and Lena Mai—and we take great care to take only enough to satisfy.

Once they are cut, all you have to do is rinse them well and carefully brush off any dried brown skin. They will stay quite fresh in the fridge for a couple of days. Although I have seen them frozen, I prefer the fresh taste and crisp texture of those that are straight from the woods.

I think that I liked fiddleheads more once I learned to cook them delicately. Old recipes suggest boiling or steaming for 10 to 15 minutes, but I simply sauté them for about 7 minutes in clarified butter and finish them with a squeeze of fresh lemon and a sprinkle of sea salt.

One recent spring, when I had some precious fiddleheads tucked away in the fridge, I brought home some scallops with their roe fresh from the sea and came up with this dish. It is very easy to make but it truly is a recipe for which the ingredients have to be pristine. It has become our favorite welcome-spring dish. All you do is sauté the fiddleheads as directed. Then, lightly coat the scallops with a bit of Wondra flour and season with salt and pepper. Reserve the left-over flour remaining on the plate. Give the scallops a quick sear in grapeseed oil so that both sides take on some color and a touch of crispness while the centers stay milky and mellow.

Remove the scallops and give a big fat squeeze of lemon to the mix of oil and brown bits remaining in the pan, and toss in the tiny amount of reserved flour. Give it all a swirl. Add a nice cube of chilled unsalted butter and some lemon zest and—voila!—a smidgen of sauce to finish the plate.

 CHRIS'S SUGGESTED WINE PAIRING
WHITE BURGUNDY WITH A TOUCH OF OAK

Scallops in the Shell

When I'm lucky enough to find fresh scallops with their roe attached still in the shell, I always prepare them the same way. I clean them up and place them, shells and all, one at a time, into a hot pan. Then I add a bit of white wine and butter to each shell, season with salt and pepper, cover the pan, and cook for just a few minutes to warm the shellfish and make a little sauce. They make an exceptionally exotic appetizer, with the barely cooked scallop to be devoured on its own and the bright orange roe slathered on some rye toast—along with some lovely New Zealand sauvignon blanc, of course!

Linguine with Clam Sauce

Why isn't this recipe in my homage-to-Italy chapter, you might ask? Well, it's because on our annual trip out to Provincetown, we have fish or shellfish every day and my inspiration does not necessarily come from whence it should. All of the seafood is so pristine that I usually serve it raw or cooked simply—why spoil something that's so delicious in its own right with sauces and such? The only exception is when I make pasta. One of our favorite dishes is linguine with clams, for which I don't really have a tried-and-true recipe—after all, I'm not an Italian grandma!

The first time I made this version, I incorporated some very sweet little yellow cherry tomatoes that we had purchased from a local farm along with a charming bouquet of nasturtiums that the farmer's dear little daughter had picked, tied with ribbon, and sold for ice-cream money. The end result was ab-

solutely *delicioso*. Here's what I did then, and do every time I can get that combination of fresh garden loveliness. There is no real measurement—just gauge how much broth you want with the amount of clams and pasta you are going to serve.

While you are making the clam sauce, cook the linguine to al dente according to package directions. For the sauce, put a nice layer of olive oil in the pot. Add a good measure of chopped garlic—I use about 8 cloves—and when the garlic starts to smell up the oil, add a cup of white wine and let it bubble for a few minutes to allow the winey flavor to mellow. Then, add a bottle of clam juice, a cup of chicken stock, and a cup or so of fresh chopped clams. Cook for a couple of minutes, or until very hot. Taste and season with pepper and, if needed, salt. Add the clams in their shells (if you have some sweet cherry tomatoes, add them along with the clams), cover, and cook until all of the clams pop open.

Stir in some chopped parsley. Drain the pasta well and toss it with a touch of extra virgin olive oil. Transfer it to a large platter with sides (so the broth doesn't run off). Pour the clams and broth over the pasta. And for the crowning glory, julienne the nasturtium flowers and leaves and sprinkle them over the dish. You can't believe what a wondrous marriage of flavors comes together with the sweet clams, winey broth, and spicy nasturtiums.

CHRIS'S SUGGESTED WINE PAIRING
PINOT GRIGIO FROM THE ALTO ADIGE

Salmon with Curried Carrot Couscous and Green Puree

SERVES 4

This dish comes from Mickey, who puts fish on the menu every Friday night. Why Fridays, I have no idea, as I'm certain he has no knowledge of the religious edict that had Catholic families eating fish every Friday for generations. This is a simple but extremely tasty and elegant dish that evolved out of Mickey's love for the combination of carrots and curry. He cooks the couscous in carrot juice and then balances the sweetness with the bitterness of an arugula puree. If you are not a salmon fan—and I'm not—you can use halibut, scallops, or any other non-oily fish.

Mickey: I like salmon to be rare in the center, but feel free to cook it to your taste. If you want to heighten the flavors a bit, dust the fish filets with freshly ground cumin. (**Judie:** "None of that pre-ground out-of-the-jar kind for Mickey.") Also, if you want a hint of heat, use half mild and half hot curry powder or add a sprinkle of cayenne pepper.

 CHRIS'S SUGGESTED WINE PAIRING
AN EARTHY PINOT NOIR

2 bunches arugula (or spinach or your bitter green of choice), washed well and dried

3 tablespoons unsalted butter or to taste

Salt and pepper

1 tablespoon olive oil

2 shallots, minced

1 cup Israeli couscous

2 teaspoons mild curry powder or to taste

½ cup diced carrots

1½ cups fresh carrot juice

1 tablespoon canola oil

4 (6-ounce) skinless salmon filets

Freshly ground cumin (optional)

1. Place the arugula in boiling water for about 30 seconds to blanch. Drain well and pat dry.

2. Transfer the blanched greens to a blender (or food processor fitted with the metal blade) and process to a saucelike consistency, adding a bit of warm water as needed to smooth out.

3. Scrape the puree into a small saucepan, add the butter, and place over low heat to warm through. Remove from the heat and keep warm. (The puree can be made in advance and reheated in a double boiler over boiling water).

4. Heat the olive oil in a saucepan over medium heat. Add the shallots and cook, stirring occasionally, for about 4 minutes, or until softened. Add the couscous and cook, stirring occasionally, for a few minutes, until the couscous takes on some color. Add a healthy dose of curry powder along with the diced carrot and carrot juice. The juice should cover the couscous by about ½ inch. Bring to a simmer. Lower the heat, season with salt and pepper, cover, and cook for about 12 minutes, or until the liquid has been absorbed and the couscous is tender. If the liquid is absorbed before the couscous has cooked, add a bit of water.

5. Remove from the heat and set aside, covered.

6. Heat the canola oil in a large frying pan over high heat.

7. Season the salmon with salt and pepper and dust with cumin. Place in the hot pan and sear, turning once, for about 6 minutes, until nicely colored on the exterior and rare in the center.

8. Place a mound of the couscous in the center of each of 4 dinner plates. Place a salmon filet on top and drizzle the puree around the edge. Serve i mmediately.

Cod Cakes

SERVES 6

Years ago I read *Cod: A Biography of the Fish That Changed the World,* **by Mark Kur**-lansky, and became fascinated with the mystery and history of the fish. Whenever I cook cod I can't help wondering if future generations will have the opportunity to experience its delicate flavor—can you imagine that schools of cod were once so thick that you could almost walk on the water? Apparently this was true for sturgeon in the Delaware River as well, where nary a fish can be found today. How much we can discover about ourselves and our history by learning how and why we eat what we eat.

As much as I love cod, I cook it rarely because Steve is allergic to any fish with scales (and, we've found, frog's legs) and I don't like to prepare a different dish for each of us. However, when we go off to Provincetown, Massachusetts, which we do at least once a year, I can't resist the beautiful catch in the local market. Since we are on the Cape, the cod is particularly pristine and I try to use it in as many ways as I can, with one of our favorites being meaty cod cakes.

In years past when I was doing restaurant consulting, one of the dishes I would al-ways test a cook on was crab cakes. Along with roasting the perfect chicken, I think that making the perfect crab cake really tests a chef's mettle. To me, there is nothing worse than a mushy fish cake made with smashed-up cooked seafood and overstuffed with breadcrumbs or potatoes. I like to think that I take my own advice and turn out a pretty mean fish cake. Rather than create just one night's dinner, I usually make a big batch so that I can have them on hand for future meals. Nothing better for a quick lunch than a crisp cod cake on top of a plate of salad greens.

Because of the addition of potatoes, all you really need to complete dinner is a sal-ad or a sautéed green veggie and a lovely glass of sauvignon blanc. You can offer some tartar or other acidic sauce if you like. I sometimes serve with a homemade horseradish mayo, but it really isn't necessary.

 CHRIS'S SUGGESTED WINE PAIRING
AN ALBARIÑO FROM SPAIN

1 tablespoon butter

1 teaspoon canola oil, plus more for frying

1 onion, diced

2 pounds cod (or other meaty white-fleshed fish),
   medium dice

2 cups mashed potatoes

½ cup sliced scallions

2 large eggs

1 tablespoon finely chopped parsley

Salt and pepper

3 cups bread crumbs

1. Heat the butter and oil in a small frying pan over medium heat. Add the onion and fry, stirring frequently, just until the onion begins to take on some color, about 5 minutes. Remove from the heat and set aside.

2. Combine the potatoes with the scallions and cooked onion in a large mixing bowl. Add the cod and stir gently to incorporate. Add the eggs and parsley and season with salt and pepper. Mix just enough to combine—you don't want to mash the fish.

3. Place the bread crumbs in a large, shallow bowl.

4. Using your hands, form the cod mix into cakes of equal size. I like mine to be about 3 inches in diameter and 1 inch thick. The mixture will be loose.

5. Working with one at a time, gently roll the cakes in the bread crumbs.

6. Lightly coat a large frying pan with canola oil. Place over medium heat and when oil is hot, carefully transfer the cakes to the pan. Do not crowd the pan. If the cakes split apart a bit, just use a spatula to keep them together. The looseness and chunkiness of the fish are what makes these cakes so delicious. Fry, turning once or twice, for about 10 minutes, or until the fish is cooked through.

7. Serve piping hot.

What Would We Do Without Pizza, Pasta, and All Things Italian?

🍷 Chris's Wine Advice

No need to break the wine bank here. Reasonably priced Italian reds offer tons of flavor and intensity. I particularly enjoy Nero D'Avola from Sicily and so does Mom. Don't hesitate to chat up your local wine merchant for suggestions from the inexpensive Italian bin; I think you'll easily find some new favorites you'll end up ordering by the case. (Judie: "Steve and I love most wines from Sicily—rarely have we had one we didn't embrace.")

Pizza

I just know that I had to be Italian in a past life as there is nothing I love more than the foods of the Italian table and the accompanying joy and love of family that meets there. I've always said that my last meal would have to be pasta with great Parmigiano-Reggiano and a bottle of red wine. (At the moment my two favorite red wines are Juan Gil, a wonderful Spanish red, and Rosso Piceno 2008 Saladini Pilastri. They go especially well with my take on pizza.) Although there is nothing better than a bubbling pizza straight from a wood- or coal-burning oven, I have learned to make a good facsimile on the grill, and in the winter I content myself with heating my ancient gas oven to infernal temperatures to produce that smoky wood flavor. The plain fact is, pizza is right up there as one of my favorite foods.

When summer rolls around, pizza is on the grill weekly. It is quite simple and easy to do—even if you don't get your act together until the late afternoon. The dough can be made just an hour before cooking and I always have my marinara sauce (page 140) in the freezer if I choose to use it. Pizza making is such fun because each one can be completely individualized with a myriad of possible toppings. I will often clean the fridge when I make pizza, putting a little of this and a little of that on each one, but a plain old pizza margarita is still my favorite (just a smear of marinara sauce topped with dabs of mozzarella and a few leaves of basil). Sometimes I make single pizzas to order and sometimes a big one to share. And sometimes I make a spectacular dessert pizza by topping the dough with fresh figs, honey, and creamy goat cheese.

This dough recipe is easy to use, whether you're making pizza on the grill or in the oven.

 CHRIS'S SUGGESTED WINE PAIRING
A NERO D'AVOLA FROM SICILY

Pizza Dough

MAKES ENOUGH FOR FOUR 12-INCH PIES

1 package instant yeast
1 teaspoon sugar
4¾ to 5 cups all-purpose flour
2 teaspoons coarse salt
⅓ cup extra virgin olive oil, plus more for
    oiling the bowl
Semolina flour for rolling

1. Combine the yeast and sugar with 1¼ cups room-temperature water. Set aside for 12 minutes.

2. Place the flour and salt in the bowl of a standing electric mixer fitted with the paddle and give a stir. With the motor running on low, alternately add the yeast mixture and ⅓ cup of the olive oil. When blended, raise the speed and beat for about 5 minutes, or until the dough is soft, a wee bit sticky, and elastic. If the dough is too stiff, you can add room-temperature water, about a tablespoon at a time, to loosen. The dough should be soft and pliable.

3. Rub the inside of a clean bowl with olive oil. Using your hands, form the dough into a ball and transfer it to the olive-oil-coated bowl. Cover and let rest for 1 hour. (You can also place the dough in a resealable plastic bag and refrigerate for up to 1 day or freeze for up to 1 month. For the latter, thaw in the refrigerator before using.)

4. If baking, place a pizza stone in the oven and preheat it to its hottest temperature. Lightly sprinkle a cookie sheet (one without sides) with semolina flour.

5. If grilling, prepare a hot grill. (I use hardwood charcoal, which adds a lovely smoky taste). Clean and oil the grate.

6. Have all of the toppings laid out either near your rolling surface or by the side of the grill.

7. When ready to roll, sprinkle a generous coating of semolina flour over a clean, flat work surface. If making large pizzas, divide the dough into 4 equal pieces; if small, divide into about 8 to 10 pieces of equal size.

8. Place a piece of dough on the prepared work surface and sprinkle semolina flour on top. Begin rolling in all directions until you have a sort of circle about 12 inches in diameter. I never roll out an even circle and it doesn't matter one bit—you could make rectangles, triangles, or any shape you like.

9. If baking, transfer the dough to the prepared baking sheet and add whatever toppings you are using. Immediately transfer to the hot oven and bake for about 10 minutes, or until the dough has puffed up a bit, any cheese you've used has melted, and the pizza is nicely charred around the edges.

10. If grilling, lift the dough circle from the rolling surface and carefully transfer it to the hot grill, pulling out the sides as you lay it on the grill.

11. Grill for 3 to 4 minutes, until the bottom is charred slightly and the dough begins to puff.

12. Turn the dough and as fast as you can, cover the grilled dough top with your toppings. If using tomato sauce, don't overdo or the pizza will get soggy very quickly.

13. Grill over direct coals for 3 to 4 minutes, until the bottom is nicely charred and the edges begin to color. Immediately pull the pizza to the cool side of the grill, cover, and bake for about 3 minutes, or until the toppings are hot and the cheese has melted.

14. Keep on making pizzas until you've used up all of the dough.

About Toppings

You really can make about any type of pizza you like. I usually like precooked toppings—roasted or grilled veggies, grilled or marinated fish—such as sardines or anchovies, and almost any cured meat or cooked sausage—unless I have some really sweet little tomatoes fresh from the garden that will just heat up and pop. Steve would be content with a little marinara sauce, a mound of grilled mushrooms, and a light sprinkle of cheese. For cheese, I use whatever I have on hand—favorites are burrata, fresh mozzarella, and ricotta salata.

Another thing to remember when making any Italian dish requiring Parmegiano-Reggiano (aka Parmesan) cheese, always and forever use the very best you can find. It will make all the difference in the world to the flavor. Plus, when of excellent quality, it makes a beautiful and tasty garnish peeled over the tops of pastas and salads.

Correcto Risotto

SERVES 6

Steve and I still laugh about the afternoon that Mickey was making his favorite corn risotto with Chris mumbling in the background, "He's not doing it right, he's not doing it right." We actually couldn't tell what it was that Mickey wasn't doing right and, having enjoyed his risotto many times, didn't think whatever it was made a great difference in taste. But, because Chris was taught to make risotto by an extraordinary Roman chef, Giovanni Perticone, we are going to go with his version for the perfect risotto and let Mickey work his magic with corn and rice in another recipe.

Chris: Giovanni's recipe is nonpareil. When we worked together, I never tired of eating his risotto—plain or with any number of additions. I carefully watched and learned, as I knew that it was something I wanted to be able to make at home. There were two rules that Gio

said could never be broken when making risotto: 1) the stock had to be kept at a rolling boil so that the temperature of the risotto would not fall with each addition of more liquid and ingredients, and 2) the final addition of the Parmigiano and butter should not be immediately folded in, but the dish should be covered and allowed to rest for exactly two minutes first. Then, once finished, Giovanni said that the risotto should be served on a plate and—this is the most important test that you've achieved the right consistency—when you tap the edge of the plate with your hand, a gentle wave should move through the rice. And, believe me, Mickey doesn't do it right!

Heather: My colleagues at work are well aware of Chris's cooking prowess as I often proudly describe a home-cooked meal from the night before and share tidbits from my "left-over" lunch. There is always some guessing of ingredients and techniques—"He makes it look so easy and effortless," I respond, knowing full well that it is the end result of growing up with a marvelous cook for a mom.

CHRIS'S SUGGESTED WINE PAIRING
A NEBBIOLO DI LANGHE FROM PIEDMONT

¼ cup plus 1 tablespoon unsalted butter,
   room temperature

1 tablespoon olive oil

1 onion, finely diced

2 quarts good-quality well-seasoned chicken stock

1½ cups Arborio rice

1 cup dry white wine

Coarse salt and freshly ground white pepper

½ cup freshly grated Parmigiano-Reggiano cheese

1. Combine 1 tablespoon of the butter with the olive oil in a large pan at least 2 inches deep. Place over medium heat and when hot and blended, stir in the onion. Cook, stirring constantly with a wooden spoon, for about 5 minutes, or until the onion is very soft and translucent. Stir in the rice and continue to cook, stirring constantly, for about 4 minutes, or until the rice is shimmering and beginning to almost toast.

2. While the onion is cooking, place the stock in a saucepan over medium-high heat. Bring to a boil and adjust the heat to keep the stock at a rolling boil.

3. Add the wine to the rice and bring to a boil. Cook, stirring constantly, for about 7 minutes, or until the wine has been absorbed by the rice. Begin adding the boiling stock, 1 cup at a time, and cook, stirring constantly, until the stock has been absorbed by the rice. Keep adding stock and stirring constantly until the rice is *al dente*. This should take about 25 minutes. Make sure the risotto isn't too thick when finished cooking as the addition of the butter and cheese will cause it to thicken further. I usually err on the side of too loose, almost always adding a little extra stock at the end.

4. Remove from the heat. Place the remaining butter along with the cheese on top of the risotto; cover and let rest for 2 minutes. Uncover and gently fold in the butter and cheese. Taste and, if necessary, season with salt and pepper.

5. Ladle equal portions into the centers of 6 warm dinner plates. Pass additional cheese at the table, if desired.

Mom's Potato Gnocchi

SERVES 6

Although I do still make homemade pasta from time to time, until recently I had for-gotten all about my mom's gnocchi. How, you might ask, did a first American-born child of Scottish immigrants come to make excellent gnocchi? Unbelievably, she was introduced to this traditional Italian dish by the mother of a friend of my brother while they were out fishing on Flathead Lake, in Montana. And that's a whole other story!

Once Mom mastered potato gnocchi, she felt that hers surpassed all gnocchi on earth. When dining out, if it was on the menu, she would order it only, I believe, to be able to say, "These are sure not as good as mine." While she was alive, I never dared to make gnocchi. And even once she had passed on, for years I didn't attempt them, probably because I was too afraid that she would come back to watch over my shoulder and say, "Those are sure not as good as mine." Anyway, eventually I did make my own gnocchi, and you know what? They weren't as good as hers. Mom's were light as air and absorbed just enough sauce—whatever she put on them—usually just lots of butter and Parmesan cheese. Here's her recipe; now it's up to you to make gnocchi as good as hers.

I serve these gnocchi as a main course, sometimes as Mom did, sometimes with pesto, and sometimes with marinara sauce. I have made one change—Mom used mashed potatoes, I use extra-large baked Idaho potatoes, for their airiness. I do, however, still press them through the food mill to make sure there are no lumps. You'll need about two pounds to yield 2½ cups.

2½ cups mashed potatoes
2 large eggs, room temperature
½ teaspoon plus 2 tablespoons salt
2¼ cups all-purpose flour, sifted
Approximately ½ cup Wondra flour for dusting

1. Lightly coat a shallow baking dish with olive oil. Lightly flour a sheet pan. Set both aside.

2. Using the Wondra, lightly flour a clean, flat workspace.

3. Combine the potatoes, eggs, and ½ teaspoon salt in a mixing bowl, beating thoroughly with a wooden spoon. When well combined, beat in 1½ cups of the flour. When blended, scrape the dough out onto the floured surface.

4. Begin adding the remaining ¾ cup flour, kneading it into the dough. This should take about 5 minutes. If the dough becomes too sticky, sprinkle the surface with additional flour; however, don't over-flour or the gnocchi will be tough.

5. Cut the dough into 6 equal pieces. Roll each piece into a long strip approximately 1 inch in diameter. Cut each strip into pieces about ⅔ inch wide. Place the pieces on the floured sheet pan as you work.

6. At this point, fill a large stockpot of water and add the remaining 2 tablespoons of salt. Place over high heat and bring to a boil.

7. You can now either leave the dough as is or roll each piece on a gnocchi paddle to form ridges which will, once cooked, serve to catch the sauce used. If using a paddle (a large dinner fork will also work), working with one piece at a time, place the dough on the paddle and, using the side of your thumb, quickly and gently press forward on the dough so that it will curl up and form a rather oval shape engraved with the linear markings of the paddle. Return the dough pieces to the floured sheet pan.

8. When all of the gnocchi have been shaped, place about a third of them in the now rapidly boiling salted water. As the gnocchi rise to the top, using a

slotted spoon or strainer, transfer them to the olive-oil-coated dish. Tent with foil to keep warm.

9. Serve hot, with lots of melted butter, Parmesan cheese, and cracked pepper; marinara sauce; or pesto—or, in fact, any sauce you like.

Butternut-Squash Ravioli

SERVES 4 TO 6

The sturdy KitchenAid stand mixer with all of its attachments has been a boon to home cooks, certainly to all members of the Choate family. The pasta attachments make homemade pasta dough a breeze. Laurel was the first of us to embrace pasta making on a weekly basis (because, she says, Mickey was too afraid to tackle something outside the French kitchen—though he says "not so" and besides "I now make all of the pasta"). Her recipe only requires all-purpose flour and two eggs, while Chris, Mickey, and I use three eggs and 00 flour (see Note, page 137). Although we take advantage of the sturdy machine, you can also roll pasta by hand—an arduous job—or use what I used for years: a small imported and very inexpensive pasta maker that works just fine.

🍷 CHRIS'S SUGGESTED WINE PAIRING
ARNEIS OR A LANGHE NEBBIOLO FROM THE PIEDMONT REGION—ALTHOUGH SOME MIGHT PREFER SOMETHING SERIOUS, LIKE A BARBARESCO OR BAROLO

1 large butternut squash
1 tablespoon unsalted butter
2 shallots, minced
Pinch of ground nutmeg
Salt and pepper
½ cup grated Parmesan cheese, plus more for garnish
1 large egg, at room temperature
1 recipe Pasta Dough (recipe follows)
½ cup (1 stick) unsalted butter, room temperature
1 tablespoon julienned sage leaves, plus more for garnish
Juice of ½ lemon

1. Preheat the oven to 375°F.

2. Wash and dry the squash. Cut it in half lengthwise and remove and discard the seeds. Place cut side down on a tray in the preheated oven and bake for about 45 minutes, or until very soft. Remove from the oven and set aside until cool enough to handle.

3. Scrape the flesh from the skin. Measure out 1 cup and reserve the remainder for another use.

4. Heat the butter in a nonstick frying pan over medium heat. Add the shallots and sauté until soft, about 4 minutes. Add the cup of squash and the nutmeg and cook, stirring, for another couple of minutes to just combine.

5. Transfer the squash mixture to a food processor fitted with the metal blade, add the cheese, and process to a smooth puree. Scrape into a clean bowl and set aside.

6. Line a baking sheet with parchment paper and set aside. If you like, you can dust the paper with semolina flour, but it isn't necessary.

7. Combine the egg with a tablespoon of cold water, whisking to combine. Set aside.

8. Very lightly dust your work surface with flour. Place a sheet of dough on the flour and, using a 3-inch biscuit cutter, cut the dough into circles. Lift off and set aside any unused dough.

9. Working with one piece at a time, drop a tablespoon of the butternut-squash mixture in the center of each circle. Dip your finger into the egg wash and carefully coat the inside edge of the circle. Fold the top half of the circle over the filling and gently press the edges together.

10. When all of the ravioli have been made, set them aside to dry for at least 30 minutes or freeze for later use. (To freeze, leave them on the baking sheet and place in the freezer until solidly frozen. Then, transfer to a resealable plastic bag. They can be frozen for up to 3 months.)

11. When ready to serve, bring a large pot of salted water to a boil over high heat. Carefully slide the ravioli into the boiling water and cook for about 4 minutes. They will rise to the top when fully cooked. If necessary, cook in batches as you don't want them to stick together as they cook, which is exactly what will happen if you crowd the pot.

12. While the ravioli are cooking, melt the butter in a large sauté pan over medium heat. Add the julienned sage and cook, stirring, just until the butter begins to color. Remove from the heat and add the lemon juice. Season with salt and pepper.

13. As the ravioli are cooked, using a slotted spoon (or a fine-mesh sieve), lift them from the water, taking care that all of the water drains off. Slide the cooked ravioli into the sage butter and toss gently to coat.

14. Serve sprinkled with sage julienne and grated Parmesan cheese.

Pasta Dough

SERVES 4 TO 6

2¼ cups 00 flour

1 teaspoon salt (or more or less as desired)

3 large eggs, room temperature

1 tablespoon olive oil

1. Set up a heavy-duty stand mixer with the pasta-rolling attachment.

2. Combine the flour and salt on a clean work surface, slightly mounding it in the center. Then, make a well in the center. Place the eggs and olive oil in the well and using your fingertips, loosen the eggs and incorporate a bit of the oil into them. Slowly pull the flour into the well, working from the inside out, moving in a circular motion. It is easiest if you use one hand to mix and the other to move the flour into the moistened mixture. Continue working in this manner until all of the flour has been incorporated into the dough. At this point the dough should easily pull into a ball.

3. Lightly coat the work surface with flour and begin kneading the dough by flattening it out and folding over and over until the dough is smooth and elastic. This might take about 12 minutes.

4. Cut the dough into 2 or 3 pieces. Wrap the piece(s) you are not using immediately in plastic film and set aside.

5. Place a small bowl of flour at hand as you might need to flour the work surface, the finished dough, or your hands to keep the dough from sticking at any point.

6. Push the remaining piece of dough into a long rectangle and begin rolling it through the pasta machine on the widest setting. Roll at least 3 times, stretching the dough with your hands as it comes out of the roller. Then, begin reducing the settings and pushing the dough through each one 2 to 3 times. Continue until you are on the thinnest setting and the dough is about ⅛ inch thick.

7. At this point, the dough is ready to be used as is or cut into shapes. Although you will continue to roll the dough using the reserved pieces, it's easier to make and fill the ravioli circles as each batch of dough is rolled. You can, of course, use this pasta dough to make any style of pasta you like. In fact, when we have left-over dough, we make it into noodles, dry it, and save for a rainy day.

NOTE: Traditionally used to make pizza and pasta dough in Italy, 00 flour is a finely ground flour with a cottony texture. Until recently it was not available in the United States. It is very easy to work with and has the perfect "mouth feel" once it's baked or cooked. It is available from Italian markets and many specialty food stores as well as online (see Sources).

Chris: I love the pasta attachment for my KitchenAid because it allows me to easily make pasta by myself. Always a messy job, but very gratifying.

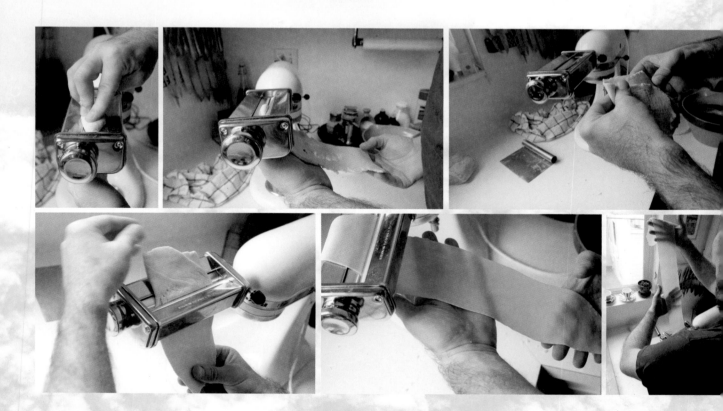

Raw Tomato Sauce

SERVES 6 OR MORE

This is Steve's favorite pasta sauce of all. Unfortunately, it can only be made when plum tomatoes are ripe and deeply sweet and meaty. In reality, this happens about three times a season, although I keep at it, trying to create a batch with the taste that he is always looking for. It is very, very easy to make and, like all simple dishes, its deliciousness depends solely on the quality of the ingredients used. The sauce freezes well, but is really no longer raw when you reheat it after freezing, though it is still pretty darn good—just different.

To make the sauce, first cover the bottom of a large sauté pan with olive oil; I use extra virgin, but it isn't a must. Then, microplane about six fresh cloves of garlic (more or less if you like) into the oil. (If you don't have a microplane, just thinly slice the garlic.) Place over low heat and cook just long enough to allow the garlic mash to soften but not color. As soon as it begins to even look like it might color slightly, remove the pan from the heat.

Peel about three pounds of rich, ripe plum tomatoes. (Or if you're as lazy as I sometimes am or as rushed, just bypass the peeling process.) Core and remove the seeds—the latter is optional, so if you don't mind a seedy sauce, by all means skip it. Cut the tomatoes into pieces and then place them along with whatever amount of basil you want to use, a few at a time, in a food processor fitted with the metal blade. Process until just chunky. Do not puree. Pour the tomatoes into the warm garlic oil. Season with salt and pepper and let rest for at least a couple of hours. Taste and, if necessary, season with additional salt and pepper.

Cook the amount of dried spaghettini or cappellini you want according to manufacturer's directions for al dente. Drain very well and place in a bowl. Add just enough sauce to nicely coat the pasta. Top each serving with a couple more spoonfuls of sauce. I like to grate some Parmesan cheese on the top but Steve thinks it detracts from the simplicity of the tomatoes, basil, and pasta. He usually drizzles a little bit of extra virgin olive oil over his.

Meatballs and Spaghetti

SERVES 6 TO 8

I hadn't made meatballs and spaghetti since the "boys" left home, until a few years ago, when Steve suddenly had a craving for the dish. Just like riding a bike, once you've made meatballs the recipe and the routine become second nature, so it didn't take long before I had a freezer full of the little guys.

I was taught to make Italian-style meatballs—we sometimes forget that there are other types—by a neighbor from Southern Italy when I was about nine or ten. The one thing that she did that I don't see in many other recipes was add a finely grated carrot—something I still do. She also used a mixture of beef and pork with a little sausage, but nowadays I use either very lean ground beef or lean ground turkey.

TIP: I make marinara sauce in batches so my freezer is always stocked with all-purpose tomato sauce. I only use and strongly recommend Pomi tomatoes for any tomato-based sauce, as there are absolutely no additives, including salt. They are available in sterile boxes from most supermarkets. For the first cooking, I simmer the sauce for just a few minutes, because when overcooked on its own it will become acidic. I always use dried basil—when in Sicily I learned that Italian home cooks always use dried herbs, so I feel I can too.

 CHRIS'S SUGGESTED WINE PAIRING
A GOOD-VALUE ROSSO DI TOSCANO

Marinara Sauce

MAKES ABOUT 4 QUARTS

¼ cup olive oil

Sliced or chopped garlic to taste (I generally use at least 10 cloves)

3 boxes Pomi strained tomatoes

3 boxes Pomi chopped tomatoes

1½ teaspoons dried basil or about ¼ cup fresh basil leaves (or more or less as desired)

Coarse salt and freshly ground pepper

Red pepper flakes (optional)

1. Heat the oil in a large Dutch oven or other large nonreactive pot over medium heat. When just warm, stir in the garlic and cook for a minute or so—do not brown. Add the tomatoes and basil. Season with salt and pepper (and red pepper flakes) and bring to a simmer. Simmer for no more than 15 minutes or just until nicely seasoned. Taste and, if necessary, add about ½ teaspoon sugar to heighten tomato flavor, salt, and pepper.

2. Use as is for a pasta sauce, as a sauce for pizza, or as a base for meat sauces, stews, and casseroles.

Meatballs

MAKES ABOUT 20

2 pounds lean ground beef or turkey or a
  mixture of ground beef, pork, and veal (you
  can add ½ pound of crumbled Italian sausage
  in place of ½ pound of the meat)

3 large eggs

1 small onion, grated

1 small carrot, trimmed, peeled, and grated

2 tablespoons minced fresh flat-leaf parsley

1 teaspoon minced garlic

1 cup fresh bread crumbs

Salt and pepper

Approximately ⅓ cup cool water

Olive oil for frying (not extra virgin)

1. Place the meat in a mixing bowl. Add the eggs, onion, carrot, parsley, and garlic, mixing lightly to begin to combine. Add the bread crumbs and salt and pepper along with about half of the water. Mix gently to just combine but don't overmix or the mixture will tighten up and the cooked meatballs will be tough. If the mixture seems dry, add the remaining water.

Gently and quickly form the meat mixture into 2-inch balls by rolling it between your palms. Set the balls aside as they are formed.

2. Heat a thin layer of olive oil in a large cast-iron or other heavy skillet. When the oil is very hot but not smoking, begin adding the meatballs without crowding the pan. Fry, turning frequently, until nicely browned on all sides, about 5 minutes. Using a slotted spoon, remove to a double layer of paper towels to drain. If necessary, wipe out the pan and add fresh oil to continue frying until all meatballs have been browned.

3. At this point, you can add them to a gently simmering pot of marinara sauce and cook for about 30 minutes, until the meatballs are cooked through and the sauce has taken on some of their flavor. Or you can freeze them for later use: place the meatballs on a sheet pan in a single layer in the freezer. When frozen, pack in containers or resealable plastic bags. Label and date and store in the freezer for up to 3 months.

Eggplant Parmigiana

SERVES 6 TO 8

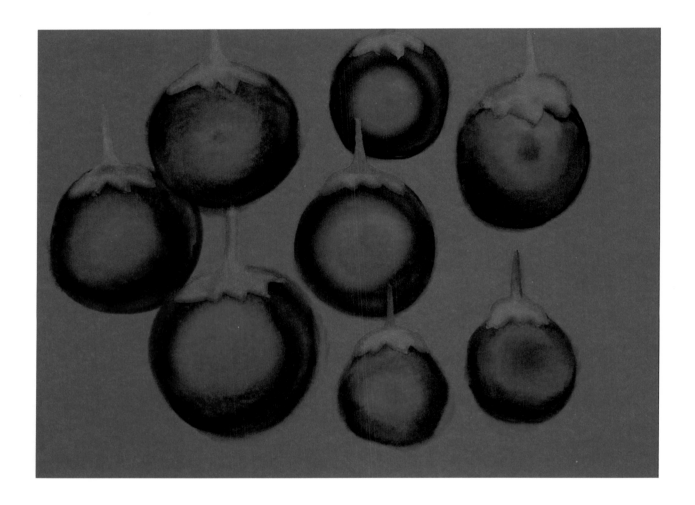

Since I always have a batch of Marinara Sauce (page 140) in the freezer, eggplant parm is my default vegetarian dish. Besides having the sauce on hand, I can count on eggs, flour, bread crumbs, and Parmesan cheese being in the pantry. That just leaves mozzarella, which is pretty easy to come by, particularly in our neighborhood, where I can buy both the plastic-wrapped commercial variety and the artisanal hand-pulled kind within a few blocks. Although traditionally made as a multilayered casserole, alternating between thinly sliced fried eggplant and cheese, I generally make only 1 layer. This cuts down the overindulgence a bit and makes it easier to turn leftovers into sandwiches.

 CHRIS'S SUGGESTED WINE PAIRING
A DOLCETTO FROM THE PIEDMONT REGION

4 to 6 cups Marinara Sauce (page 140)

1½ cups Wondra flour

3 large eggs

3 cups bread crumbs

1 cup cornmeal

1 large (or if layering, 2 large) eggplant

¼ cup olive oil, plus more if needed

1 to 1½ pounds mozzarella cheese, cut crosswise into ¼-inch-thick slices

1 cup grated Parmigiano-Reggiano cheese

1. Preheat the oven to 350°F.

2. Line a baking sheet with parchment paper. Set aside.

3. Generously coat the bottom of an 11 by 7-inch baking pan with marinara sauce. It will probably take about 2 cups. Set aside.

4. Set 3 large, shallow bowls in a row. Place 1 cup of the Wondra flour in the first bowl, whisk the eggs with 2 tablespoons of water in the second, and combine the bread crumbs, cornmeal, and remaining Wondra flour in the third.

5. Peel the eggplant and cut it crosswise into thick slices (somewhere between ¼ and ½ inch).

6. Working with one slice at a time, place the eggplant in the plain flour, follow with a dip in the eggs, and finally, coat both sides in the bread-crumb mixture. As each slice is coated, lay it on the baking sheet.

7. Heat the olive oil in a large frying pan over medium heat. When hot, begin frying the eggplant. You don't have to cook it through, but both sides should be golden brown and crisp. Turn carefully as you don't want to crack the coating. And don't crowd the pan or you will, for sure, crack the coating.

8. As they are fried, place the eggplant slices on a double layer of paper towels to drain.

9. Carefully place a layer of eggplant in the bottom of the sauce-lined pan. Now this is where you decide whether you want to be piggy or not. You can either cover the slices with a thin coating of sauce followed by a thin layer of mozzarella cheese and then repeat the process (except the second time you use a little more sauce and a lot more mozzarella), OR you can do just one layer of eggplant, sauce it, and add a nice layer of mozzarella. With either method sprinkle the top with grated Parmigiano cheese.

10. Place in the preheated oven and bake until bubbling and lightly browned on the top, about 20 minutes for one layer; 35 minutes for two .

11. Remove from the oven and let rest for about 5 minutes before cutting into it. The resting period allows the cheese to firm a bit.

We Can't Forget the French

The French make some of the greatest examples of wine on the planet—Champagne, Bordeaux (cabernet and merlot), red (pinot noir) and white (chardonnay) Burgundies—but to drink these great wines you have to have very, very deep pockets. However, Southern France is now producing really terrific values that are often labeled by varietal. Our family tends to drink the finer French wines only on special occasions, like Christmas, but Mickey would drink them every day if he could.

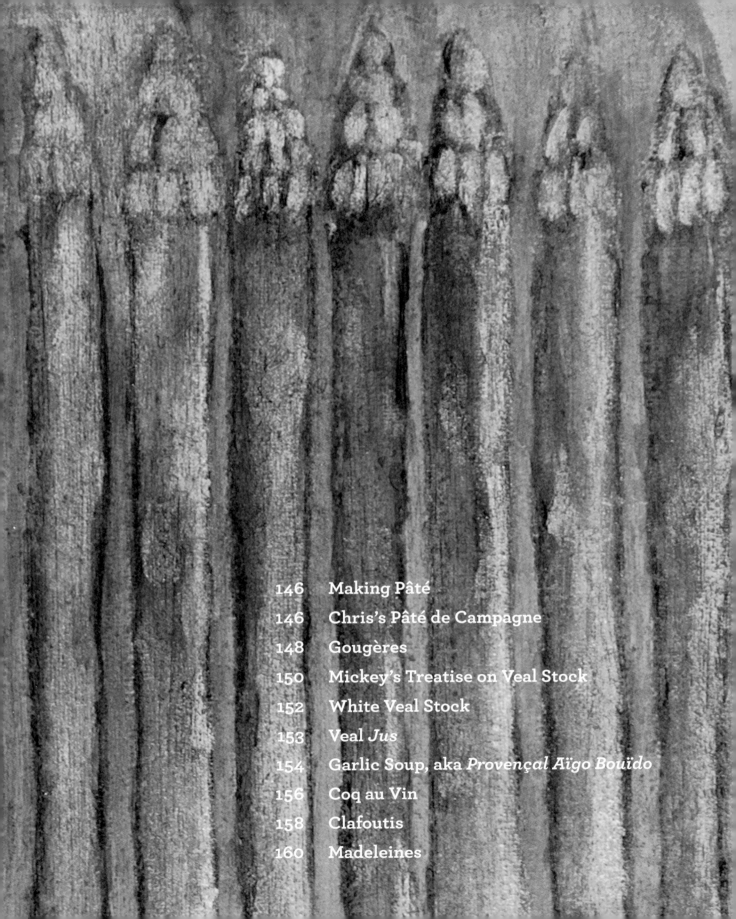

Making Pâté

When we had a catering business within our original MOM, TOO take-out store (an
adjunct to our MOM bakery and, I believe New York City's first all-American prepared-
food store) one of my favorite dishes to feature on party menus was a classic pâté de
campagne. In those days, there were very few specialty food retailers and a tiny company
called Les Trois Petits Cochon (it has grown to be not so tiny at www.3pigs.com) had only
just begun producing and selling classic French pâtés and charcuterie in Manhattan, so

making your own was about the only way to go. I probably found my first recipe in an Elizabeth David cookbook and then, through trial and error, made it
my own. My base was boneless, skinless chicken and slab bacon with the addition of cubes of smoked ham and pistachios. It was pretty much the same
as the pâté Chris now makes, except I lined my pan and covered the loaf with
thin slices of ham or, when I could get it, prosciutto. Both of us serve our pâté
with cornichons, a variety of mustards, and baguette toasts.

The most important thing about making pâté is to weight it evenly and
heavily in the mold, so that it compacts into a firm loaf. Otherwise it will be
very difficult to cut.

Chris's Pâté de Campagne

MAKES ONE 1½ QUART TERRINE MOLD—EASILY SERVES A CROWD

CHRIS'S SUGGESTED WINE PAIRING
A LOVELY ROSÉ FROM PROVENCE

2 pounds pork butt, cut into pieces and well chilled

¼ pound chicken livers, chilled

½ cup flat-leaf parsley

¼ cup diced onion

1½ tablespoons minced garlic

2 tablespoons coarse salt

1 teaspoon freshly ground white pepper

½ teaspoon pâté spice (see Note)

2 large eggs

½ cup heavy cream

2 tablespoons all-purpose flour

2 tablespoons brandy

1. Preheat the oven to 300°F.

2. Line a 1½-quart terrine mold (with a lid) with plastic film, leaving about 3 inches of overhang. Set aside.

3. Set up a heavy-duty stand mixer with the grinder
attachment fitted with the coarse plate.

4. Place a large metal bowl filled with ice under the
end of the grinder; then, place another bowl into
the ice.

5. Push the cold pork through the coarse setting
into the chilled bowl. When all of the pork has been
ground, add the chicken liver, parsley, onion, and

garlic along with the salt, white pepper, and pâté spice, tossing to blend. Keep chilled.

6. Remove the coarse plate and replace it with the fine plate.

7. Remove the chilled bowl from the ice and replace it with the large bowl of the mixer. Immediately begin pushing the chilled pork mixture through the fine plate into the clean chilled mixer bowl.

8. When all of the pork mixture has been finely ground, remove the grinder attachment. Replace it with the paddle attachment and fit the bowl into the stand.

9. Add the eggs, cream, flour, and brandy, and mix on low to blend completely.

10. When completely blended, scrape the mixture into the prepared mold, smoothing out the top with a spatula. Bring the overhang up and over the meat mixture to completely cover. Place the lid on.

11. Place a large baking pan with sides into the preheated oven. Transfer the terrine to the larger pan and add enough water to come halfway up the sides of the terrine mold.

12. Bake for about 1 hour, or until an instant-read thermometer reads 160°F when inserted into the center.

13. Remove from the oven and uncover. Place a weight on top of the loaf to evenly weigh it down. You want to compact the meat while still hot. Allow to cool slightly before transferring to the refrigerator to chill for at least 8 hours or overnight.

14. When ready to serve, remove from the fridge. Take off the weight and lift the pâté from the mold.

15. Place on a wooden board, cutting a few slices from one end. Garnish the board with cornichons and little bowls of mustards and set a basket of toasts at the side.

NOTE: Pâté spice comprises 1 teaspoon each of ground cloves, nutmeg, ginger, coriander, and cinnamon plus 1 tablespoon of freshly ground white pepper.

Gougères

MAKES ABOUT 3 DOZEN

Of all the cherished recipes in this book, I can think of none more beloved by the entire Choate family than this one. Gougères (or cheese puffs) are on the menu every Christmas at Mickey's and throughout the year whenever we gather for a Champagne toast. They are nothing more than a simple *choux* paste (*pâte à choux* is the proper French term) of butter, flour, water, and eggs that has been flavored with sharp cheese. For us, the cheese is Gruyère, but Emmenthaler, Comté, or Cheddar can also be used. We always have a basket lined with a linen napkin ready to receive them hot from the oven, but no sooner do they hit the basket than multiple hands reach in to grab them. The gougères never last long in our house. Up until recently, making the Gougères was my only Christmas dinner obligation, but I've now turned the reins over to the girls.

 CHRIS'S SUGGESTED WINE PAIRING
A CREMANT DE BOURGOGNE

4 large eggs, room temperature
1 cup water
½ cup unsalted butter, cut into pieces and chilled
Pinch of salt
15 tablespoons all-purpose flour
1 cup grated Gruyère or any other sharp cheese you like

1. Preheat the oven to 400°F.

2. Lightly spray 2 cookie sheets with nonstick baking spray or lightly butter and flour. Set aside.

3. Set up a heavy-duty standing electric mixer fitted with the paddle.

4. Have all of your ingredients ready to go.

5. Crack the eggs into a bowl and whisk to blend.

6. Combine the water with the butter and salt in a heavy-bottomed saucepan over high heat. Bring to a boil, stirring occasionally.

7. Immediately remove from the heat and quickly add the flour all at once, beating vigorously with a wooden spoon. Continue to beat until the dough lifts away from the inside of the pan.

8. Return the mixture to low heat and continue to beat for 1 minute to dry it somewhat. Then, scrape the dough into the bowl of the standing electric mixer and begin mixing on low.

9. Raise the speed to medium-high and slowly add the beaten eggs along with half of the cheese. The dough should become the consistency of thick mayonnaise.

10. Scrape the dough into a pastry bag fitted with the ½-inch plain tip. Pipe the dough into mounds, no larger than 2 inches in circumference, onto the prepared baking sheets, leaving about 2 inches between each mound.

11. When all of the mounds have been made, sprinkle the tops with the remaining cheese.

12. Place in the preheated oven and bake for about 20 minutes or until puffed and golden brown. If possible, do not open the oven door or the puffs might deflate somewhat or dry out.

13. Remove from the oven and serve warm.

Mickey's Treatise on Veal Stock

MAKES ABOUT 3 DOZEN

Mickey: If there is one dish that sums up my cooking style it is veal stock. You see the French connection here? If you asked me, I would say that stocks and sauces are the ultimate expression of any cooking. But from my point of view it is the preparation of sauces that makes French cooking stand out above all other cuisines. It is the long, slow melding of meat bones and scraps into an aromatic liquid that does it. Because once you have that stock, you have the base for a myriad of sauces.

Here is the story of the revelatory experience that led me to the exultation of veal stock and how it turned me on to the beauty of perfectly cooked fish (which, up to that point, I had generally avoided). Some twenty-five years ago I had the opportunity to eat quite often in one of New York's top restaurants when Mom was working on a cookbook with the chef. (**Judie:** "It was Aureole, chef Charlie Palmer's premier restaurant and the focal point of one of my most favorite writing experiences.") We had a great many extraordinary meals, but one dish in particular blew my mind and became a touchstone for my future home cooking. It was a halibut T-bone that had been cooked in a hot oven in veal stock. The dish opened my eyes to just how good properly cooked fish could be and how veal stock could elevate a dish to four-star caliber. The halibut T-bone—a thick center piece cut from the spot where the cartilage that makes up the halibut's spine divides the filets—was seared in a pan and then bathed in garlic and a rich veal stock reduction. The pan was thrown into a very hot oven and a line cook would periodically spoon the reduction over the fish while it finished cooking. (Halibut is a big, meaty fish with dense, snow-white flesh that can withstand high-heat cooking, and when fresh [as it certainly was in this instance] has absolutely no "fishy" taste). Once plated, the fish glistened with a dark brown coating of meat *jus* atop a mound of braised cabbage with a carrot dice. WOW! Need I say more? Plus, I learned that a great red wine can go extremely well with fish!

Now, at home, I typically make two types of veal stock (as well as chicken, lamb, and duck, among others) which are in my freezer at all times; a basic traditional rich, dark sauce consisting of veal bones, some sort of tomato product (usually tomato paste), *mirepoix* (carrots, onions, celery, and leeks), thyme, and bay leaf; and a white veal stock. In the "old" days I'd roast the bones for the dark stock, but I now skip that step since learning that most contemporary four-star chefs feel the addition of the tomato product is enough to add the desired dark color, richness, and depth of flavor.

For white veal stock, no tomato product is added. I use this stock more often because it offers a more neutral backdrop for so many sauces. Unlike a dark stock, there is no assertive sweet/acidic tomato flavor and the star ingredients of a sauce can shine. It is this stock I use to make a veal *jus* for veal chops or loin. Although it sounds fancy, a *jus* is nothing more than a sauce made by reducing a stock (or even water) over the bones and scraps of the particular protein you are preparing. So, for veal *jus*, you simply sauté or roast a couple of pounds of veal neck, stew, or breast with some onion, garlic, and thyme (no need to add carrots unless you want a note of sweetness). Deglaze once with a cup or so of water; then pour on a quart or two of white veal stock when the meat scraps are nicely browned. Sit back and let it cook down until the liquid is syrupy and very flavorful. Then, just cook a little more until it thickens a bit more and is so sticky that it coats your finger like glue when you dip it into the pot. You can add other ingredients like herbs or mushrooms depending upon what type of sauce you are making, or you can pour in a splash of wine or a fortified wine after deglazing with water. I really do believe that in a previous life I must have been a saucier in an elegant Parisian restaurant.

White Veal Stock

MAKES ABOUT 2 QUARTS

8 pounds of meaty veal bones, such as neck or marrow

3 onions, peeled and diced

3 carrots, peeled and diced

2 leeks, washed well, trimmed of most of the green part, and diced

A couple of sprigs of fresh thyme (or 1 teaspoon dried)

1 bay leaf

Some parsley sprigs (if you have them)

1. Place the bones in boiling water for about 5 minutes, or just until a good measure of scummy stuff comes to the top. Remove from the heat and drain well. This step isn't necessary, but it does cook off some of the scum.

2. Place the drained bones, onions, carrots, leeks, thyme, and bay leaf in a large stockpot. (If you want a dark stock, add a 6-ounce can of tomato paste along with the vegetables.) Add 5 quarts of cold water (the bones should be covered by at least 2 inches) and place over high heat. Bring to a boil; then, lower the heat and cook at a bare simmer for 6 hours, skimming the top frequently to remove the detritus that rises to the surface. Skimming is probably the most important thing you can do when making stock. I keep a large bowl of cold water next to the stockpot and use a wire mesh skimmer to transfer the scum to the water.

3. Remove from the heat and strain through a fine-mesh sieve into a clean container. Place the container in an ice-water bath to cool quickly. Then, pour into small containers, cover, label, and freeze.

Veal *Jus*

MAKES ABOUT 1 CUP

2 to 3 pounds veal neck bones or cut-up
  pieces of veal breast
1 onion, diced
Half a head of garlic IF you want a strong
  garlic infusion
3 sprigs fresh thyme
1 bay leaf
2 quarts white veal stock

1. Place the veal bones in a large saucepan over medium-high heat. Cook, stirring frequently, for about 10 minutes or until browning. Add the onion, garlic, thyme, and bay leaf, and cook, stirring frequently, just until the onion begins to soften, about 4 minutes. Add a cup of water and stir up the brown bits on the bottom of the pan. Cook, stirring, for a few minutes to deglaze the pan. Add the stock and bring to a boil. Lower the heat and cook at a gentle simmer, skimming frequently, for 1 hour.

2. Remove from the stove and strain through a fine-mesh sieve into a clean saucepan. Return the strained liquid to medium heat and bring to a simmer. Simmer, skimming as necessary, for about 30 minutes, or until it reaches a saucelike consistency.

3. You can use the *jus* immediately or chill in an ice bath and then transfer to small containers and freeze (labeled, of course, with name and date) for the future. I always have small containers of *jus* ready to fancy up an everyday dinner.

About stocks!

Though I am not as disciplined as Mickey is about keeping every possible type of stock in my freezer at all times, I do generally keep chicken stock and sometimes vegetable. All meat and poultry stocks are made in about the same way Mickey makes his veal stock—white stocks with raw bones and trimmings and brown with roasted. Fish stock is made from the bones of white fishes and shellfish stocks are made with the shells and peelings of lobster or shrimp; either type calls for a light infusion of leeks and onions and dry white wine.

Garlic Soup aka *Provençal Aïgo Bouïdo*

We love garlic in all its forms—I keep roasted garlic on hand throughout the year to add depth and savor to all kinds of dishes and always have a few bulbs of fresh in the onion basket. Other than adding a bit of roasted garlic to sauces and braises to insert that hint of sweet pungency, my favorite way of using fresh garlic is to grate raw cloves (using my trusty rasp grater) into sauces, soups, salad dressings, and breads. I grate garlic so often that I have a permanent scrape at the base of my thumb, which I can only assume is an allergic reaction to the oil.

A number of countries have a garlic soup all of their own—Spain has *sopa de ajo*, Portugal its *AÃsorda*, Italy the wondrous *zuppa all'aglio*—but my favorite is this French one known as *Provençal Aïgo Bouïdo*. It is a warming fall or winter dish and filling enough to be a main course (when you add the cheese and bread). The aroma coming from the kitchen will make you ravenous—extra bread, a lovely frisée salad, and a bottle of chilled light white wine complete what is, to me, the perfect meal.

Fresh Garlic

Store-bought garlic really can't compare with freshly picked. And here is the reason why. Almost all of the garlic in our supermarkets comes from China; brought in daily by the container load! Lord only knows how old it is. Angelo Zingone, my local green grocer (see Sources), recently told me that when he began selling fruits and vegetables, all garlic came either from local farmers or from California, then it started coming from Mexico, and now he can only get China-grown. This is inexplicable to me, as garlic is so easy to grow. At the end of every summer in Upstate New York, for instance, you'll find gardeners urging you to take baskets-full for free.

3 heads of very fresh garlic

1 medium sweet onion, such as Vidalia, peeled and chopped

2 bay leaves

2 cloves

2 fresh sage leaves

2 sprigs fresh thyme

Salt

3 large egg yolks, room temperature

¼ cup extra virgin olive oil

Freshly ground pepper (optional)

1 teaspoon chopped fresh flat-leaf parsley

1 teaspoon chopped fresh chives

Freshly grated Parmigiano-Reggiano, for serving

1 baguette, sliced on the diagonal and toasted, for serving

1. Place 2 quarts of water in a large saucepan and bring to a boil over high heat.

2. While the water is coming to a boil, using your fingers, push all the dry, loose skin from the garlic heads. Coarsely chop the heads, skin and all.

3. When the water is boiling, add the chopped garlic along with the onion, bay leaves, cloves, sage leaves, and thyme sprigs. Add some salt and return to a low simmer. Simmer for about 25 minutes, or until the garlic is mushy.

4. While the broth is simmering, prepare the thickener (*liaison* in French culinary terms, and since we're in the territory we might call it as we should). Place the egg yolks in a small mixing bowl. Using a whisk, beat until very light and quite thick. Whisking constantly, add the oil in a slow, steady stream, beating until the mixture comes to a mayonnaise-like thickness. (Since we're in the classic mode, I've suggested doing this by hand, but you could just as easily do it in a food processor.) Cover and set aside until ready to use.

5. When the garlic is mushy, remove the broth from the heat, and strain through a fine-mesh sieve, discarding the solids. Taste and, if necessary, season the broth with salt and pepper.

6. Return the strained liquid to the saucepan and set aside.

7. When ready to serve, return the garlic broth to medium heat and bring to a boil.

8. While the broth is heating, scrape the *liaison* into a soup tureen or large serving bowl. Once the broth has come to a boil, remove it from the heat and, whisking the *liaison* constantly, slowly pour about a cup of the hot broth into the *liaison*; then, pour in the remaining broth. Sprinkle chopped parsley and chives over the top. Serve individual portions with a healthy dose of Parmigiano over the top and plenty of toasted baguette slices to dip into the broth.

Roasting Garlic

Preheat the oven to 350°F. Use either unpeeled whole heads of garlic (if serving whole on a platter with grilled meats, take a nice, neat slice off the top) or peeled individual cloves. Lightly coat the heads or cloves with olive oil, wrap in aluminum foil, and place in a baking pan in the preheated oven. Whole heads will take about 25 minutes and individual cloves about 12 minutes to become soft and aromatic. To make roasted garlic puree, roast whole heads and then unwrap them, cut off the tops, and squeeze out the lush, soft flesh. One large head will usually yield about 2 tablespoons of garlic puree.

Coq au Vin

On a visit to Paris many years ago I had the deepest, darkest, richest coq au vin I've ever tasted in a little neighborhood bistro on the Left Bank. Through the years I've tried to replicate it many times. But I've never had true success at reaching the almost-black sauce of that Parisian experience, so I content myself with my own take on the classic French dish, which has gone through many evolutionary turns to become downright traditional.

Some of my attempts came about while writing about coq au vin. Years ago I did a book with Christian Delouvrier, one of the finest French chefs I've known. His coq au vin packed a double whammy as it was made with a coq au vin stock (you can find the recipe in his book *Mastering Simplicity*). Another recipe I tried a few times came from my friend Linda Arnaud's book *The Artful Chicken*. It is made with vin jaune, a yellow, slightly sherry-tasting wine from the Jura region of France—the bottle was pricey (around $50, as I recall) and the result not much more interesting than one made with a decent red wine. In the end I knew I just wasn't going to be that French—either with a special stock or wine, so I dredged up memories of my early dependence on Julia Child and went back to tradition. Should a big pot of chicken in red wine sauce appeal to your winter sensibilities, this is a very good recipe. I usually serve it with a big mound of mashed potatoes in the center, but buttered noodles would do just as well.

CHRIS'S SUGGESTED WINE PAIRING
A SIMPLE CÔTE DE RHONE

1 (3-pound) chicken, cut into serving pieces, rinsed well and dried

Approximately ½ cup all-purpose flour

Salt and pepper

¼ pound slab bacon, medium dice

3 to 4 tablespoons butter, room temperature

¼ cup cognac

3 cups dry red wine

2 cups chicken stock (or nonfat low-sodium chicken broth)

2 teaspoons tomato paste

1 teaspoon minced garlic

1 bay leaf

1 sprig fresh thyme

1 sprig fresh oregano

1 package button mushrooms, rinsed, trimmed, and quartered

½ bag frozen pearl onions, thawed and patted dry

1. Lightly dredge the chicken in flour and season with salt and pepper. Set aside.

2. Place the bacon in a Dutch oven over medium heat. Add a cube (about a tablespoon) of butter and fry, tossing frequently, for about 15 minutes or until all of the fat has rendered out and the bacon is brown and crisp. Using a slotted spoon, transfer the bacon to a double layer of paper towels to drain.

3. Drain off and reserve half of the fat. Return the pan to medium-high heat. Add the chicken, a few pieces at a time, and sear, turning frequently, until nicely colored on all sides, about 5 minutes. Add

additional fat if the pan gets too dry and sticky as you continue to sear all of the pieces. Using tongs, transfer the seared pieces to a platter as they are done.

4. When all of the chicken has been seared, drain off any excess fat from the pan. Keep the pan on medium-high heat and add the cognac. If you are not fearful, carefully light the cognac with a kitchen match and let some of the alcohol burn off. Otherwise, just bring it to a boil and let it bubble for a minute or so. Scrape any brown bits from the bottom of the pan and then add the wine along with the stock (or broth), tomato paste, and garlic. Bring to a simmer; then, add the bay leaf, thyme, and oregano and cook for a few minutes. Add the reserved chicken, season with salt and pepper, and again bring to a simmer. Lower the heat, cover, and cook for about 30 minutes or until the chicken is cooked through but not falling off the bone. Taste and, if necessary, season again with salt and pepper.

5. While the chicken is cooking, divide the reserved fat between 2 sauté pans. Add a tablespoon of butter to each pan. Place the pans over medium heat. When hot, add the mushrooms to one and the pearl onions to the other. Season with salt and pepper and sauté for about 10 minutes or until lightly colored and cooked through. Combine the mushrooms and onions and set aside.

6. When the chicken is cooked, add the reserved mushrooms and onions and cook for another 5 minutes. Transfer to a serving platter and sprinkle the top with the reserved bacon bits.

Clafoutis

SERVES 8 TO 10

Once upon a time I asked a French friend what she thought was the homiest of all French desserts and, without thinking, she said, "Clafoutis." I'd never tasted one before, but being a lover of nursery desserts, I immediately hunted down a recipe and took a stab at making it. The result was my idea of dessert heaven and it quickly rose to the top of my list when longing for a simple sweet.

The main ingredient in the traditional Limoisin recipe is black Bing cherries complete with their pits. Folklore says that leaving the pits in enhances the flavor during baking. Being all too familiar with the dentist's chair and the cost thereof, I choose to take on the arduous task of pitting the little gems and have not found the flavor to be any less deep or rich.

Once cherries disappear I use other fruits and berries—soft ripe plums and berries, wild and tame; juicy pears are a favorite. I even make one with cranberries for the fall and winter holidays that ends up being rather like an upside-down cake, but it is delicious and a perfect finale to a fall meal. Only recently did I learn that when made with fruit other than cherries, a clafoutis is called a *flaugnarde*. But I still call it clafoutis and so can you.

1½ pounds ripe Bing cherries, pitted

¾ cup granulated sugar

¼ cup unsalted butter, melted

Zest of 1 lemon

3 large eggs, separated

Pinch of salt

¼ cup Wondra flour (or sifted all-purpose flour)

¼ cup heavy cream, at room temperature

1 teaspoon pure vanilla extract

A couple of tablespoons confectioners' sugar for dusting

1. Preheat the oven to 375°F.

2. Place the cherries in a shallow baking dish (either round or a 9- to 10-inch rectangle). Add ½ cup of the sugar along with the melted butter, tossing to mix. Place in the preheated oven and bake just until the cherries begin to soften, about 5 minutes. Remove from the oven, stir in the lemon zest, and set aside. Do not turn the oven off.

3. Combine the egg yolks with the remaining ¼ cup of sugar and the salt in the bowl of a standing electric mixer fitted with the paddle. Beat on low to blend; then, raise the speed and beat for about 4 minutes, until light and airy. Add the cream, flour, and vanilla and beat to blend. Remove the mixing bowl from the mixer and set aside.

4. Using a handheld electric mixer (unless you're a glutton for punishment and want to beat the egg whites with a whisk in a copper bowl), beat the egg whites until soft peaks form. Carefully fold the beaten egg whites into the egg batter until just barely blended. Pour the batter over the warm cherries.

5. Transfer to the preheated oven and bake for about 25 minutes, or until the top has puffed up and is golden brown. Remove from the oven and sprinkle with confectioners' sugar. Serve warm.

Madeleines

MAKES ABOUT 4 DOZEN

I guess that anyone who loves food eventually makes the pilgrimage to Paris and then forever carries with them reminiscences of that delicious city. Mickey proposed to Laurel during dinner at Tour D'Argent and that's a truly lasting memory! Our most unforgettable experience is not quite so romantic but it is equal to Proust's madeleines in its food association. On a rainy February night we headed off to the venerable Parisian brasserie, L'Ami Louis with confirmed reservations and no cabs. We arrived late, only to be gruffly told by the maitre d' that *"no reserve."* We could clearly see that the restaurant had empty tables—noticeably one set for four nestled against the front window. The neighborhood was deserted, we were starving since our entire day had been spent saving ourselves for the night's blow-out, and the maitre d' had absolutely no interest in bailing us out.

I hemmed and hawed; then, I summoned up a few tears and humbled myself before his haughty self. Finally, when nothing else would work, I explained that one of my dinner companions was a very famous American chef from Texas (this was true, we were celebrating a momentous birthday of our friend, Dean Fearing). It was the Texas part that got him. Now convinced that we were millionaires who could make his week, he immediately seated us.

What was unexpected from us "Texans" was the enthusiasm with which we ordered just about everything offered—leg of lamb, the famous Bresse chicken, the foie, the pommes frites. On and on we ordered, stopping to sip our not inconsequential wines. And I don't care that its detractors say that L'Ami Louis has lost its grandeur: the multicourse meal we lingered over that night was without comparison. Straightforward and delicious and oh-so memorable. Even the madeleines and tiny bowl of succulent cherries and the one mangosteen that finished the meal are indelible in my recollections.

As our evening slowed, a neighboring table asked to join us. They were Brazilian bankers who had been eavesdropping on our ribald conversation and couldn't resist the Texas twang. They ordered the brandy—which, of course, Louis (or whatever his given name is) told us was from his special cellar and not available to "just anyone." We closed the place with Louis singing songs and the Brazilians giving us investment advice. I could only assume that they had some idea of our bill and thought we might need a little financial help in the future. I could never hope to replicate that meal, but I can offer up some lovely madeleines upon which you can build your own memories.

1½ cups unsalted butter
4 large eggs, room temperature
1½ cups granulated sugar
1 teaspoon freshly grated lemon zest
1 teaspoon pure vanilla extract
2 cups all-purpose flour, sifted
Confectioners' sugar (optional)

1. Melt the butter in a saucepan over low heat and then continue cooking until the foam disappears from the top and a light brown sediment forms on the bottom of the pan. The melted butter should now be a clear, golden yellow. Remove the butter from the heat. Using a spoon, carefully skim off and discard any brown crust from the top. Set aside to cool.

2. When cool, carefully pour the clear yellow liquid into a clean container, taking care that all of the brown sediment remains in the pan. Set aside.

3. Preheat the oven to 450°F.

4. Generously butter the molds in madeleine pans. Set aside.

5. Place the eggs, granulated sugar, and lemon zest in the bowl of a standing electric mixer. Place the bowl in hot water and let stand, whisking occasionally, until very warm.

6. When warm, place the bowl in the mixer stand fitted with the paddle attachment. Beat on low for a minute or so and then raise the speed to high and beat until the mixture is light, fluffy, and tripled in volume. Add the vanilla and beat to mix. Fold in the flour, followed by the reserved clarified butter, taking care not to beat or the batter will fall.

7. Transfer the batter to a large pastry bag fitted with the large, plain round tip. Carefully pipe the batter into the prepared molds, filling about two-thirds full.

8. Place in the preheated oven and bake for about 10 minutes, or until the cakes are lightly colored on the top and a hint of brown is seen around the edges. Immediately remove from the oven, turn the pans upside down, and gently tap the little cakes out onto wire racks to cool.

9. If necessary, again butter the molds, refill with batter, and bake and cool as above.

10. When the cakes are cool, lightly dust with confectioners' sugar if desired.

Grilled Cheese and Tomato Soup Days

Impromptu Soups

Impromptu soups are not pantry soups with recipes but are soups that are made out of whatever happens to be in the fridge—a left-over platter of crudité, a chicken carcass, some greens that are no longer fresh enough for salad, and on and on the possibilities grow. All you need is a pot, some water, and a sense of adventure. They are particularly well suited to winter, when nasty weather keeps you from wandering the supermarket aisles, the farmers market is pitiful, and the refrigerator seems to have accumulated a little of this and a lot of that. And they are economical to boot, 'cause you use up all the things that might otherwise go out the door.

I discovered impromptu soups years ago, while still a working cook. I was always disheartened by the amount of waste produced at catered events. In the aftermath of a cocktail party, for instance, one would usually find the once-beautiful crudité basket sitting, slightly askew, in unappetizing disarray with otherwise perfectly good vegetables beginning to wilt. One day, the lightbulb went on and I thought, "Why can't I make soup?" Ever after, when a party ended, I would always find the largest pot in the kitchen and throw all of the crudité vegetables in, add a bit of water and any herbs that had been used for garnish, season the mixture well, and leave it to simmer while I tidied up the kitchen. By the time we were ready to depart, a nice pot of soup was ready for the host. If I was still feeling energetic, I would hunt up a blender or food processor and puree the mixture. If not, I'd simply call it chunky vegetable soup and be done with it. But, just in case the host was a novice cook, I always left a note giving instructions for reheating and/or storing.

Impromptu soups can also be made from veggies that have seen better days. How many times do you discover a wrinkled eggplant, a bag of limp carrots, or a wilting cabbage hiding in the back of the cooler bin in the fridge? With eggplant, because it is such a beautiful fruit (it is actually a berry) I am forever buying a selection of types (Japanese, African, Chinese, Italian—green, purple, lavender, white, striated, and on and on the list of exotica goes) to pile in a bowl for table décor. It eventually starts to wrinkle and since

Steve doesn't like eggplant very much it ends up disguised in a soup. I just roast up the eggplant (this adds some depth of flavor) and then cook the roasted flesh with some veggie broth, aromatics (shallots are great), and herbs. I puree the mess with an immersion blender, garnish with some cream or yogurt, and I have a very elegant soup.

This idea always comes into play when I find a roast chicken carcass (along with the remaining carrots, onions, potatoes, garlic, and juices left in the pan) in the freezer, or bits and pieces of leftover chick-

en in the fridge. Here's what you do: Throw the carcass and its accompaniments into a soup pot along with a cup or two of frozen stock. If you don't have stock, use canned nonfat low-sodium chicken broth or forget about the extra chicken flavor and use water. Cover the mix with a couple of inches of cold water, add some chopped onion (1 small), 2 or 3 cloves of garlic, a bay leaf, a few sprigs of parsley, and half of a lemon if you have it. If you are fighting a cold, add some immunity-boosting fresh ginger. Put the pot on the fire and let it simmer away for an hour or so. After about 30 minutes, if you have any chicken parts—a breast, a leg, or a thigh or two—add them to the pot.

When it begins to smell so aromatic and inviting that you can't wait for a steaming bowl, take it off the stove and drain, reserving the broth. Pick off whatever meat is still clinging to the carcass and set it aside. If you added chicken parts, remove the skin, cut the meat into small pieces, and mix it into the carcass meat.

Ladle off the fat and return the broth to the pot. Dice up whatever vegetables you have on hand—a few carrots, an onion, leeks, chard, kale—anything will do except strong green veggies, such as broccoli, unless, of course, they are what you like. Add a good amount of any kind of grain or pasta—fregola sarda, a wonderful Sardinian pasta that resembles Israeli couscous, is one of my favorites—and put it on to simmer. Within 15 to 30 minutes you will have the most delicious, belly-warming meal. Serve it in large shallow soup bowls with a mound of the chicken meat in the center and grated Parmesan cheese over the top. Add a loaf of crunchy bread and a drizzle of extra virgin olive oil along with a bottle of inexpensive (but delicious) pinot noir and you will also have created an elegant one!

Black-Bean Soup

SERVES 6 TO 8

Years ago, black-bean soup was a specialty of the Coach House, a venerated New York restaurant owned by Leon Lianides that was "the" place to go when you wanted to celebrate. (I also remember an occasion there where my children's father asked the waiter for a "chateaubriand for two, for three" which remains a family dining-out joke). The Coach House closed in the early nineties and its space is now the home of Mario Batali's much-admired Babbo, but serious diners of a certain age will always mention black-bean soup when remembering that now extinct restaurant.

I don't know why I've gone on about it because my recipe is not taken from the Coach House, but comes straight from one of my out-of-print books, *The Rediscovered Bean*. It is, however, a good one and will serve you well throughout the year as it is delicious either hot or chilled. When hot, it's great garnished with some hard-boiled egg; when it's chilled, I prefer it straight up or with a dollop of crème fraîche or plain yogurt and a sprinkle of candied orange zest or crystallized ginger. The soup will keep for a few days in the fridge, or it can easily be frozen for another day.

1½ cups dried black beans

2 medium carrots, peeled and chopped

Peel of 1 orange (preferably organic)

1 cup chopped winter squash or pumpkin

1 cup chopped onions

1 cup chopped celery, leaves included

2 tablespoons chopped fresh flat-leaf parsley

2 teaspoons minced garlic

1 small smoked ham bone (optional)

½ pound pancetta (optional)

1 tablespoon fresh lemon juice

1 tablespoon ground cumin

½ teaspoon fresh thyme leaves

Salt and pepper

½ cup dry sherry

⅓ cup finely chopped or sieved hard-boiled egg whites (optional)

Lemon slices, chopped chives, or other garnish (optional)

1. Place the beans in cold water to cover by 1 inch and set aside to soak for 8 hours or overnight.

2. Drain the beans and transfer to a Dutch oven. Add water to cover by 3 inches, along with the carrots, orange peel, squash, onions, celery, parsley, and garlic. Place over medium-high heat, stirring to blend. Add the ham bone and bring to a boil. Lower the heat and cook, at a gentle simmer, for 2 hours, or until the beans are very soft. If necessary, add water to keep the mixture from drying out.

3. About a half hour or so before the beans are done, place the cubed pancetta in a cold frying pan over medium-low heat. Fry, turning frequently, for about 12 minutes, or until the fat has been rendered and the meat is nicely browned. Using a slotted spoon, transfer the meat to a double layer of paper towels to drain.

4. When the beans are very soft, remove and discard the orange peel and the ham bone. Stir in the lemon juice, cumin, and thyme. Taste and season with salt, if necessary, and pepper. Return to medium heat and simmer for another 30 minutes.

5. Remove from the heat. Transfer to a blender—in batches, if necessary—or food processor fitted with the metal blade, and process to a smooth puree.

6. Return the puree to a clean saucepan. Stir in the sherry and place over medium heat. Cook just until heated through.

7. Remove from the heat and stir in the pancetta. Taste and, if necessary, adjust the seasonings.

8. Ladle into hot shallow soup bowls. If desired, garnish the top with the egg white and a lemon slice, minced chives, or a dollop of crème fraîche, plain yogurt, or whatever you have on hand that will look spectacular against the lovely soft black soup.

Butternut-Squash Soup

SERVES 6 TO 8

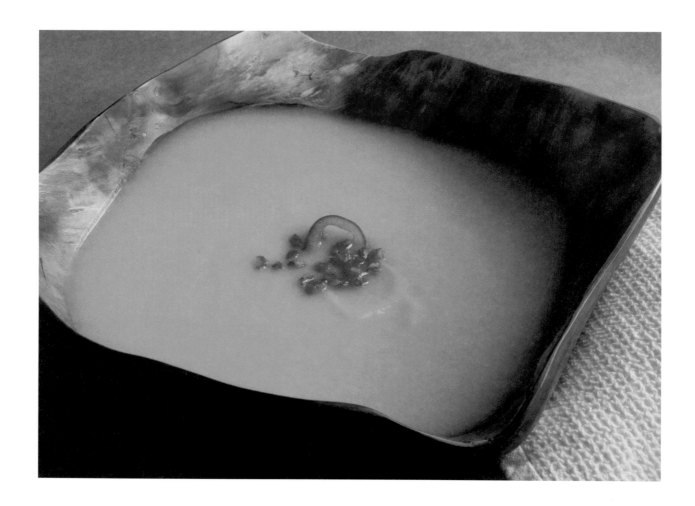

I think that the thing I like best about winter squash is their names—Sweet Mama, Long Island Cheese, Blue Banana, Marblehead, Turk's Turban, Red Bonnet, Sweet Dumpling, Pawpaw—to mention just a few. Even their scientific name, *cucurbita*, is fun to say. The way they look is pretty neat, too. Warty, streaked, lumpy, sectioned, striped, dotted, scalloped—they are all magnificent moments of natural beauty. And they are deliciously sweet and silky on the tongue. You can use almost any hard winter squash to make this soup. It is wonderful throughout the cold months, but can be just as delicious served chilled as the weather warms.

CHRIS'S SUGGESTED WINE PAIRING
A RICH DOMESTIC CHARDONNAY

2 medium butternut squash, peeled, halved, seeded, and cubed

1 cup chopped sweet onion

1 teaspoon grated fresh ginger or galangal

Approximately ¾ cup maple syrup (or other sweetener)

¼ teaspoon ground nutmeg

¼ teaspoon ground cinnamon

¼ teaspoon ground cardamom

4½ cups homemade chicken stock (or nonfat low-sodium chicken broth)

Coarse salt and freshly ground pepper

¼ cup heavy cream (optional)

1 tablespoon minced fresh chives or parsley (optional)

1. Combine the squash cubes, onion, and ginger in a steamer basket placed over boiling water. Cover and steam for about 15 minutes, until the squash is very tender.

2. Divide the syrup in half. Set aside.

3. Working in batches, place the squash mixture in the bowl of a food processor fitted with the metal blade. Using half of the syrup, place some of the syrup along with a portion of the nutmeg, cinnamon, cardamom, and the stock into each batch. Process to a smooth puree. You should use up all of the stock and spices. As the squash is pureed, transfer the mix to a soup pot and season with salt and pepper.

4. Place over medium heat and bring to just a simmer. Taste and, if necessary, add all or part of the remaining syrup to achieve the desired degree of sweetness. (The soup may be made up to this point and stored, covered and refrigerated, for up to 3 days or frozen for up to 2 months.)

5. Serve hot, garnished with a swirl of heavy cream and a sprinkle of chives, if desired.

Ideas for Cooking Squash

Although most squash have an innate sweetness, many recipes add a little sugar (brown or white), honey, or maple syrup to accent the positive—my favorite is maple syrup. Some type of squash soup is always on our fall menu, but never in the summer or spring. When I'm not making soup out of fall's bounty, I stuff it for an easy everyday meal. I have no single recipe, but make a stuffing out of whatever I have on hand. Sometimes I use a little bit of meat—prosciutto, chicken, sausage (even soy sausage), sometimes not—just some grains, nuts, and aromatics. Sometimes I serve the squash with a sauce—marinara, curry, green— sometimes not. I find that all winter squashes make a great canvas for culinary artistry. Plus, they usually do not cost much, are extremely filling, and are nutritious to boot.

Corn Chowder

SERVES 6 TO 8

Although there is just about nothing in the vegetable world as sweet and delicious as summer corn, I always have to remind myself that there are so many other things to do with it than eat it straight off the cob. One of my favorites is corn chowder, but unfortunately I don't make it in the summer because it just seems too rich for a warm-weather meal. But give me a couple of below 85-degree days and I go right to it. It's filling, delicious, and is easily frozen to use on another day.

 CHRIS'S SUGGESTED WINE PAIRING
NAPA VALLEY SAUVIGNON BLANC

10 ears fresh corn, shucked

6 cups whole milk (you can use 2-percent, but it won't be as rich)

3 cups chicken stock or nonfat low-sodium canned chicken broth

½ pound slab bacon, small dice

3 leeks, some green part, washed well and finely diced

1 red bell pepper, stemmed, seeded, membrane removed, and finely diced

¾ pound potatoes, peeled, medium dice

Salt and pepper

1. Using a sharp knife or corn-kernel remover, remove all of the kernels from the corncobs, separately reserving the kernels and cobs.

2. Combine the cobs with the milk and stock in a stockpot. Place over medium heat and bring to a simmer. Simmer for 15 minutes.

3. While the cobs are infusing the liquid, place the bacon in a medium frying pan over low heat. Fry, stirring occasionally, until the bacon bits are brown and crisp, about 12 minutes. Using a slotted spoon, remove the bacon from the pan and place on a double layer of paper towels to drain.

4. Pour off most of the bacon fat from the pan and return it to medium heat. Add the leeks and bell pepper and sauté just until slightly softened, about

4 minutes. Again, using a slotted spoon, remove the vegetables from the pan and place on a double layer of paper towels to drain.

5. Remove the cobs from the liquid and place on a platter to rest until cool enough to handle.

6. Add the potatoes, along with the leeks and bell pepper, to the corn-infused liquid. Season with salt as necessary (remembering the bacon and its fat) and lots of black pepper. Bring to a simmer; then lower the heat and cook at a bare simmer for about 12 minutes, until the potatoes are just about soft.

7. Using a sharp knife, scrape the cooled cobs to extract all of the milky residue from the kernels. Add the residue to the liquid along with the reserved corn kernels. Raise the heat and bring to a simmer. Simmer until the kernels are just tender, about 5 minutes.

8. Remove about 2 cups of the soup from the pot and transfer to a blender. Process to a rough puree. Return the puree to the pot and simmer for another 5 minutes. Remove from the heat and stir in the reserved bacon bits. Taste and, if necessary, season again with salt and pepper.

9. Serve hot, garnished with a bit of whipped cream, sour cream, yogurt, minced chives, or more crisp bacon.

Talking About Sandwiches

I'm not a sandwich person and I never have been—except for one sandwich, which, to my great dismay, I can't eat anymore. Not because I no longer like it, but because it is composed of some of the great cardiac patient no-nos. I first sampled this winning sandwich many years ago at a Greek diner near my office—yes, I did once have a traditional 9-to-5 job (well, sort of). Teddy, the owner, concocted it for me especially because he wanted to turn me into a sandwich lover. And so he did—with an egg-salad BLT. The egg salad has to be really, really heavy on the mayonnaise with just a hint of fresh dill, the tomatoes have to be ripe, the lettuce iceberg, and the bacon thick, crisp, and double layered—one under the egg salad and one on top. Trust me, it is the most delicious sandwich you can imagine.

Steve, on the other hand, loves sandwiches and is perfectly happy to have one for dinner. In the summer he frequently requests a turkey-bacon BLT for dinner and, when the tomatoes are perfection, he might also order one for breakfast. At other times, he will take a mix of whatever leftovers I have on hand—chicken salad, meatloaf, grilled veggies—it doesn't really matter as long as I can wrap it between two slices of bread.

Thin Yellow Boys

SERVES 4

These were a favorite of my mom's. I have no idea where the name Thin Yellow Boys came from, it's just what she called them. Perhaps it came from her Scots family or perhaps she just made the name up. I didn't ask and now I will never know. I would guess that they must have evolved from pub food as they do go awfully well with beer or ale. Steve forgoes the latter for a glass of rosé, but he loves these little sandwiches.

6 hard-cooked eggs, peeled and chopped

1 tablespoon minced sweet onion

1 tablespoon minced sweet pickle

1 tablespoon minced flat-leaf parsley

1 teaspoon minced fresh dill

1 tablespoon Dijon mustard

1 tablespoon Worchestershire sauce

1 tablespoon white wine vinegar

Coarse salt and freshly ground pepper

8 slices warm white toast, preferably homemade or homemade-style

1. If you don't have a microwave (and I don't), preheat the oven to 350°F.

2. Combine the eggs with the onion, pickle, parsley, and dill in a mixing bowl, stirring to blend. Add the mustard, Worcestershire sauce, vinegar, and salt and pepper, stirring to combine.

3. If you have a microwave, combine the egg mixture in a microwavable bowl and microwave on high for about 15 seconds, or until warm. If using the oven, transfer the mixture to a casserole, cover lightly, and place in the preheated oven. Bake for about 10 minutes or just until warm.

4. Place equal portions of the warm egg mixture on 4 slices of toast, smoothing to make an even layer. Top with another slice and cut into triangles. Serve warm.

Really, Really Good Grilled Cheese Sandwiches

This is a grown-up grilled cheese sandwich that I often make myself for lunch when it's just me. If you don't have goat cheese, use any cheese you might have on hand, even good ole American slices if that's what you like. But, the better and more interesting the cheese, the better the sandwich. If tomatoes aren't great, use roasted red or yellow peppers, eggplant caponata, olive paste—well, you get the idea, this is a sandwich you can put your own stamp on.

1 English muffin, split and lightly toasted
Honey mustard
¼ cup arugula leaves, washed and dried
1 very ripe tomato, peeled, sliced, seeds removed
Salt and pepper
1 teaspoon extra virgin olive oil
½ cup crumbled fresh goat cheese
1 tablespoon fresh bread crumbs

1. Preheat the broiler.

2. Place the English muffin, split side up, on a baking sheet of a size that will fit under the broiler.

3. Generously coat the top of each piece of muffin with honey mustard. Place some arugula leaves on each one and then a slice or two (depending on the size of your tomato) of tomato on top. Season with salt and pepper.

4. Using a pastry brush, lightly coat the top of the tomatoes with olive oil.

5. Transfer the baking sheet to the broiler and broil for about 3 minutes or just until the tomatoes are beginning to soften. Remove from the broiler and sprinkle generous equal portions of the cheese over the tomatoes, following this with a sprinkling of the bread crumbs.

6. Return the muffins to the broiler and broil for an additional 5 minutes, or until the cheese has melted and the bread crumbs are golden brown. Remove from the oven and serve immediately.

Panini for Lunch

Some years ago Chris got a panini maker for Christmas and went on a sandwich-making frenzy and then, as far as I can tell, he forgot all about it except, perhaps, at Super Bowl time, when he is famous for his Cubanos. I, on the other hand, being no lover of gadgets, have continued to make my pressed sandwiches on the stovetop in a nonstick frying pan with my metal press on top (see Chicken Under a Brick, page 88).

In case you don't know what makes a panino different from a grilled sandwich, neither do I. Well, that's not exactly true, as I believe that in Italy a panino is made with rustic bread and a pressed sandwich is made with presliced bread; however, *panino* is really the word for "small roll." So, go figure! Whatever you call it or however you make it, this sandwich is a tremendous lunch treat and one you can take liberties with—just use some cured meat and something veggie and tasty with some horseradish for a little heat.

For each sandwich:

2 slices rustic artisanal bread (such as peasant, ciabatta, or country)

A few slices of prosciutto, country ham, jamón serrano, capicola or any dry-cured meat you like

¼ cup (or as much as you like) caponata (store-bought will do, or make your own)

A touch of bottled horseradish

Extra virgin olive oil for brushing the bread

1. Place a slice of bread on a clean work surface. Layer a good amount of meat on it and then top the meat with the caponata, spreading it out to cover. Sprinkle a little horseradish over the caponata and top with a slice of bread.

2. Using a pastry brush, lightly coat the bread with the olive oil.

3. Preheat a nonstick pan over medium heat. Place the sandwich in the hot pan and cover with a press (or place into your panini press following the manufacturer's instructions).

4. Cook for about 4 minutes, or until it begins to brown. Turn and cook for an additional 3 to 4 minutes, or until the filling is hot and the bread is brown and crisp.

5. Remove from the pan, cut in half, and serve piping hot.

Country Cooking

Newsom's Country Ham

A couple of years ago I was lamenting my inability to get a holiday ham from Col. Bill Newsom's Aged Kentucky Country Hams. The late Col. Bill was a nephew of my uncle by marriage (a friend loves to tease me: "You always say, he/she is a cousin, a cousin by marriage, a second cousin once removed—in other words, everyone you know is a relative"—and even when they're not, I like to make them so). When Col. Bill's daughter, Nancy Mahaffey, got wind of my lamenting, I was put on the list for a Christmas ham.

Came the week before Christmas and, as promised, the UPS guy delivered my ham. When I opened the package, I was floored. The ham weighed in at 13.74 pounds but it looked like it weighed 50! I had no idea what container I could possibly have that would hold the bugger completely covered in cold water for the 12- to 18-hour soak required. I ended up scrubbing out my kitchen garbage can, which served very nicely, thank you.

The cooking process began a couple of days before Christmas Eve. I did just as I was instructed: I soaked the ham in cold water for twelve hours, then rinsed it with a mixture of warm water and white vinegar, scrubbed it with a wire brush, placed it in a large roasting pan along with some water, vinegar, and brown sugar, covered it with foil, and baked it for almost six hours (25 minutes per pound). Then, I cut off the skin, glazed it with a mustard/honey/orange zest mixture, coated it with bread crumbs, and baked it again to a nice golden crust. When all was said and done, I had an exquisite ham that could feed a multitude. It's quite salty and must be very, very thinly sliced (think prosciutto), so only a wee portion was consumed on Christmas Eve. I shared the leftovers with many friends and we had a number of ham and red-eye-gravy breakfasts (page 218). Steve got a bit tired of having ham in every salad, sandwich, and omelet for days to come, but Col. Bill Newsom's Aged Country Kentucky Hams have stayed on our holiday menu ever since; they are just too perfect a reminder of days gone by.

CHRIS'S SUGGESTED WINE PAIRING
EITHER A GRENACHE (FOR A RED) OR A RIESLING (FOR A WHITE)

Fried Chicken

How many photographs of fried chicken do you think have appeared on the covers or in the pages of the various food magazines over the years? Thousands, I would guess. And yet, does anyone really make fried chicken anymore? It's just too easy to pick up a bucket at one of the many chains and local joints that specialize in frying up the "holy bird." In New York City, the go-to spot has long been Charles' Southern Style Kitchen, now known as Pan-Fried Chicken. And recently, many folks seem to head to Harlem's Red Rooster, where Marcus Samuelsson, a Swedish chef, serves his take on this classic American dish. With all the commercial fried chicken available, standing in front of a couple of hot pans of bubbling fat just doesn't hold much appeal to most home cooks.

For years and years I made what came to be known as "the best fried chicken in the city," or—when the speaker was feeling really expansive—"the world." It was in fact baked—not fried—and it was moist, crispy, and crunchy, and not too greasy. Steve's Auntie (that's what we always all called her, never Anna, her given name), a Southern gentlewoman of a certain age, always felt that I screwed up a good thing with too much fussing. She simply did "a mess of chicken" lightly coated with flour, seasoned with salt and pepper, and deep-fried in a couple of inches of hot vegetable shortening. No soaking or breading for her.

When Steve says, "Let's have a down-home picnic"—little matter that "down-home" was Brooklyn—I know that he means: "Fry some chicken, please!" And he means fry, not bake, just as Mama (his grandmother) and Auntie did. So I cut up a chicken and put it to soak in sour milk (made with a bit of vinegar added to whole milk when I don't have any fresh or powdered buttermilk on hand) for a couple of hours. I always use buttermilk or sour milk, as my mom said that it insures moist, tender fried chicken. (I don't know if this is actually true but my chicken is never dry.) Then, I put a good amount of all-purpose flour in a large resealable plastic bag with just enough salt and lots of black pepper. I heat up some blended oil—I'd say almost ½ inch—in my extra-large cast-iron skillet. Then I work fast. I quickly pull the chicken pieces from the milk, shake off the excess, and put a few pieces at a time in the flour. I seal the bag and give a couple of tosses to coat the chicken well. I place all of the pieces in the pan (mine is a huge one) and, over medium-high heat, I quickly

brown all sides and then turn down the heat and fry, turning frequently, for about 20 minutes. The chicken gets a beautiful crust—crisp, slightly salty, with a bite of pepper—and the meat is deliciously moist. If you don't want to make the greasy-top-of-the-stove mess that frying chicken results in, use my recipe for not-fried; I promise it's just as good and no one will know the difference.

My Famous Not-Fried Chicken

SERVES 6 TO 8

🍷 CHRIS'S SUGGESTED WINE PAIRING
CHAMPAGNE IF YOU'RE NOT ON A BUDGET; PROSECCO IF YOU ARE

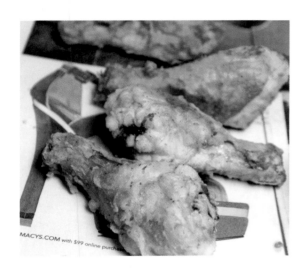

MACYS.COM with $99 online purchase

2 (3-pound) frying chickens, cut up, rinsed,
   and patted dry

2 cups whole milk

½ cup plain yogurt

2 large eggs

4 cups all-purpose flour

½ cup fine ground cornmeal

1 tablespoon freshly grated lemon zest

1 teaspoon dried tarragon

1 teaspoon paprika

Coarse salt and freshly ground black pepper

2 to 3 cups canola oil, peanut oil, or vegetable shortening

1. Place the chicken in a large resealable plastic bag.

2. Whisk the milk and yogurt together in a mixing bowl. Whisk in the eggs and blend well. Pour the mixture over the chicken, seal the bag, and shake to coat well. Refrigerate for at least 30 minutes and up to 2 hours.

3. Combine the flour, cornmeal, lemon zest, tarragon, and paprika, and add some salt and pepper as desired, in a large resealable plastic bag.

4. Remove the chicken from the fridge and lift the chicken pieces, one at a time, from the soaking liquid, shaking to allow excess liquid to drip off.

5. Place a few pieces of chicken at a time into the seasoned flour, seal the bag, and shake to coat well. As coated, place the chicken pieces on a sheet pan. Do not crowd, or the coatings will stick together and then pull off when you lift up each piece.

6. When all of the chicken has been coated, cover lightly, and refrigerate for at least 2 hours and up to 8 hours.

7. When ready to cook, preheat the oven to 500°F.

8. Divide the oil between two shallow baking pans. Place in the preheated oven until very hot.

9. Add the chicken pieces to the hot oil without crowding the pans. Bake for about 15 minutes, or until one side is golden and crisping. Using tongs, turn and bake for another 20 minutes or until the chicken is golden brown and very crisp. If chicken is getting too brown, lower the oven temperature to 350°F. If concerned about the degree of doneness, insert an instant-read thermometer into the thickest piece. It should read 160°F to meet most safety requirements. Not to brag—well maybe a little bit—I don't use a thermometer for most meat or poultry cooking and I rarely over- or undercook. Remove from the oven and, using tongs, immediately transfer the chicken to multiple layers of paper towel or newspaper to drain well.

10. Serve hot or at room temperature.

Making Sausage

One Thanksgiving in San Francisco, Chris and I decided to try our hand at making sausage. Years ago I had frequently made sausage with my mom using her hand-cranked grinder (which I still have and use), but I had little remembrance of the actual task. I have no idea where she got the casings we used (perhaps from a local farmer) but Chris got his at the Golden Gate Meat Company at the Ferry Building, where we also picked up the chicken and pork for the sausage base.

We totally did the job "on the fly," as they say in the restaurant business. We had absolutely no idea what to do, but we had courage. First we tried a chicken-apple mix. We sautéed a large sweet onion with just a clove or two of garlic and some minced fresh thyme and sage. Chris neatly cut a couple of apples into a fine dice. We ground a couple of pounds of skinless, boneless chicken and then mixed the cooled onion mix and apples into it and seasoned it well with salt and pepper. The apple dice was a little bit too big, but we managed to force it into the casing (which we had soaked in lukewarm water for about an hour) through the tube on the KitchenAid attachment. From the grimaces on our faces, you'd think we were mining coal. We didn't quite have the technique down, but we had some laughs and the sausage tasted pretty darned good. Good enough that we went on to make pork sausage seasoned with roasted peppers and basil in much the same way.

The meat should be ice cold when you begin, and if the mixture gets too warm as you stuff, place it in the freezer to chill down. The chilling makes your job much easier. You will need sausage casing if you want to make links, but you can also make individual patties if you can't find it.

Homemade Chicken Sausage

MAKES ABOUT 4 POUNDS

2 tablespoons canola oil (chicken fat would be great if you have it)

1 large onion, chopped

3 cloves garlic, chopped

1 teaspoon minced fresh sage

1 teaspoon minced fresh thyme

4 pounds skinless, boneless chicken thighs, just a tad frozen

2 tart apples, peeled, cored, and very finely diced

A pinch of ground nutmeg

Salt and pepper

1. A few hours before you want to begin sausage making, put the casing in a big pot of warmish water to soak. Drain and add fresh water a couple of times. Leave soaking until you are ready to use.

2. Heat the oil in a large frying pan over medium heat. Add the onion, garlic, sage, and thyme. Cook, stirring frequently, until soft and fragrant. Remove from the heat and set aside to cool.

3. Fit the grinding attachment with the medium disk to your KitchenAid mixer or set up a hand-cranked grinder that has a sausage-stuffing attachment. For hand cranking, the stuffing attachment is not necessary *IF* you are content to make sausage patties.

4. While the onion mixture is cooling, push the chicken through the medium grind disk on the attachment. Then, combine it with the cooled onion mixture and the apples. Season with nutmeg, salt, and pepper, and mix with your hands, combining thoroughly.

5. Fit the sausage-stuffing piece into the stand mixer and lightly coat it with canola oil. Attach the end of the casing to the opening. Feed the chicken mixture into the chute and carefully push it down into the opening. Here's where the fun begins. Hold the casing to the opening with your hands as you watch it fill with air—try to release the air before the meat mixture begins to fill the tubing. Keep the sausage mixture coming as you simultaneously keep the air out, your fingers from slipping, and holes from bursting open in the casing. You'll get a lot of laughs—don't despair.

6. When the sausage seems to be about the length you are aiming for, twist the casing a few times to close it off and begin making the next link. Continue in this fashion, twisting the casing in the opposite direction after each fill. That is, if you twist right the first time, twist to the left the next and so on. Continue making sausages until all of the meat has been used.

7. Use immediately or divide into serving-size portions and place in resealable plastic bags, label, and freeze for later use.

Fried Green Tomatoes

SERVES 6

Green tomatoes are a sure sign that the summer's tomato crop has been bountiful. I always ask farmers to pick some for me even when the crop is slight. Green tomatoes are a special treat in our house—both fried and in relish. I often make them for a celebratory breakfast, but they are equally good as a side dish for chicken or ribs. You can enjoy them as is or accent them with relishes of all kinds—we particularly like those made by our friend's mom, a South-Asian master cook, Neeta.

5 large green tomatoes, washed, cored, and cut crosswise into ½-inch-thick slices

2 large eggs

½ cup buttermilk

1 cup Wondra flour

1 cup stone-ground cornmeal

Salt and pepper

Oil for frying (I use canola)

1. Place the tomato slices on a double layer of paper towels to drain slightly.

2. Whisk the eggs and buttermilk together in a large, shallow bowl.

3. Combine the flour, cornmeal, and salt and pepper in another large, shallow bowl.

4. Heat a thin layer of oil in a large frying pan over medium heat.

5. Working with one tomato slice at a time, dip it into the milk mixture and then into the flour mixture, pressing down to coat evenly. Shake off excess and place in the hot oil. Fry each slice for about 3 minutes. Turn and fry for another 3 minutes, or until crisp and golden on both sides.

6. Using a slotted spatula, lift the slices from the oil and place on paper towels to drain. Serve hot with a spritz of fresh lemon or any tart or spicy relish or condiment you have on hand. Or, if you like, make a cream gravy in the pan (work some flour into the fat in the pan and when blended, whisk in some milk or cream, and cook until thick—season with salt and pepper, of course) and drizzle over the tomatoes.

Corn Fritters

SERVES 4 TO 6

One summer, many, many years ago, we were a little short on cash but long on fresh corn on the cob. My mom and I devised about as many ways as you could possibly imagine to turn corn into the center of the meal. Chowders, stews, salads, puddings, and fritters alternated throughout the season. As you might have guessed, after that year, a couple of fresh ears of corn were about all I could manage to eat come summer's crop. But as time has passed, I have often gone back to retrieve some of the recipes we created during those lean months, corn fritters being one of the favorites. I like mine with a little dab of sour cream and Steve likes his for breakfast wrapped around a couple of slices of turkey bacon (lots of people also like them with maple syrup). Fritters can be used as a breakfast or brunch treat or as a side dish for roasts, grills, or braises.

2 cups fresh corn kernels

2 large eggs, separated

¾ cup milk

3 tablespoons melted butter

½ teaspoon minced hot chile or ¼ chopped onion (optional) (you can also add a good handful of chopped ham or cooked bacon)

1 cup cornmeal (I like the coarse-ground style)

½ cup all-purpose flour

Salt and pepper

Clarified butter, peanut oil, or nonstick vegetable spray for frying

1. Place the corn in a mixing bowl. Stir in the egg yolks, milk, and melted butter. When blended, stir in the cornmeal and flour, along with the chile or onion, and ham or bacon. Season with salt and pepper.

2. Put the egg whites in a small mixing bowl and, using a handheld electric mixer, beat until stiff peaks form. Carefully fold the beaten egg whites into the batter.

3. Place a nonstick skillet or griddle over medium-high heat. Add whatever fat you are using. When hot, ladle in just enough batter to make 4 cakes (or whatever number your skillet/griddle can easily fit), each about 2 to 2½ inches in diameter. Cook for about 4 minutes, or until golden and beginning to set. Turn and continue cooking for another 3 to 4 minutes, or until golden and cooked through. (Some cooks like to put a fair amount of fat into the pan, particularly butter or bacon fat, so that the cakes absorb quite a bit of it—I don't really like this as you have more taste of the fat and less of the corn.) Remove from the skillet and serve hot.

Digging Ramps

The first time I had the opportunity to dig ramps I had no idea that I was going to get a cardio workout. What's the big deal about pulling up some wild things? I thought. Well, with pitchfork, rubber gloves, and trowel in hand, Steve and I had managed, many hours later, to dig up enough to pickle a couple of jars and have a supper of farm eggs scrambled with ramps and bacon. Not a celebration-worthy amount, but plenty to turn us into ramp lovers. Plus, we really did enjoy the time spent in the woods. From that point hence, we have looked forward to our annual spring dig.

Nowadays, my best buddy Lynn, along with her canine pal and our best friend in the whole wide world, Lena Mai, or as we affectionately call her "Leaner" ('cause that's what she does), venture out into the woods at the first appearance of the lily-of-the-

valley–like leaves that signal ramps have arrived. Lynn usually maps out the ramp clumps so we don't have to go searching high and low for a green mass in the awakening spring forest. Deer almost always get there first and nip off many of the succulent leaves. We harvest selectively and tell no one of our secret spots so that next year the clusters will return and we will, once again, embrace one of the season's great tastes.

Although often described as tasting strongly like onion, I find that the smell of ramps is far more aggressive than the flavor. I'm told that in Upstate New York in the old days, boys would go out early in the morning and dig ramps so that the smell on their hands and clothes would have the teacher sending them home from school for the day—that's just how overpowering the odor can be. I almost prefer the soft, lightly garlicky taste of the leaves over the shallot-like taste of the white part of the bulb, but both add wonderful character to all kinds of dishes. I usually cook them very simply: I chop up the lot, greens and all, and sauté them with some morels if they have popped up alongside the ramps, or button mushrooms if I haven't been so lucky. Add a poached egg on top, and you have a light and lovely meal. Or for something a bit more substantial, this quick and easy pasta dish combines ramps with fava beans—another great spring vegetable that is not so quick and easy to begin with.

Pasta with Ramps, Pancetta, Mushrooms, and Fava Beans

SERVES 4

🍷 CHRIS'S SUGGESTED WINE PAIRING
AN ETNA ROSSO FROM SICILY

½ cup finely diced pancetta

1 cup chopped ramps, white part only

About 8 button mushrooms, cleaned, stemmed, and sliced

1 cup vegetable stock

About 1 teaspoon fresh thyme leaves

1 cup fresh fava beans, blanched and peeled

½ cup heavy cream

Salt and pepper

2 large handfuls of ramp greens, julienned

About ½ box spaghetti or other dried pasta, cooked al dente according to package directions

Freshly grated Parmigiano-Reggiano, as topping

1. Fry the pancetta in a large nonstick frying pan over medium-low heat, stirring frequently, for about 10 minutes, or until crisp and all of the fat has been rendered out. Add the ramps and sauté for a couple of minutes. Stir in the mushrooms and cook, stirring frequently, for about 5 minutes or until the mushrooms begin to brown. Add the stock and thyme and continue to cook for another 5 minutes, or until the liquid has begun to evaporate a bit. Stir in the fava beans, followed by the cream. Taste, and season with salt and pepper. Toss in the ramp greens.

2. Pour the sauce over the pasta and toss to blend. Serve immediately with a good sprinkling of freshly grated Parmigiano-Reggiano.

Waffles for Dinner

MAKES 6 WAFFLES

When I was a little, my mom would occasionally make waffles for dinner complete with a side of bacon and lots of maple syrup just as we would normally have for a weekend breakfast. I still make those waffles, as do Mickey and Chris for their families, though generally not for dinner. Some years ago, recalling my childhood breakfast-for-dinners, I decided to take it a step further and turn it into a savory experience. The waffles are a riff on Mom's original recipe (page 221) while the ragout can be made with whatever you have on hand. I like a mix of mushrooms and greens, but you could make a meat-based gravy, a savory veg mix like caponata, or even a curry.

2 cups all-purpose flour
½ cup rolled oats
¼ cup cornmeal
1 tablespoon baking powder
½ teaspoon each salt and pepper
2 large eggs, separated
2 cups 2-percent milk
¼ cup olive oil
Easy Mushroom Ragout (recipe follows)

1. Combine the flour, oats, cornmeal, baking powder, salt, and pepper in a mixing bowl.

2. Combine the egg yolks with the milk and olive oil. Set aside.

3. Using a handheld electric mixer, beat the egg whites until they hold soft peaks.

4. Add the egg-yolk mixture to the dry ingredients and, again, using the mixer, beat until just combined. When blended, fold in the beaten egg whites until just barely incorporated.

5. Heat a waffle iron. Add batter according to manufacturer's directions and bake until golden brown and crisp. Serve with the ragout on the side or over the top.

Easy Mushroom Ragout

2 tablespoons olive oil

2 large shallots, minced

1 clove garlic, minced

4 cups sliced mushrooms—any type will do

1½ cups chicken stock or low-sodium, low-fat chicken broth

1 tablespoon tomato paste

Dried thyme

Salt and pepper

1 cup shredded beet greens, kale, mustard greens, or Swiss chard

1. Heat the oil in a large frying pan over medium heat. Add the shallots and garlic and sauté for about 3 minutes, or until just soft. Add the mushrooms and cook, stirring frequently, for about 5 minutes, or until the mushrooms have exuded moisture and begun to color.

2. Add the chicken stock and tomato paste, stirring to blend well. Season with thyme, salt, and pepper, and cook, stirring occasionally, for about 10 minutes, or until the mushrooms are quite soft and the mix is nicely flavored. Stir in the greens and cook for an additional couple of minutes until just wilted. Serve warm.

Annie's Brown Bread

MAKES 3 LOAVES OR 2 DOZEN MUFFINS

This is a typical Irish bread taught to me by my almost-daughter, Annie. Annie's dad, Kevin, sent her off from Ireland to America with the recipe and she has now made it her own. Ideally, the bread should hang around the kitchen for a day before cutting into it. I never let that happen—I'm slicing off pieces and slathering them with sweet butter as soon as it is cool enough to handle. The loaves make great toast and are a complete breakfast in a few bites. In fightin' Irish fashion, Annie says her dad's routine goes something like this: bake a few loaves, insult your children, start a massive family fight, and then go down to the pub and complain about your lousy wife and kids to all of your cronies. If you do this, you'll have a true McDonagh recipe. However, this is definitely not what happens when Annie and I bake together!

Nonstick baking spray

4 cups plus 2 tablespoons buttermilk

1 large egg, room temperature

4 cups (21 ounces) all-purpose flour

3½ cups (1 pound) whole-wheat flour

½ cup steel-cut oatmeal

½ cup wheat bran

½ cup oat bran

½ cup wheat germ

3 heaping teaspoons baking soda

3 teaspoons sea salt

2 to 3 teaspoons Demerara sugar (or dark brown sugar, if you can't find Demerara)

1. Preheat the oven to 400°F for loaves or 365°F for muffins.

2. Using a nonstick baking spray, lightly coat the pans. Set aside.

3. Combine the buttermilk with the egg in a small mixing bowl, whisking to blend completely. Set aside.

4. Combine the all-purpose and whole-wheat flours with the oatmeal, wheat bran, oat bran, wheat germ, baking soda, salt, and sugar in a large mixing bowl, stirring to blend. Add the buttermilk mixture and, stirring with a wooden spoon, mix thoroughly.

5. Spoon the dough into the prepared pans, filling either the loaf pans or muffin tins no more than two-thirds full. Transfer to the preheated oven and bake the loaves for 10 minutes. Then, lower the heat to 365°F and continue to bake for 50 minutes (35 minutes for muffins) or until a toothpick inserted into the center comes out clean.

6. Remove from the oven and tap the breads from the pans and place on a wire rack to cool. The muffin tins can be placed directly on wire racks and the muffins left in the pans to cool.

7. Allow to rest for a day before eating.

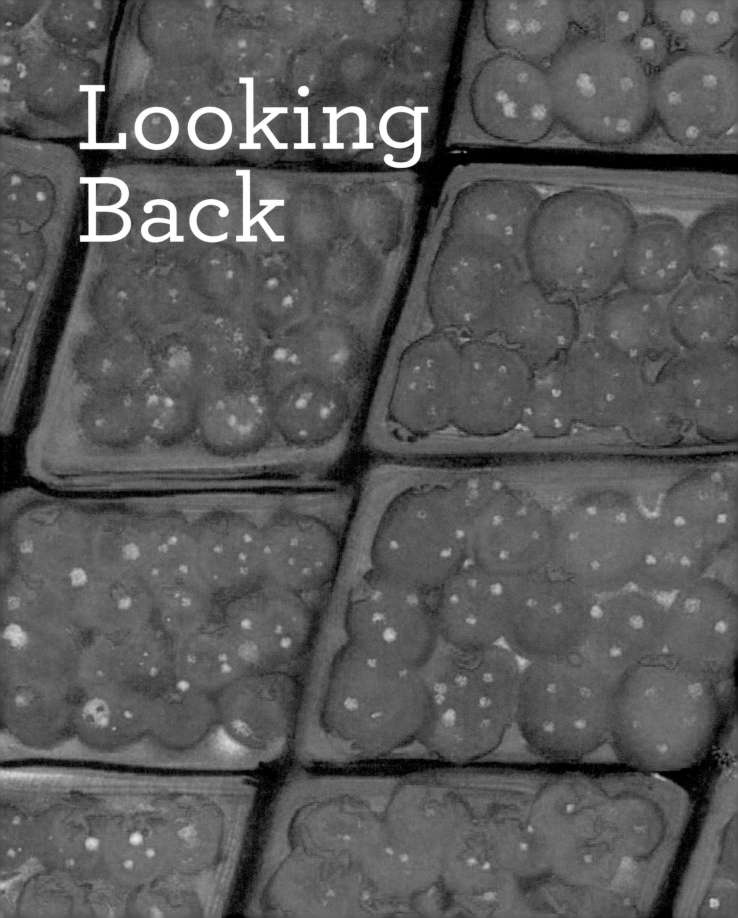

Looking
Back

Chris on Vinegar

Chris: For years, I simply poured the last remains of opened wine bottles down the drain. As the volume of left-over wine increased from the almost daily tastings I did for my staff and our customers, I decided that I should try to make vinegar. Partly it was a matter of economy, as I hated to waste all that great (and sometimes not so great) wine; partly it was to create something of my own; but perhaps most of all I wanted to give something homemade and special to my friends and business associates at Christmastime—much as I had seen Mom do throughout my life.

When I first started, it was simply pouring the remaining wine from a mix of bottles into a clean glass container. That led to buying a barrel and all of the vinegar-making accouterments. Then Canada joined in and created a label for our brew. Our vinegar has been a great success—we are now getting requests for refills. The pleasure that we take in creating something that is ours alone is even more rewarding. (**Judie:** "This is where I get prideful—it is just so gratifying to see that some of my old-fashioned ideas live on through the 'boys.'")

Pickled Asparagus

MAKES 4 TO 6 QUARTS, DEPENDING UPON THE SIZE OF THE SPEARS

When I was a little girl (don't you just love a paragraph that begins like that?) in southeastern Colorado, every spring I would accompany my mom and Aunt Frances to pick the bountiful asparagus that grew wild along the local irrigation ditches. I don't know if it was the fact that it sprouted next to muddy water or that it smelled so pungent, but it was the one vegetable that I didn't like. (Yes, I even liked beets and spinach!) As the years passed, asparagus remained on my "well, I'll eat it but…" list. Just within recent memory has it, unexpectedly, become one of my favorite spring treats.

When I have the opportunity to pick wild asparagus or when the local crop is expansive, I pickle it using the same recipe that my mom and aunt shared so many years ago. I rarely have enough to do an all-out canning, so I just seal and refrigerate the few jars I manage—a couple for our use and a couple to share with friends. Although a traditional recipe, pickled asparagus makes a sophisticated hors d'oeuvre (wrapped with some thinly sliced speck or prosciutto), a great addition to a summer salad, or a perfect side with grilled fish.

5 cups white or rice wine vinegar

½ cup coarse salt

4 pounds very fresh asparagus, tough ends cut off to make a neat end (do not peel, as you want firm stalks)

As many fresh garlic cloves as you like for each jar

1 sprig fresh dill per jar

½ teaspoon mustard seed per jar

1 small hot chile per jar (optional)

1. Make an ice-water bath in a large, shallow pot or bowl. Set aside.

2. Combine the vinegar and salt with 5 cups of water in a heavy, nonreactive saucepan over high heat. Bring to a boil. Working with a few spears at a time, blanch the asparagus in the boiling liquid for 45 seconds. Using tongs, transfer the blanched asparagus to the ice-water bath. As cooled, place on a double layer of paper towels to drain.

3. Keep the vinegar mixture at a bare simmer once all of the asparagus has been blanched.

4. Pack the cooled, blanched spears in clean, sterilized quart jars, tips up. Into each jar, put some garlic cloves, a sprig of fresh dill, the mustard seed, and chile. Cover with the hot vinegar mixture, leaving about a ¼-inch space at the top. Screw on lids and, if refrigerating, set aside to cool. Store, refrigerated, for up to 1 month.

5. If canning, place the jars in a boiling-water bath (the water must cover the jars by 1 inch) and boil for 5 minutes. Remove from the boiling water and tighten the lids. Set aside on wire racks to cool before storing.

Easy Refrigerator Pickles

MAKES ABOUT 4 QUARTS

One thing you can count on in our house is that as soon as Kirby cucumbers arrive in early summer at the farmers market, I will be making my Easy Refrigerator Pickles. I have been preparing these crisp, refreshing pickles for many, many years and we never seem to tire of them. The recipe couldn't be simpler and they keep in the refrigerator for about three weeks before they start to get soggy. If your family members aren't big pickle eaters, you can always make less or just share them with friends and neighbors.

4½ pounds Kirby cucumbers, washed and, if large, cut in half lengthwise
4 dried hot red chilies
16 to 20 fresh garlic cloves
1 cup sugar
3 tablespoons kosher salt
4 cups white vinegar
12 sprigs fresh dill

1. Combine the cucumbers, chilies, and garlic in a large nonreactive bowl. Add the sugar and salt, tossing to coat. Add the vinegar and 4 cups of water and set aside, stirring frequently, for about 30 minutes or until the sugar and salt are dissolved.

2. Pack the cukes into sterilized quart jars, adding an equal number of garlic cloves, 1 chile, and 3 dill sprigs to each jar. Pour in enough liquid to cover the cukes. Cover and refrigerate for at least 3 days before eating. The pickles keep, refrigerated, for quite a long time but they do soften and develop stronger flavor as they sit.

Making Old-Fashioned Relish

My canning sometimes leaves a bit to be desired. I never plan ahead, tending to just tackle the job when I have more produce than I know what to do with—which also means that I don't follow the good cook's rule of making sure I have everything on hand. However, all of these relishes come from my mom's recipe book, so you can be assured that they work.

Nana's Pepper Relish is Steve's favorite condiment. My mom introduced him to it and, of course, hers was much better than mine could ever possibly be! But without Mom to make it any longer, my relish has to suffice as the zest needed to brighten grilled chicken or meat or add flavor to a winter's everyday lunch sandwich or salad. I always go straight to the farmer for my peppers, often Parson's Farm Stand in Sharon Springs, New York. When I tell Kenyon, the farmer, that I need eighteen of each color along with sixteen onions, out to the fields we go so I don't deplete the roadside stock piled in baskets. Sneaky of me, but could anything be fresher? I don't think so!

Green tomato and corn tie for a close second on the favorite relishes list. It's not always easy to get enough green tomatoes to make relish, unless you have a garden or an agreeable farm stand nearby. If you can manage to lay your hands on a bundle, put up a few jars of this tangy condiment. It's excellent on grilled meats, fish, sandwiches, and tossed into salads. I will give you Mom's recipe, but you can really add and subtract ingredients as you wish.

I'll be perfectly honest with you—I never can anything with high sugar or high acid content. My mom didn't, my aunts didn't, and so I don't either and I've never had a batch spoil. The only high-acid product I would can is tomatoes, as childhood memories have jars of tomatoes exploding in the basement. However, the USDA rules now require that every home-canned recipe has to be finished in a boiling-water bath, so I give you those instructions. As I've said, I have never had my relishes, pickles, or jams spoil, but I would get in trouble if I didn't tell you to follow the rules.

Nana's Green-Tomato Relish

MAKES APPROXIMATELY 8 PINTS

8 to 9 pounds green tomatoes, washed and cored

4 large sweet onions, peeled and trimmed

3 red bell peppers, washed, stemmed, and seeded

2 green bell peppers, washed, stemmed, and seeded

1 jalapeño chile, stemmed and seeded (optional)

3 cups sugar (or more or less as desired)

3 cups white vinegar

¼ cup coarse salt (or more or less as desired)

1 tablespoon mustard seed

1 teaspoon dry mustard powder

1 teaspoon celery seed

½ teaspoon ground turmeric

¼ teaspoon ground nutmeg

1. You can deal with the vegetables in any way you wish—hand grate, grate on the grating blade of a food processor, or do as my mom did: push them through the shredding blade on a hand grater.

2. Once shredded, put all of them into a large nonreactive saucepan or canning pot. Add the sugar, vinegar, salt, mustard seed, dry mustard powder, celery seed, turmeric, and nutmeg, and place over high heat. Bring to a boil; then, lower the heat and simmer for about 30 minutes or until slightly thickened and well seasoned. Depending on your plans, either transfer to clean containers with lids, cover, and let cool (and then store, refrigerated, for up to 6 weeks), or if canning, remove from the heat, pack into hot, sterilized jars, seal, and place on a rack in a canner (or other large pot) filled with boiling water. Boil for 10 minutes; then, using tongs, invert the jars on a wire rack to cool before storing.

Nana's Pepper Relish

MAKES ABOUT SIXTEEN 8-OUNCE JARS

18 red bell peppers, cored, seeded, and
   membrane removed
18 green bell peppers, cored, seeded, and
   membrane removed
16 onions, cut into chunks
4 hot red or green chilies, stemmed and seeded
8 cups (2 quarts) white vinegar
5½ cups sugar
2 tablespoons coarse or pickling salt

1. Run the peppers, onions, and chilies through the medium blade of a food grinder or, alternately, through a food processor fitted with the shredding blade. Put the pepper mixture in a large heatproof bowl and cover with boiling water. Let stand for 5 minutes. Drain well, discarding the liquid.

2. Transfer the pepper mixture to a large canning kettle or stockpot. Add 4 cups of the vinegar and 4 cups of cold water. Place over high heat and bring to a boil. Immediately remove from the heat and drain well, discarding the liquid.

3. Return the pepper mixture to the kettle and add the remaining 4 cups of vinegar along with the sugar and salt. Place over high heat and bring to a simmer. Lower the heat and continue to cook at a gentle simmer, stirring occasionally, for 30 minutes.

4. Remove from the heat and pack into hot, sterilized jars. Seal and place on a rack in a canner (or other large pot) filled with boiling water. Boil for 10 minutes; then, using tongs, invert the jars on a wire rack to cool before storing.

Corn Relish

MAKES APPROXIMATELY 4 PINTS

6 cups fresh corn kernels

2 cups finely shredded green cabbage

2 cups chopped onions

1 cup diced red bell pepper

2 teaspoons celery seed

1 teaspoon mustard seed

1 teaspoon ground turmeric

1 teaspoon dry mustard powder

¾ cup sugar

1 cup white vinegar

1. Combine the corn with the cabbage, onions, bell pepper, celery seed, mustard seed, turmeric, mustard powder, and sugar in a large heavy-duty pot. Stir in the vinegar and place over high heat. Bring to a boil; then, lower the heat and simmer for 20 minutes.

2. Remove from the heat and pack into hot, sterilized jars. Cover tightly and either invert them and cool on wire racks before refrigerating, or place them in a canning pot and process in a boiling-water bath for 10 minutes. Remove from the canner with tongs, invert, and cool on wire racks.

Fresh Fig Relish

MAKES ABOUT 4 CUPS

Growing up in California, we had a generous neighbor with two fig trees. He wasn't a great fan of the fruit, so, come each fall, we were often overloaded with the bounty from his trees. My mom was particularly taken with pickling the figs, especially when they

were on the firm side. I, on the other hand, loved nothing better than to stuff my face with the luscious fruit straight from the branch. Nowadays, I rely on one of my most favorite chef buddies, Jimmy Canora (known as Shoes) who has an array of relatives in Queens, New York, with fig trees in their yards. (Throughout New York City neighborhoods that were once [and sometimes still are] predominantly Italian, you will often find fig trees and grape vines producing prodigious amounts of fruit.) Shoes will often ring my bell late in the evening bearing a shopping bag full of ripe and ready figs. There is nothing to do but put on an apron and devise yet another relish or chutney. The following recipe keeps well—you could also preserve it—and is terrific as a garnish for roasted meat or poultry as well as a great accompaniment to all kinds of curries.

3 pounds fresh ripe figs, washed, stemmed, and cut, crosswise, into thin slices

2 cups sugar (or more or less as desired)

½ cup freshly squeezed orange juice

1 teaspoon freshly grated orange zest

½ teaspoon freshly grated lemon zest

6 whole cloves

2 whole allspice berries

1 cinnamon stick, chopped into pieces

½ cup sherry wine vinegar

1 cup toasted slivered almonds

¼ cup dried currants

1. Combine the figs with the sugar in a large mixing bowl, tossing to coat. Stir in the orange juice along with the orange and lemon zests. You could add some liqueur here if you like. Cover and set aside to marinate for 3 hours.

2. Tie the cloves, allspice, and cinnamon pieces in a cheesecloth bag.

3. Transfer the marinated figs along with all of the juices to a heavy saucepan. Add the spice bag and place over medium heat. Bring to a boil; then, lower the heat and add the vinegar. Simmer for about 30 minutes, or until quite thick.

4. Remove from the heat and stir in the almonds and currants.

5. Store, covered and refrigerated, for up to 1 month. Or, if you like, transfer to sterilized canning jars and process in a boiling-water bath for 10 minutes.

Making Jams

From the first fruits and vegetables of spring—think strawberries and rhubarb—to the last hard squash of fall, you will find me at some point during every week in the kitchen with my preserving pots, sterilized jars and lids, or pickling crocks. I don't really have room to store all that I preserve, so a great deal of my "putting by" goes to friends. I have been doing this for as long as I can remember; it seems to keep me connected to my past as well as help me stay tied to the land, since I am not much of a gardener. I certainly don't do it to save money, as often my cost—particularly when buying organic ingredients from the farmers market—is greater than the expense of purchasing commercial jams and pickled vegetables. But I do so love the whole process, particularly

when I have the opportunity to pick the produce myself. I love the solitude of meandering through the woods filling a bucket with wild berries, sitting in the middle row of a friend's garden picking beans or peas in the hot sun, or, best of all, wandering the back 40 of Lynn and Doug's acreage along with Lena Mai, my very best doggie pal.

On that back 40, the wild blackberries and raspberries are absolutely glorious and abundant most years, and when I'm not with them, Lynn and Lena Mai pick and pick and have the freezer filled with bags of them. The blackberries are tight and not very juicy and the raspberries tiny but sweet as sugar. Lena Mai can pick them right off the bush and often finishes an outing with her head and muzzle covered in berry juice. When I tire of making jam we throw the left-over berries into a giant canning jar along with some vodka, sugar, and other flavorings, and make Hootch (page 32).

During the winter months, I tend to clean out the freezer or, when I'm lucky, get some overripe berries or fruit from Uncle Nick at Zingone Brothers and turn my bounty into jam. I put the fruit into a pot with a little bit of sugar, some flavoring if I think it can use it, and lemon juice, and let it cook down while I make dinner. When it is good and jammy I pack it into some Weck food storage jars. I love to use them as they are so eye-pleasing. Though they are not made for long-term preserving, they are just fine for fridge storage. I hand out the filled jars all winter with strict

instructions to keep the jam refrigerated and to return my jars ASAP if they ever want to get another gift from my kitchen.

I always have at least one box of unused canning jars and a couple of packages of tops and lids on hand. You can reuse the jars and the screw-top closures—which I do since they are expensive—but you can't reuse the sealing lids. And you must take care that the jars are sparkling clean and boiling hot when you fill them. I put the jars in one large pot and the lids and screw tops in a small pan, cover them with water, and bring to a boil. I keep them at a low simmer while the jam cooks and lift them out of the water as I fill to insure that no bacteria have time to grow. I wipe off any drips or spillage on the jar with a clean cloth and immediately place the lid and screw cap on.

If you want to speed things along, you can use commercial pectin to make jam. Every brand comes with instructions, which you must follow exactly or the end result may not be what you hoped. When making jam as I do, without the addition of pectin, you have to cook it longer and take care that it doesn't stick and burn on the bottom of the pot. The more sugar you use, the more likely this is to happen; the less sugar you use, the longer the jam will take to jell.

Raspberry Preserves

MAKES ABOUT EIGHT ½-PINT JARS

10 cups raspberries
1 tablespoon fresh lemon juice
4 cups sugar

1. Wash your jars and lids thoroughly.

2. Combine the berries and lemon juice in a large heavy-bottomed pot. Stir in the sugar and bring to a boil over high heat, stirring constantly. Lower the heat to a bare simmer; cook for about 45 minutes or until the jam begins to congeal somewhat when spooned onto a cold plate. You can also test consistency by filling a spoon and watching how the jam drops off of it back into the pot. If the last drops linger before they fall, the jam is ready.

3. Remove from the heat and pack into hot, sterilized jars. If canning, seal and place on a rack in a canner (or other large pot) filled with boiling water. Boil for 10 minutes; then, using tongs, invert the jars on a wire rack to cool before storing.

Boston Brown Bread

MAKES 6 NO. 303 CANS OR ABOUT 5 SMALL LOAF PANS

Whenever I decide to do a lot of cooking for gift giving I always return to my mom's recipes. Boston Brown Bread was an original of hers and one of her most favorite breads to share, particularly at Christmastime. When I was a young mother, it became my favorite too, usually made with my mom working by my side. Then, for some reason I just quit making it. One explanation might have been Mom's requirement that it be baked in gold-lined No. 303 cans. I had all but stopped using commercially canned products, so I no longer had any cans on hand (Mom saved hers from year to year) in which to bake it. But a few years ago I went on a scavenger hunt and came up with cans I thought would do the job. Being of a cautious nature (well, sometimes) I still kept some small loaf pans within reach when I made my first return batch. The photo shown here, which always makes me laugh, should give you a good idea of my failure to find the right can on my first try.

8 ounces dark raisins

2 teaspoons baking soda

2 cups sugar

2 tablespoons unsalted butter, room temperature

2 teaspoons pure vanilla extract

2 large eggs, room temperature

4 cups sifted flour

1 teaspoon salt

1 cup chopped walnuts

1. Place the raisins in a heatproof bowl and cover with 2 cups of boiling water. Stir in the baking soda and set aside to cool to room temperature.

2. Preheat the oven to 350°F.

3. Combine the sugar, butter, and vanilla in the bowl of a standing electric mixer fitted with the paddle. Beat on low to lighten. Raise the speed to medium and beat until blended. With the motor running, add the eggs, one at time, and beat to blend. When well blended, add the flour and salt and beat until well incorporated. Then, add the raisins along with their soaking water and beat to combine. Remove the bowl from the mixer and, using a wooden spoon, stir in the nuts.

4. Carefully scoop the mixture into the cans, filling each one about half full. If you are using loaf pans, either coat them with a nonstick baking spray—like Baker's Joy—or butter and flour them.

5. Put the cans in the preheated oven and bake for about 45 minutes, or until the breads begin to pull away from the sides of the cans. Remove from the oven and place on wire racks for 10 minutes before removing the bread from each can by running a small, sharp knife around the interior and then popping the bread out.

6. Serve warm or at room temperature with butter or cream cheese or alongside Boston baked beans.

Banana Bread with Canada

MAKES ONE 9-INCH LOAF OR THREE 5-INCH LOAVES

Canada, my eldest grandchild, has been my kitchen assistant for a very long time. For most of her young life, she has spent a good part of her summers with me and Steve. Our shared kitchen times have enabled us to get to know each other in the best of all possible ways. On her own, Canada now makes delicious and beautifully decorated cakes—far fancier than mine—but she still seems to enjoy my simple approach, too. I absolutely love baking with her as it brings remembrances of me baking with my mom—it was the closest I ever felt to her. I hope that Canada, years from now, has the same warm feelings as she mixes, kneads, and ices with her children and grandchildren, hopefully still turning out recipes that we once made together. Even though Canada refuses to eat a banana straight out of the skin, this recipe for banana bread (which I learned from my mom) is one of our favorites.

1¾ cups sifted all-purpose flour

2 teaspoons baking powder

¼ teaspoon baking soda

¼ teaspoon salt

⅓ cup unsalted butter, at room temperature

⅔ cup sugar

2 large eggs, room temperature

3 very ripe bananas, mashed

1 teaspoon pure vanilla extract

1 cup walnut pieces

1. Preheat the oven to 350°F.

2. Lightly coat the interior of your loaf pan(s) with nonstick baking spray. Set aside.

3. Sift the flour, baking powder, baking soda, and salt together. Set aside.

4. Put the butter in the bowl of a standing electric mixer fitted with the paddle. Mix on low until just softened. Add the sugar, raise the speed to medium, and beat until light and creamy. Beat in the bananas and vanilla. Slowly add the flour mixture, beating to incorporate. Remove the bowl from the mixer and using a rubber spatula, fold in the nuts.

5. Scrape the batter into the prepared pan(s). Place in the preheated oven and bake for about 45 minutes for a large pan, 30 minutes for small pans—or until a cake tester inserted in the center comes out clean and the top is golden brown. Remove from the oven and tip out of the pan(s) onto a wire rack to cool.

6. Serve warm or at room temperature. May be stored, well wrapped and frozen, for up to 3 months.

Making Bread

For almost all of my life I have loved two kitchen chores—making bread and canning.
No matter the weather (well, maybe not in hot and humid August) I try to turn out at least six loaves a week for eating and sharing. And in the summer, canning becomes an almost daily ritual as I try to make use of whatever fruit or vegetable is ripening. I know that for many cooks both of these activities are true chores—that is, tasks to be avoided as much as possible. I imagine this is because the execution seems daunting to most, whereas I find both bread making and canning so easy and relaxing that they've become the perfect way to quiet my soul.

Bread is something that I make by feel—it's so hard to give a recipe. Since I've been at it so long, I often make it with whatever I have on hand or, sometimes, stuff I need to finish off—like that half container of fat-free sour cream that's about ready to grow some fuzz, or the quarter cup of cornmeal left at the bottom of the bag. But I always begin with King Arthur flour (see Sources)—a combination of white and white whole wheat. I will give you my method and try to offer a "sort of" recipe. The thing to remember is just to get right in there and fall in love with the dough—I promise if you do, it will love you back!

Here's the method and the recipe: first fill a large bowl with a mix of white and white whole-wheat flour—it's probably somewhere around 14 cups (8 to 10 of white and the remainder white whole wheat). Then, add 3 packages instant-rise yeast; whatever amount of sugar you like—I generally use about ½ cup or so; a tablespoon or so of coarse or sea salt; and some flax meal, cornmeal, oatmeal, or whatever extra fiber you like (or not, this really doesn't matter)—about 1 to 2 cups. Heat about 3 cups of 2-percent milk to about 115°F—it can get a bit hotter, as the yogurt will cool it down. Whisk in 2 cups nonfat yogurt to a smooth mix. Pour the warm milk-yogurt mixture into the flour mixture. Mix with a wooden spoon for as long as you can; then, scrape the dough out onto a clean surface and knead with your hands, adding flour as needed until the dough is blended, soft, and pliable, but still a bit sticky. I have found that slightly wet dough yields a more tender bread.

Scrape the dough into a buttered bowl large enough to allow it to double in size. Cover and set aside in a draft-free spot for at least an hour or until it has doubled in size.

Preheat the oven to 350°F.

Generously butter the interior of six 8-inch loaf pans or whatever pans you have—it can be small loaves or even free-form round or oval loaves. Fill each pan about two-thirds full. Place in the preheated oven and bake for about 40 minutes or until beautifully risen and golden brown. Remove from the oven, tap from the pans, and place on wire racks to cool.

I can guarantee that even if your first batch isn't perfect, it will still be edible. And if you keep practicing, you will soon discover it's the most soothing way to meditate and the cheapest way to fill the house with fragrance—and you will never have to buy a loaf of sandwich bread again.

A Short-Order Cook, Or Isn't Breakfast Great?

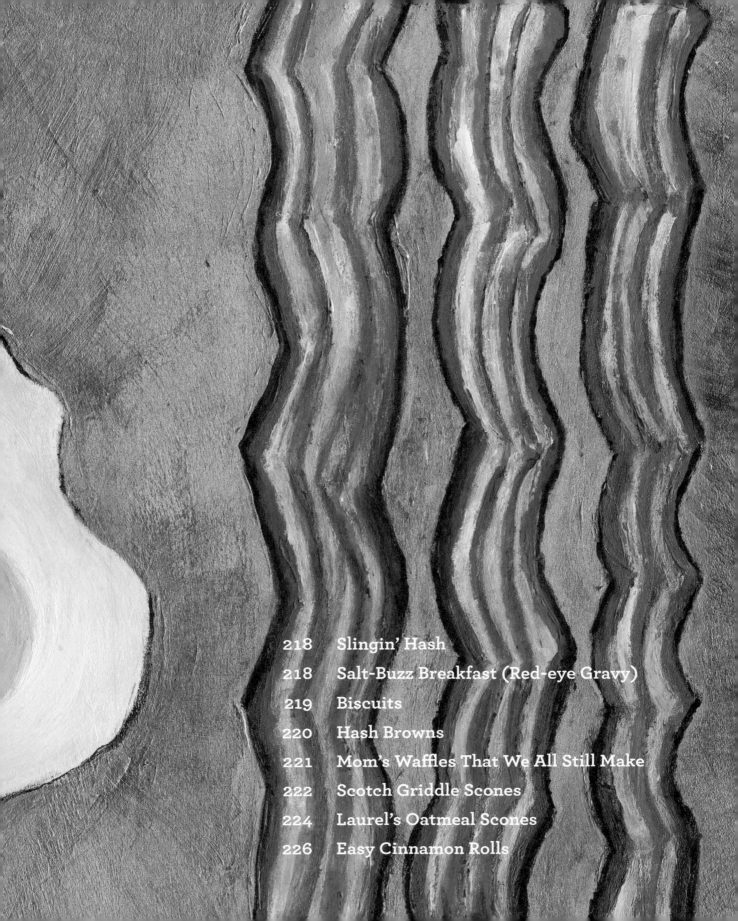

Slingin' Hash

When I was very little, and even into my early school days, my breakfast of choice was a slice of my mom's Devil's-Food Cake (page 235) and a big glass of milk. It didn't exactly cover all of the food groups, but Mom didn't seem to object (only because her sweet tooth was even bigger than mine). Then, in my teen and early adult years, breakfast simply wasn't in my plan—a cup of coffee on the run did it for me. But once I had children, I tried to prepare a healthy breakfast every morning; sometimes egg in the middle, or french toast made with thick slices of homemade white bread, or waffles (pages 214 and 221), and then there was the usual array of boxed cereals on the shelf. However, from the boys' dad, a full-on English breakfast, with kidneys (or some type of fish), fried eggs, grilled tomatoes, smashed potatoes, and toast, was a frequent request. It was then that I realized that I loved "slingin' hash" and would have had a ball being a short-order cook. Nowadays, we mostly aim for fruit, granola, and yogurt to start our days, but on the weekends or on holidays, I pull on my apron and start slingin'! I enjoy nothing more than getting the biscuits in the oven, grits on to boil, potatoes browning with onions, and then covering the entire top of the stove with my pans to take individual orders for "sunny side up," "scrambled, well," "over easy," or whatever style of eggs is a personal favorite.

Salt-Buzz Breakfast

There is nothing better than a good ole Southern breakfast featuring slices of fried, deliciously salty country ham; creamy grits; red-eye gravy; biscuits; and sliced garden tomatoes. The tomatoes are essential, as they become the buffer for the salty ham and gravy. Everyone always lets out a gasp when I serve up this bounty, yet the plates always come back clean.

Red-eye gravy is nothing more than about ½ cup of strong, hot coffee stirred into the fat remaining in the pan after frying country ham. It can't be made any other way. But I like to whisk in ¼ cup or so of heavy cream and a liberal dose of freshly ground black pepper just to gild the lily.

Biscuits

MAKES 1 DOZEN

My biscuits are acclaimed. They are the same ones my mom made and she probably learned to make them from her mother. I used to bake them almost every morning, but they are now just a weekend treat.

2¼ cups all-purpose flour, sifted

1 tablespoon fine cornmeal

4 teaspoons baking powder

1 teaspoon sugar (or more or less as desired)

½ teaspoon salt (or more or less as desired)

⅓ cup vegetable shortening

About ⅔ cup milk

1 tablespoon butter

1. Preheat the oven to 450°F.

2. Put the flour, cornmeal, baking powder, sugar, and salt in the bowl of a food processor fitted with the metal blade and, using quick on-and-off turns, process to just blend. Add the shortening and again, using quick on-and-off turns, process until just combined. With the motor running, add the milk and process quickly to make a soft dough.

3. Lightly flour a clean work surface and scrape the dough out onto it. Using your hands, lightly push on the dough to form a circular shape about ¾ inch thick. Using a 2-inch round biscuit cutter (or a drinking glass of about that size), cut out as many biscuits as you can. Then, pat the scraps together and again cut out biscuits. If you have just a small dab left, form it into a tiny biscuit.

4. Place the butter in a cast-iron skillet or baking pan in the preheated oven. Heat to melt; do not burn. Remove from the oven and nestle the biscuits into the pan, edges touching. Return to the oven and bake for about 12 to 15 minutes or until lightly browned and slightly risen.

5. Serve hot with butter and honey (or jam) or split with red-eye gravy spooned over.

Hash Browns

SERVES 6

When you hear *hash browns*, what comes to mind? Shredded potatoes in a freezer pack, Greek-diner greasy potatoes mixed with bits of green pepper and onion, half-cooked sliced potatoes in an oil slick? Or do you think of crisp, golden brown cubes with

a bit of char around the edges, just a hint of onion, and a good dose of salt and pepper? It's the latter that makes the cut in our house. Although I occasionally make them for dinner, they are most frequently on the breakfast table. I cook them exactly the way my mom did, always with raw potatoes (although if you have left-over boiled potatoes please do use them—just cut down on the cooking time). It might seem as though the recipe calls for too many potatoes to feed six, but I guarantee that you could fry double the amount and you still won't have any leftovers.

TIP: You can also add to the hash browns ¼ to ½ cup diced onion and/or diced green or red bell pepper or 2 tablespoons diced jarred pimentos. If you want to give the potatoes a contemporary taste, season with pimenton (smoked Spanish paprika) instead of the chili powder.

2 tablespoons olive oil or vegetable oil with 2 tablespoons unsalted butter or ¼ cup bacon fat (my preference when the fat patrol isn't looking)

2 pounds all-purpose potatoes, peeled and cut into small cubes

Salt and pepper

½ teaspoon chili powder (or more or less as desired) (optional)

1. Heat the oil and butter or bacon fat in a large frying pan over medium-high heat. Add the potatoes and season with salt and pepper, stirring to blend well. Cover and cook for about 15 minutes.

2. Uncover, and using a wooden spatula, toss and turn to break up the potatoes. Add the chili powder and continue to fry, occasionally tossing and turning, for about 10 minutes or until potatoes are cooked, crisp, and golden brown with some charring around the edges.

3. Serve hot.

Mom's Waffles That We All Still Make

MAKES 6

Mom's recipe card for waffles: "2 eggs, separated, 3 t baking powder, 5 Tbsp sugar, ½ t salt, 2 cups milk, 2 cups flour, Add beaten egg whites last. Melted butter" (written in by hand—no quantity; when asked how much butter, she'd say, "Oh, about the size of an egg"). That's it, no more instructions necessary.

To make Mom's waffles, sift the dry ingredients together, beat in the milk (I use 2-percent milk), egg yolks, and melted butter (only on really special occasions do I use butter, it's generally canola oil), and then fold in the beaten egg whites. Bake in a hot waffle iron according to manufacturer's directions.

The waffle iron I grew up with made the best waffles. It had been given to my mom in 1928 as a gift from my father when my brother was born. I passed it on to Mickey, who, sadly, threw it out when the cord no longer worked. I still miss it and have, from time to time, picked up old waffle irons at garage sales, but none has done the job that my mom's did.

My mom wrote her recipes on index cards and kept them in a metal box on the kitchen shelf. She had very small, neat handwriting that was easy to read, but when she got a typewriter all of these lovely cards were transferred to type. I too had a recipe box for many years and then, after writing so many cookbooks, I abandoned the box for my files and threw most of my cards away. Of course, now everything is found on the computer—a far less warm experience than sifting through a box of handwritten cards or pieces of notepaper stained with the makings of the dishes. I still have some of those cards from Mom's box as well as a few sent to me by my aunts or their friends from my earliest days of cookbook writing. The recipes

written in the early 1900s (and before) are much as this waffle recipe is—ingredients (and sometimes those were a bit vague, also) with minimal instruction. Women were expected to know how to cook unless they were extremely wealthy, and then their cook had the know-how.

Scotch Griddle Scones

MAKES 1 DOZEN

This is my oldest family recipe. Unfortunately, I did not know my mom's mother, who brought the recipe with her from Scotland, where it had been taught to her by my great-aunt Ann. These scones would not be recognizable as such in modern bakeries that turn out giant, fluffy, fruit-filled varieties. These are flat, griddled gems that are somewhere between pancakes and biscuits. In fact, the recipe card says: "Have griddle same heat as for pancakes and fry on a dry griddle." They should be eaten hot off the stove with sweet butter and homemade jam.

3 cups all-purpose flour
1 teaspoon baking powder
1 scant teaspoon baking soda
Sugar
Salt
2 tablespoons butter
Enough buttermilk to make a soft dough,
    usually about 1 cup

1. Combine the flour, baking powder, and baking soda in a mixing bowl. Add some sugar and salt—I use about 2 tablespoons of sugar and no more than ¼ teaspoon of salt. Cut in the butter using your fingertips.

2. Slowly add the buttermilk, beating with a wooden spoon until a soft dough forms.

3. Lightly flour a clean work surface.

4. Scrape the dough out onto the work surface and divide it in half. Pat each half into a fairly neat circle about ¼ inch thick and then cut each circle into 6 wedges.

5. Place the griddle over low heat until very hot.

6. Add the scones, a few at a time, and cook for 3 minutes, just to set. Then, increase the heat slightly and cook for another 4 minutes, or until the dough begins to puff up a bit and the underside has begun to color. Using a spatula, turn and cook for an additional 6 minutes, or until golden brown and cooked through. Watch carefully, adjusting the heat as necessary, to keep the scones from burning.

7. Remove from the heat and serve hot with butter and jam.

Laurel's Oatmeal Scones

MAKES 1 DOZEN

Although Mickey does most of the cooking in his household, I think Laurel took over scone making right after they married. I remember Alexander and Clara clamoring for Mama's chocolate-chip scones about as soon as they could talk. Laurel's scones are much tastier than my grandmother's, often filled with sweet tidbits that make them extra special, particularly for the kids. And this recipe even adds some fiber to an out-of-hand breakfast.

Laurel: I have been, for a long time, totally addicted to these scones—there is nothing as wonderful as beginning the day with an oatmeal scone and a cup of tea. I guarantee that these are so much better than the types featured at Starbucks or Au Bon Pain that once you start making mine, you'll never be satisfied with commercially made ones again. If you want bigger scones, just cut them into eight instead of twelve pieces. They freeze very well and can be reheated until just warm in a microwave.

1½ cups all-purpose flour

⅓ cup sugar

2 teaspoons baking powder

½ teaspoon ground cinnamon

½ teaspoon salt

½ cup plus 2 tablespoons chilled unsalted butter, cut into pieces

1½ cups old-fashioned rolled oats, toasted (see Note)

¾ cup cinnamon-flavored chips

¼ cup skim milk

¼ cup heavy cream

1 large egg, room temperature

1 tablespoon cinnamon-sugar

1. Preheat the oven to 450°F.

2. Line a baking sheet with a silicone liner or parchment paper. Set aside.

3. Combine the flour with the sugar, baking powder, cinnamon, and salt in the bowl of a food processor fitted with the metal blade. Process, using quick on-and-off turns, to blend. Add the butter and process quickly for a few seconds, just until the mixture resembles coarse cornmeal. Scrape the mixture into a mixing bowl.

4. Set aside 2 tablespoons of the toasted oats and pour the remaining oats into the flour mixture along with the cinnamon chips.

5. Put the milk, cream, and egg in a small bowl and whisk vigorously. Remove and set aside 1 tablespoon of the liquid to brush on the tops of the scones to make a glaze.

6. Pour the milk mixture into the flour-oat mixture, and using your hands, knead until the dough comes together.

7. Sprinkle half of the reserved toasted oats on a clean work surface. Scrape the dough out into the

center and flatten slightly. Sprinkle the remaining tablespoon of oats on top and gently pat the dough out to about a 7-inch-round circle. It doesn't have to be perfect.

8. Using a dough scraper or a large knife, cut the pastry circle into 12 wedges of equal size. Transfer the wedges to the prepared baking sheet.

9. Using a pastry brush, lightly coat all of the surfaces with the reserved milk mixture. Sprinkle the top with cinnamon-sugar.

10. Place in the preheated oven and bake, watching carefully as the chips hanging off the edges or on the bottom can easily burn, for 12 minutes, or until golden brown.

11. Remove from the oven and place on a wire rack to cool slightly before serving.

NOTE: To toast the oatmeal, place it in an even layer in a baking pan with sides in a preheated 375°F oven and bake for about 5 minutes, or until very aromatic, golden brown, and a bit crunchy.

Easy Cinnamon Rolls

MAKES 1 DOZEN

Is there any aroma more enticing than that of cinnamon coming from the baker's oven? How many times have I been lured by the Cinnabon kiosk in a mall or at a rest stop on the New Jersey Turnpike ... I'm a complete sucker even though I don't actually much like the flavor of commercial cinnamon buns and usually eat only a bite or two before returning it to its little paper box. Part of the reason I get snookered is the deep memory of my mom's early-morning baking—huge, fluffy, nutty, spiced, and gently iced yeast-risen cinnamon swirls were her special treat. I can still taste the yumminess of my sticky fingers after I'd devoured that first warm bun.

For years, I supplanted Mom's buns with an easy-to-make cinnamon coffee cake, only because I was too impatient for the necessary dough rise. But a couple of years ago, I decided to try to make an inviting cinnamon bun in a hurry. After a number of tries, I finally came up with the solution—a rather firm biscuit-type dough that can be rolled out and filled. My friend Mary says that I should market the results. Instead of taking my brand to market, this recipe will let you make your own.

3 cups all-purpose flour

¼ cup sugar

1½ teaspoons baking powder

½ teaspoon baking soda

¼ teaspoon salt

1¼ cups sour milk or buttermilk (see Note)

¾ cup plus 2 tablespoons melted unsalted butter, cooled slightly

Brown Sugar Filling (recipe follows)

2 tablespoons unsalted butter

Orange Glaze (recipe follows)

1. Preheat the oven to 400°F.

2. Combine the flour, sugar, baking powder, baking soda, and salt in a mixing bowl. Stir in the sour milk and ½ cup of the melted butter, mixing until just combined.

3. Scrape the dough out onto a lightly floured surface and, using your hands, work the dough until it comes together and is smooth. If the dough is too sticky, add additional flour, a bit at a time.

4. Lightly flour a clean surface. Transfer the dough to it and gently pat it out to a rectangle shape. Using a rolling pin, roll the dough out to a rectangle about 12 inches long by 9 to 10 inches wide, oriented in landscape format in front of you. Using a pastry brush, lightly coat the entire surface of the dough with the 2 tablespoons of the remaining melted butter.

[*recipe continued on next page*]

5. Spoon the brown sugar filling in an even layer over the surface of the buttered rectangle, leaving a ½-inch border uncovered along the (long) side of the rectangle farthest away from you. This will give the dough the ability to seal itself together. Lightly push the filling into the dough.

6. Starting at the long side closest to you, begin rolling the dough up, cigar fashion. Do not roll too tightly or too loosely—the roll should be just barely coming together. When the roll reaches the uncovered edge, lightly press on it to seal the edge to the roll. Tidy up the ends, making sure that all of the filling remains inside the roll. Using a sharp knife, cut the roll crosswise into slices about ½ inch thick.

7. Place the 2 tablespoons of butter in a 10-inch cast-iron skillet in the preheated oven. When the butter has melted but not browned, carefully place the dough slices in the pan.

8. Using a pastry brush, lightly coat the tops of the rolls with the remaining 2 tablespoons melted butter. Place in the preheated oven and bake for about 30 minutes, or until the buns have risen, oozing some of the filling, and are golden brown.

9. Remove from the oven and set on a wire rack to cool for 10 minutes. Drizzle the orange glaze over the top and let rest for about 10 more minutes. Serve warm.

NOTE: A trick I learned from my mom: If you don't have buttermilk or other sour milk, you can make it by adding 1 teaspoon white vinegar or lemon juice to whole milk. Stir well and set aside for 10 minutes before using.

Brown Sugar Filling

1 cup light brown sugar

¼ cup granulated sugar

1 tablespoon ground cinnamon

3 tablespoons unsalted butter, melted and cooled slightly

1 cup walnut pieces (or any nut you prefer)

1 cup dark raisins

Combine the brown and granulated sugars with the cinnamon. Stir in the melted butter to make a slightly crumbly mixture. Stir in the nuts and raisins. Use as directed in the recipe.

Orange Glaze

1 cup confectioners' sugar

3 to 4 tablespoons fresh orange juice,
    strained of all pulp

Mix the sugar and juice together until smooth. It
should be slightly thick. Use as directed in the recipe.

We All Love Dessert

 ## Chris's Wine Advice

Dessert wines have many different styles, production methods, and levels of sweetness. They can be enjoyed on their own or as a terrific complement to a dessert. Unfortunately, I've found that diners are often reluctant to try these delicious and remarkably complex nectars. You need high-acid grapes to make dessert wine so that the sweetness is balanced and the wine does not taste cloying. I personally love dessert wines that are a by-product of "noble rot," or botrytis, a mold that grows under specific conditions and pierces the skin of the grape, making the sugars and inherent flavors of the fruit more concentrated. The Château d'Yquem that I mention elsewhere in the book undergoes this process. For this particular wine, the grapes are individually hand-harvested in small baskets during many passes through the vineyard to select only the perfect fruit. This is why the wine is so, so expensive. Cost aside, I recommend all wine drinkers try this singular wine at least once in their lifetime. That being said, in our family we usually have port, the famous Portuguese fortified wine, at the end of special dinners simply because it is Mickey's favorite.

Judie: A little Château d'Yquem story: at some point in his late teens, Mickey discovered a small bottle (which had been a gift to me) in the fridge that I had put aside for a celebration I was planning. I came home to listen to him tell me about that really, really sweet wine he had opened and poured out 'cause something had to be wrong with it. Years later, I can assure you that he lamented its loss, but no more so than I did at that moment.

Chocolate Chess Pie/Cake

MAKES ONE 9-INCH PIE OR CAKE

When I spent my days making pies at MOM, I started out selling savory pies only. But after the first year or two, so many customers asked for dessert pies that I caved and added them to my repertoire. I didn't want to do cream or meringue pies, so I researched old cookbooks so that we could expand the menu from the standard fruits. Chess pies came up time and again, probably because they are made from basic, always-on-hand ingredients—eggs, butter, sugar, and a flavoring—baked in a single bottom pastry shell.

Although Southern in origin, variations of this simple mix are found in many areas of the country. Some chess pies have cornmeal added to the basics while others have vinegar and consequently are known as vinegar pie. This version is my take on tradition and it was the most requested dessert pie in the bakery for years. And once the bakery closed, customers and friends still asked me to make it for them or teach them how to make it. Although for years I made this mix as a pie, I now almost always make it as a cake. My good friend Aris Mixon has tried to master it, but always calls me at the last minute to go through the recipe again. So, for Aris, here it is once again.

If you want to make a pie, you will need a 9-inch-deep uncooked pastry shell (you can use my pastry on page 70, make your own, or use a commercially prepared pie shell). If you want to make a cake, generously butter and lightly flour a 9-inch round cake pan. If you want to make elegant, individual servings, generously butter and lightly flour 8 to 10 small ramekins. This is an extremely rich mix and small servings are all you need; even the 9-inch pie should feed at least 10 to 12 people.

1 cup unsalted butter

1 ounce unsweetened chocolate

2 cups sugar

¾ cup Dutch-processed cocoa powder—
   the better the quality, the better the cake

¼ cup all-purpose flour, sifted

4 large egg yolks, room temperature

2 large whole eggs, room temperature

6 tablespoons water

2 teaspoons white vinegar

1. Preheat the oven to 350°F.

2. Combine the butter and chocolate in a small pan over low heat. Warm, watching carefully, until the butter and chocolate are melted. Stir to combine and set aside to cool slightly.

3. Combine the sugar, cocoa powder, and flour in a small mixing bowl. Set aside. Combine the egg yolks, whole eggs, water, and vinegar in the bowl of a standing electric mixer fitted with the paddle. Beat until light and airy. Add the cooled, melted butter mixture and mix to combine. Add the reserved dry ingredients, beating to blend well.

4. Pour into your pie shell or pan and place in the preheated oven. Bake for about 35 minutes or until the center is set and the top is crisp.

5. Remove from the oven and set on a wire rack to cool slightly. Serve warm or at room temperature dusted with confectioners' sugar or with a dollop of whipped cream, ice cream, frozen yogurt, crème fraîche, or Greek-style plain yogurt.

Devil's-Food Cake

MAKES ONE 9-INCH ROUND 2-LAYER CAKE OR 8-INCH ROUND 3-LAYER CAKE

Devil's-food cake was my childhood favorite breakfast—a big slice of cake with a glass of farm-fresh milk. Perhaps that's why I was buying my dresses in the "Chubbette" section! My mom always topped her cake with the traditional 7-Minute Frosting, which she made in a double boiler; I share her recipe as well as a quicker, easier version. With the latter, a heavy-duty standing electric mixer will speed the process considerably. In our family, Canada has now made this cake her own, and it is quite wonderful for me to see it find a place in the heart of the next generation.

Nowadays, the favorite American bakery specialty appears to be red velvet cake, which is nothing more than this old-fashioned cake with a mad dash of red food coloring. Mom's recipe lacks the bright scarlet hue, but is moist, deeply flavored, and absolutely homemade delicious. And it's inexpensive to make and keeps extremely well—if you don't eat it for breakfast!

2½ cups all-purpose flour, sifted

½ cup Dutch-processed cocoa powder

1½ teaspoons baking soda

¼ teaspoon salt

¾ cup unsalted butter, at room temperature

1 cup granulated sugar

½ cup light brown sugar

3 large eggs, at room temperature

1½ teaspoons pure vanilla extract

1½ cups sour milk (see Note)

7-Minute Frosting or Quick 7-Minute Frosting (recipes follow)

1. Preheat the oven to 325°F.

2. Lightly spray two 9-inch round or three 8-inch round cake pans with nonstick baking spray (or butter and flour them). Line the bottom of each pan with a parchment paper round and lightly coat the paper with the baking spray (or with butter).

3. Sift the flour, cocoa, baking soda, and salt together. Set aside.

4. Place the butter in the bowl of a standing electric mixer fitted with the paddle. Beat on medium until softened. Add the granulated and brown sugars and beat on medium-high until light and fluffy. Add the eggs, one at a time, beating well after each addition. Add the vanilla and beat to blend.

5. Lower the speed to medium and begin adding the sifted dry ingredients alternately with the sour milk, scraping down the sides of the bowl and beating until well combined. Place equal amounts of the batter in the prepared pans, gently smoothing the top of each one.

6. Place in the preheated oven and bake for about 25 minutes or until a cake tester inserted into the center comes out clean.

7. Remove from the oven and let stand for 5 minutes. Then, invert onto wire racks to cool completely. Remove and discard the parchment paper.

[recipe continued on next page]

8. When cool, place one layer, bottom up, on a cake plate. Coat with frosting and top with the final (or second) layer. If making a two-layer cake, completely cover with the remaining frosting. If making a three-layer cake, coat the top of the second layer with frost-ing and place the final layer on top. Then, completely cover the entire cake with the remaining frosting.

9. Serve at room temperature. Do not refrigerate or the frosting will turn sticky and wet.

Traditional 7-Minute Frosting

3 large egg whites, at room temperature
1⅓ cups superfine sugar
¼ cup water
2 tablespoons light corn syrup
½ teaspoon cream of tartar
1 teaspoon pure vanilla extract

1. If you have a double boiler large enough to hold the frosting, use it. Otherwise, fill a pot that is large enough to hold the heatproof bowl you will be using to make the frosting with enough water to cover about ⅓ of the bowl. Place over high heat and bring to a simmer.

2. Combine the egg whites with the sugar, water, corn syrup, and cream of tartar in a large heatproof bowl. Place over the simmering water and, using a hand-held mixer, beat on low until well blended. Raise the speed and continue to beat until the mixture reads 140°F on an instant-read thermometer. Add the va-nilla and continue to beat until the mixture is glossy and holds stiff peaks when lifted, about 7 minutes. Remove from the heat and continue to beat for about 5 minutes, until cooled slightly. Use immediately.

Quick 7-Minute Frosting

3 large egg whites, at room temperature
¼ teaspoon salt
⅜ cup superfine sugar
1⅛ cups light corn syrup
2 teaspoons pure vanilla extract

Place the egg whites and salt in the bowl of a stand-ing electric mixer fitted with the whip. Beat on low until frothy. Raise the speed to high and beat until fluffy. Add the sugar and beat until glossy. Then, add the syrup and vanilla and continue beating for about 5 minutes or until frosting is very glossy and holds a stiff peak when lifted. Use immediately.

Pineapple Upside-Down Cake

MAKES ONE 9-INCH CAKE

I've never seen anybody turn down a slice of this old-fashioned dessert, so I always keep a can of sliced pineapple on hand to make it when spur-of-the-moment dinners demand a quick dessert and fresh fruit or berries and ice cream are not on hand. This is another recipe that my mom made (always in a cast-iron skillet) and it remains the best I have ever tasted. It is much lighter than most upside-down cakes with the beaten egg whites folded into the batter. I have, from time to time, used fresh pineapple, but I honestly prefer canned.

¼ cup unsalted butter, at room temperature

1 cup light brown sugar

Approximately 7 canned pineapple rings with their juice

Approximately 2 tablespoons dried cherries or cranberries

¼ cup walnut or pecan halves (optional)

3 large eggs, separated

1¼ cups granulated sugar

1 teaspoon pure vanilla extract

1½ cups sifted all-purpose flour

1½ teaspoons baking powder

½ cup water

1. Preheat the oven to 350°F.

2. Place the butter in a 9-inch round cast-iron frying pan or heavy metal round cake pan over very low heat and stir until melted. Add the brown sugar and ¼ cup of the pineapple juice and continue stirring until well blended. Remove from the heat.

3. Place the pineapple rings in the sugar mixture in a decorative pattern. Put a bit of the dried fruit in the center of each ring or in any pattern you desire. Place nut halves in any of the empty spaces. Set aside, but keep warm.

4. Put the egg yolks in the bowl of a standing electric mixer fitted with the paddle and beat until frothy. Add the granulated sugar and continue beating until thick and lemon colored, about 5 minutes. Stir in the vanilla.

5. Sift the flour and baking powder together and add to the egg mixture alternating with the water.

6. Using a handheld mixer, beat the egg whites until stiff peaks form; then, fold the egg whites into the batter, blending to just combine.

7. Spoon the batter over the pineapple rings in the prepared pan, smoothing the top slightly. Place in the preheated oven and bake for about 30 minutes, or until a cake tester inserted in the center comes out clean, the top is golden, and the caramel is bubbling up around the edges.

8. Remove from the oven and let rest for 5 minutes. Invert the pan onto a serving platter and gently tap the cake loose. It should come out with the pineapple pattern intact. Serve warm with whipped cream or ice cream.

Laurel Makes Everybody's Birthday Cake

MAKES ONE 8-INCH ROUND 3-LAYER CAKE

Although Laurel and Mickey share the cake-making chores, Laurel usually gets the designated cake-making kudos, even though Mickey often says, "But I made the cake."

There are two favorite cakes—an old fashioned 1-2-3-4 cake (1 cup butter, 2 cups sugar, 3 cups cake flour, and 4 large eggs) and a 3-layer white cake with chocolate frosting that comes from *Chocolate Chocolate*, a book by Lisa Yokelson, a master baker, much-lauded cookbook author, and client of Mickey's. It is the latter that is almost always used as a birthday cake. It is a light, airy cake that Laurel tops with one of Lisa's rich, glossy chocolate frostings. Thank you, Lisa, for giving the Choate family a classic!

3 cups plus 2 tablespoons bleached cake flour

3 teaspoons baking powder

¾ teaspoon salt

¾ cup (12 tablespoons/1½ sticks) unsalted butter, room temperature

2 cups superfine sugar

2½ teaspoons pure vanilla extract

1⅓ cups plus 2 tablespoons ice-cold water

4 large egg whites

¼ teaspoon cream of tartar

Laurel's Favorite Chocolate Frosting (recipe follows)

1. Preheat the oven to 350°F.

2. Lightly butter or grease three 8-inch round cake pans. Line each with a circle of parchment paper and then grease the paper. Set aside.

3. Sift the flour, baking powder, and salt together onto a sheet of waxed paper. Do this twice to insure lightness.

4. Place the butter in the bowl of a standing electric mixer fitted with the paddle and beat until light and creamy. Add the sugar in 3 batches, beating for a minute after each one. Add the vanilla and beat to blend.

5. With the mixer running on low speed, alternately add the dry ingredients and water, beginning and ending with the dry. Don't forget to scrape down the edges of the bowl frequently to make sure all of the ingredients are properly mixed.

6. Beat the egg whites with a handheld mixer (or if you have the luxury of an extra bowl for your standing electric mixer, use it). When they are just beginning to gain some volume, add the cream of tartar and continue to beat until firm but not stiff.

7. Stir about a quarter of the beaten egg whites into the batter to lighten it. Then, fold in the remaining egg whites until completely blended into the batter.

8. Spoon equal portions of the batter into the prepared cake pans. (**Judie:** "Laurel and Mickey weigh each one—a level of patience I, unfortunately, lack.")

9. Place in the preheated oven and bake for about 30 minutes, or until a cake tester inserted into the center comes out clean.

10. Remove from the oven and set on wire racks to cool for 10 minutes. Then, invert the cakes onto the wire racks and set aside to cool completely.

[recipe continued on page 243]

11. Tear off four 3-inch wide strips of waxed paper and place them in a square shape around the edge of your cake platter.

12. Place one cooled layer in the center of the platter, slightly covering the strips. Spread a layer of the frosting over the top of the layer, using an offset spatula to smooth it. Top with another layer and spread a layer of frosting over it. Then, top with the final layer and frost the top and sides of the 3 layers with the remaining frosting. Remove the waxed paper strips and you will serve the most perfect old-fashioned birthday cake that you can imagine.

Laurel's Favorite Chocolate Frosting

5 ounces unsweetened chocolate
½ cup (1 stick) unsalted butter, room temperature
½ cup whole milk
6½ cups confectioners' sugar
⅛ teaspoon salt
2 teaspoons pure vanilla extract
¼ cup heavy cream, plus more as needed

1. Combine the chocolate and butter in a heavy-bottomed saucepan over low heat. Cook, stirring constantly, until melted. Remove from the heat and set aside to cool until tepid.

2. Heat the milk in a small saucepan over low heat until barely warm. Remove from the heat and set aside to cool slightly. Both the chocolate mixture and the milk should be just tepid or lukewarm.

3. Sift the confectioners' sugar and salt together. Transfer to the bowl of a standing electric mixer fitted with the paddle attachment. Begin beating on low as you add the chocolate/butter mixture, milk, and vanilla. Continue to beat on low until the mixture is blended; then, raise the speed slightly and continue to beat, scraping down the sides of the bowl from time to time, for about 4 minutes, or until very smooth.

4. Begin adding the heavy cream, increasing the speed to medium-high; beat for 3 minutes or until very creamy and slightly increased in volume. If the frosting is too thick, add more heavy cream a tablespoonful at a time. If too thin, add confectioners' sugar in the same amount until the mixture reaches spreading consistency.

Lemon Meringue Pie

MAKES ONE 9-INCH SINGLE-CRUST PIE

Right after we closed the bakery, I swore I'd never make another pie, but that vow was short-lived. Oh, there might have been a few years when pie, savory or sweet, was not on the menu, but once I reached for my rolling pin again, pies came back with a vengeance. After all this time, I'd say I now make pastry equal to my mom's, and both Mickey and Chris keep the pastry artistry alive in their kitchens. To me, lemon meringue pie is, after brownies and chocolate-chip cookies, the quintessential American dessert—even more so than apple. This recipe is a combination of the recipes used by my mom and my aunt Frances, both now gone from the kitchen, but remembered always through their love of feeding family and friends.

½ recipe Nana's Flaky Pie Pastry (page 70), chilled

Wondra flour for dusting

1 large egg white

LEMON FILLING:

1½ cups sugar

¼ cup cornstarch

⅛ teaspoon salt

Juice of 3 lemons

3 large eggs, separated, room temperature (you will use the whites for the meringue)

¼ cup (½ stick) unsalted butter, cut into pieces

2 teaspoons freshly grated lemon zest

Aunt Frances's Never-Fail Meringue (recipe follows)

1. Preheat the oven to 400°F.

2. Lightly flour a clean, flat surface with Wondra flour. Place the chilled dough in the center and using a rolling pin, begin rolling the dough out to a circle about 10 to 12 inches in diameter—large enough to fit into a 9-inch pie pan and leave an edge for fluting.

3. Transfer the dough to the pie pan and carefully push on it to make a neat fit, leaving the edges overhanging the pan. Fold the excess dough under the rim and then, using your thumb and forefinger, crimp the dough into a decorative edge. Using a table fork, randomly prick the bottom of the pie shell.

4. Place the egg white into a small bowl and whisk in 1 tablespoon of cold water. Using a pastry brush, lightly coat the bottom of the pie shell with the egg-white wash.

5. Cut a piece of parchment paper to fit the pie pan and fit it into the shell. Layer the bottom with pie weights, dried beans, or rice. Place in the preheated oven and bake for about 15 minutes, or until the pastry has set and is lightly browned. Remove from the oven and set aside on a wire rack to cool. Do not turn off the oven.

6. Make the filling while the shell is baking. Combine the sugar, cornstarch, and salt in a heavy-bottomed saucepan. Stir in 1¾ cups of cold water and place over medium heat. Cook, stirring constantly, for about 6 minutes, or until thickened. Stir in the lemon juice and remove from the heat.

7. Place the egg yolks in a small bowl and gradually whisk in about ½ cup of the lemon mixture to temper. Quickly whisk the egg-yolk mixture back into the hot lemon mixture. Return to medium heat and, whisking constantly, beat in the butter and lemon zest. Cook

for another couple of minutes, until thick. Remove from the heat and set aside to cool slightly.

8. While the pastry and filling are cooling, make the meringue.

9. When cooled slightly, pour the filling into the pastry shell, smoothing out the top with an offset spatula.

10. Spoon most of the meringue on top of the center of the filling and spoon small amounts of the remaining meringue around the edges. Using an offset spatula or wide knife, gently spread the meringue out from the center to meet the edge, making sure that the entire top is covered and the edge is sealed.

11. Place the pie in the preheated oven and bake for about 10 minutes, or until the meringue is golden brown. Remove from the oven and set aside to cool for at least 30 minutes before cutting.

Aunt Frances's Never-Fail Meringue

MAKES ENOUGH FOR ONE 9- TO 10-INCH PIE

1 tablespoon cornstarch dissolved in 1 tablespoon cold water
3 large egg whites, at room temperature
6 tablespoons superfine sugar

1. Combine the cornstarch mixture with ½ cup cold water in a small saucepan over medium heat. Cook, stirring constantly, until the liquid is clear, about 3 minutes. Remove from the heat and set in a pan of ice water to cool quickly. Stir frequently to keep the mixture liquid.

2. Place the egg whites in the bowl of a standing electric mixer fitted with the whip. Begin beating on low to froth. Increase the speed and continue to beat, alternately adding the cooled cornstarch mixture and the sugar, until stiff and shiny. Use as directed in the pie recipe or for any dessert requiring a stiff meringue.

Shaker Lemon Pie

MAKES ONE 9-INCH SINGLE-CRUST PIE

More than a few years ago, when we had our bakery, MOM, I tried about every combination of flavors I could imagine in both savory and sweet pies. One of the pies that I could never master was from a Shaker cookbook (I had fallen in love with the simplicity of their lives, their furniture, and the sophistication of their food) culled from recipes devised in the American Shaker colonies of the 1800s. It is a very, very simple pie, but difficult to make without pristine, exceedingly thin-skinned lemons. Back then I could never find lemons that would do the trick.

Nowadays, we have beautiful Meyer lemons, both in the markets and pulled from the backyard trees of our California friends, that are sweet-sour, with delicate skin—the perfect specimens to make that longed-for pie. It couldn't be more different from our beloved lemon meringue pie, but it is tongue-teasing and a conversation piece to boot. Here's the recipe, should you find a generous friend or be lucky enough to live somewhere in Meyer-lemon territory. You can make your own pastry, buy refrigerated commercial pie dough, or use my recipe (page 70).

The filling is, surprisingly, quite sweet, so I serve the pie with a dollop of thick Greek-style yogurt.

3 or 4 very thin-skinned organic lemons,
  washed well and dried
2½ cups sugar (superfine is best, but regular
  granulated will do just fine)
6 eggs
One 9-inch unbaked pie or tart shell

1. Using a mandoline, Japanese vegetable slicer, or very sharp knife, slice the lemons crosswise, paper thin.

2. Place the lemons in a shallow bowl and cover with the sugar. Toss to blend. Cover with plastic film and refrigerate for 12 hours.

3. Preheat the oven to 350°F.

4. Place the eggs in a mixing bowl and beat until light and fluffy. Add the marinated lemons along with the sugar and stir to blend. Scrape into the pie (or tart) shell and gently smooth the top, making sure that some lemon slices are evident.

5. Place in the preheated oven and bake for about 45 minutes or until the top is golden brown and the center is set. Remove from the oven and set on a wire rack to cool before serving.

Strawberry-Rhubarb Pie and Some Others

Who doesn't like strawberry-rhubarb pie? Besides Steve, that is. He eats a bowl of strawberries and cream while we all dive into the first luscious pie of the season. Unfortunately, in Upstate New York, when rhubarb pops up, strawberries are still a month or so behind, so we have to purchase our berries to make this perennial favorite, but make it we do. We also freeze a good amount of rhubarb to have on hand when local berries eventually come in. Next to my mom's Lemon Meringue Pie (page 244), this is Mickey's favorite.

When I was a kid, asparagus and rhubarb both grew wild alongside the irrigation ditches that ran throughout the tiny towns of southeastern Colorado. My mom and aunt made good use of them—both in our daily meals and for canning—pickled asparagus was a favorite (see page 198) and strawberry-rhubarb jam was on the table year round for spreading on toast, pancakes, and waffles. But more than anything, I loved my aunt Frances and mom's strawberry-rhubarb pies, especially topped with a scoop of homemade vanilla ice cream. They also used this same combination to make a cobbler, as I often do too.

I also use just plain rhubarb all by its lonesome in pies or to make what I call sweet pizza, which is really nothing more than pastry dough rolled out quite thin and placed on a pizza stone or pan with a nice rolled edge. I slice the rhubarb (or whatever fruit I am using) paper thin on a mandoline, season it with sugar and orange zest, add a little flour to hold it all together, and then cover the pastry with a thin layer of the fruit. If you're feeling fancy, you can place the fruit in slightly overlapping circles so that the end result looks like the work of a professional pastry chef. Bake at 375°F for about 40 minutes or until the crust is golden and the fruit is bubbly and lightly colored.

I use my mom's pastry (page 70) for all pies and tarts. I sometimes make fancy tarts à la the French but I usually opt for more rustic-looking ones, which are so easy to pull together. I roll out a large almost-circle of pastry and place it on a flat baking sheet. I sweeten the fruit with sugar—white or light brown depending upon the flavor I want—and a bit of spice or fresh ginger, herbs, or chilies. Then, I mound fresh fruit in the center and pull the edges of the pastry up over the outside of the fruit making a little ruffle flourish all the way around. I bake it at 375°F for about 45 minutes or until the top of the fruit is glazed and bubbling and the pastry is golden. Sometimes, just before the fruit is cooked through, I pour about ½ cup of heavy cream over it and bake for another 10 minutes or so.

TIP: If you are in a hurry and don't mind cheating, you can buy those refrigerated Pillsbury pastry rounds to use for pies or tarts—nobody will know that you didn't do it all yourself. Except for the fact that they really don't taste as good as homemade. And, you can't make a rustic tart, as the commercial pastry circle is too small to make a statement! I usually make a lattice top on berry pies; I never worry about them being perfect and you shouldn't either.

Strawberry-Rhubarb Pie

MAKES ONE 9-INCH DOUBLE-CRUST PIE

Nana's Flaky Pie Pastry (page 70)
2½ cups diced fresh rhubarb
2½ cups whole hulled strawberries
1 cup sugar
1 teaspoon ground cinnamon
½ teaspoon grated fresh ginger
¼ cup instant tapioca
3 tablespoons unsalted butter, melted
Egg-white wash (1 large egg white whisked
    with 1 tablespoon cold water) (optional)
Cinnamon-sugar for dusting (optional)

1. Make the dough and divide it into two equal pieces. Wrap each piece in plastic film and refrigerate for about 30 minutes before rolling.

2. Preheat the oven to 400°F.

3. Mix the rhubarb and strawberries together in a mixing bowl. Add the sugar, cinnamon, and ginger and toss to coat. Add the tapioca and again toss to incorporate. Drizzle with the butter.

4. Line a baking sheet with aluminum foil or parchment paper. Set aside.

5. Remove the pastry from the refrigerator and lightly flour a clean work surface. Using a rolling pin, roll each piece of pastry into a 10-inch round. Fit one piece into a 9-inch pie plate.

6. Mound the fruit filling into the pastry shell. Fold the top crust in half over the rolling pin, lift, and place over the filling. Unfold to cover the filling and attach to the bottom crust by pressing the excess dough from the edge of the top and bottom crust together with your fingertips. Fold the pressed dough edge up and inward, making a rim around the edge of the pie. Starting at the edge opposite you, pinch the dough between your thumb and index finger around the edge of the pie at about ¾-inch intervals, forming a fluted design.

7. If you want to make a lattice top, using a pastry wheel (or a small sharp knife) cut the pastry round into strips about ¼ to ½ inch wide. Using the longest strips for the center and working out to the edges, lay half the strips horizontally across the top about ¾ inch apart. Working in the same manner, lay the remaining strips vertically. If you are ambitious, lay on one strip at a time and weave them into a perfect lattice or angle them for a diamond pattern. Trim off the ends of the strips, pull the excess dough from the bottom up, and flute the edge as above.

8. Place the finished pie on the prepared baking sheet. This just makes for easy cleanup, as the pie is sure to bubble over in the oven and drip.

9. Brush the top with the egg-white wash and sprinkle with cinnamon-sugar. Transfer to the preheated oven and bake for 10 minutes; then, lower the heat to 350°F and bake for about 35 minutes, or until golden brown and bubbling.

10. Remove the pie from the oven and place on a wire rack to cool for about 20 minutes before cutting into it. The resting allows the filling to set slightly.

Apple Pizza

MAKES ONE LARGE PIZZA

This is my go-to fall and winter dessert; it never fails to please. I think I began making it when we owned MOM, our pie shop, and I would tire of making the same 3- or 9-inch double-crust pies. Since we were an all-American shop, I didn't want to do a classic French tart, so I devised this presentation. I cut the apples by hand, so unfortunately, each one has its own shape, but I do try to keep all of the slices fairly thin. I use whatever apples are local and in season that seem to be crisp and a bit tart, but I particularly like very large Honeycrisps. You can make the pie in a metal pizza pan or directly on a pizza stone.

Nana's Flaky Pie Pastry (page 70)

2 tablespoons Wondra flour, plus more for dusting

2 teaspoons ground cinnamon

Approximately 1½ pounds crisp, tart apples, peeled, cored, and thinly sliced

Juice of 1 lemon

3 tablespoons apple cider

3 tablespoons melted unsalted butter

1. Preheat the oven to 375°F.

2. Lightly flour a clean, flat workspace using Wondra flour.

3. Place the dough in the center of the work surface and lightly flour the top of the pastry, again using Wondra flour. Using a rolling pin, roll the dough out to a circle about 1 inch larger in diameter than your pizza pan. Carefully fold the dough over the rolling pin and transfer it to the pan. Gently fold in the edges and crimp.

4. Mix the 2 tablespoons Wondra flour with the cinnamon.

5. Place the apples in a large mixing bowl and sprinkle with the flour/cinnamon mixture. Add the lemon juice and cider and gently toss to coat. Drizzle in the butter and again toss to coat.

6. Carefully arrange the seasoned apple slices in slightly overlapping concentric circles over the entire top of the pastry.

7. Place in the preheated oven and bake for about 40 minutes or until the crust is golden and the apples are tender, caramelized, and beginning to crisp on the edges. Remove from the oven and let rest for about 15 minutes before cutting into wedges. Serve as is or with vanilla, caramel, cinnamon, or dulce de leche ice cream, whipped cream, or vanilla Greek-style yogurt.

Chocolate-Chip Cookies

MAKES ABOUT 2 DOZEN

Oreos might be up there on the list, but I would bet that American's number-one favorite cookie is homemade chocolate chip. In our family, Laurel and Clara don't like nuts in theirs, so I always have to make a double batch of dough, nuts in one, no nuts in the other. Every time I make them, I begin to wonder just how many chocolate-chip cookies I have baked in my lifetime. Since I began cooking when I was about five and I have more than one foot into those "golden" years, I would guess it must be up in the thousands, or even hundreds of thousands. And you know what? I still lick the raw dough off the beaters and I still test the first batch out of the oven. I don't think that my basic recipe has changed much over time except I now use bittersweet chocolate chips. I wonder if cookbook readers really need another recipe, but it wouldn't be our American family without it.

2½ cups all-purpose flour
1 tablespoon Dutch-processed cocoa powder
1 teaspoon baking soda
½ teaspoon baking powder
1 cup unsalted butter, room temperature
1 cup packed dark brown sugar
½ cup granulated sugar
1 tablespoon pure vanilla extract
2 large eggs, room temperature
As many bittersweet chocolate bits as you like
    (I generally use about 3 cups)
1½ to 2 cups toasted pecans or walnuts

1. Preheat the oven to 375°F.

2. If you don't have nonstick cookie sheets, lightly coat 2 sheets with nonstick baking spray or cover them with parchment paper or reusable silicone pan liners. Set aside.

3. Sift the flour, cocoa powder, baking soda, and baking powder together. Set aside.

4. Combine the butter with the dark and granulated sugars in the bowl of a standing electric mixer fitted with the paddle. Beat on medium until light and slightly airy. Beat in the vanilla, followed by the eggs. When well blended, add the flour mixture, a bit at a time, beating to blend.

5. Remove the bowl from the mixer and, using a wooden spoon, stir in the chocolate bits and nuts until evenly distributed throughout the dough.

6. Using a tablespoon, drop the dough onto the prepared pans by the heaping spoonful, leaving about 2 inches between each one.

7. Place in the preheated oven and bake for about 12 minutes or until slightly crisp around the edges, golden on top, and still a bit soft in the center. Remove from the oven and let rest on the pan for 3 minutes.

8. Using a spatula, transfer to wire racks to cool, but test one hot, runny chocolate cookie to make sure you've got it right once again.

NOTE: If you want the cookies to be even more chocolatey, replace ½ cup of the flour with cocoa powder.

Ginger Cookies

MAKES ABOUT 5 DOZEN

I do love ginger—fresh or dried—and I particularly love ginger cookies. For years I looked for the perfect recipe, but never found one that met my requirements for crispness that was still chewy, sugary, and just biting enough, with a gentle swath of heat. Working on my own, I finally came up with a version that has become the most requested recipe of my kitchen-made Christmas gifts.

1 cup granulated sugar

¾ cup white sanding sugar

5 cups all-purpose flour

3½ tablespoons ground ginger

1½ tablespoons ground cinnamon

1½ tablespoons baking soda

1 pound (4 sticks) unsalted butter, room temperature

1 pound (2 cups) dark brown sugar

½ cup unsulphured molasses

2 large eggs, room temperature

1 tablespoon freshly grated orange zest

1 teaspoon fresh lemon juice

1 cup finely chopped crystallized ginger

1. If you don't have nonstick cookie sheets, lightly coat 2 sheets with nonstick baking spray or cover them with parchment paper or reusable silicone pan liners. Set aside.

2. Place the granulated sugar in a large shallow bowl. Set aside. Place the sanding sugar in another shallow bowl. Set aside.

3. Combine the flour, ginger, cinnamon, and baking soda. Set aside.

4. Place the butter in the bowl of a standing electric mixer fitted with the paddle. Beat, on medium, to soften. Add the dark brown sugar and beat until light, scraping down the sides of the bowl a couple of times to insure even creaminess. When creamy, beat in the molasses. Add the eggs, one at a time, and beat to incorporate. Beat in the orange zest and lemon juice.

5. Now, here you really should have a splashguard or the flour will go flying everywhere. Begin adding the flour mixture, a bit at a time, and beat on low until all of the dry ingredients have been blended in. Do not overbeat or it will dry out the dough. Fold in the crystallized ginger.

6. Scoop out about a large tablespoon of dough and roll it between your palms into a smooth ball. Roll the ball in the reserved granulated sugar and then push one side into the sanding sugar. Place the ball, sanding-sugar-coated side up, on the prepared cookie sheet. Continue making cookies, setting them about 2 inches apart on the cookie sheets.

7. Transfer to the preheated oven and bake for 10 to 12 minutes, or until just barely colored around the edges and slightly rounded in the center. Do not overbake UNLESS you want crisp, dry cookies. You will probably have to bake a few batches to figure out exactly how much baking is required in your oven to get the optimal crisp exterior and chewy interior. Or, at least, I do; it seems to change every time I bake them. When crisp, the cookies are great dunkers, though! Remove from the oven and transfer to wire racks to cool.

Poached Pears

MAKES 6

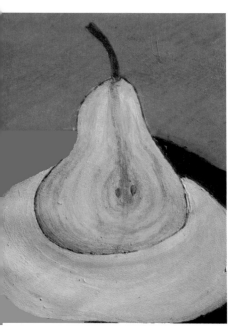

When company's coming, my first plan of attack is to get dessert done.
If I'm in a hurry it is always some version of Chocolate Chess (page 232);
if I'm feeling ambitious, it's profiteroles (nothing more than choux paste
[Sidebar, page 257] baked up into large puffs, filled with vanilla ice cream,
and drizzled with homemade bittersweet chocolate sauce). But when
winter comes and I'm cooking rich, filling stews or braises, I don't want to
end with an over-the-top dessert. So I have come to rely on poached pears
to bail me out.

You can make the poaching liquid out of almost anything—red wine,
white wine, fruit juices, cider, even water if you have some citrus to add
a little flavor. You just need enough liquid to cover the pears completely
and a pan of a size that will hold them standing straight up so that the
fruit can be completely submerged. The amount of liquid you will need
depends upon the size of the pan you use.

I prefer a highly spiced poaching liquid—I usually use red wine with
some added orange juice and brown sugar for sweetness, and lots of black
peppercorns (about 1 tablespoon), an inch or so of fresh ginger, four bay
leaves, a couple cinnamon sticks, a teaspoon of coriander, and a few strips
of citrus peel. But the mix of flavorings is really up to you, and whatever you have on
hand that will nicely flavor the pears can be thrown in.

I save the liquid and reuse it a number of times, but I generally take off a cup or
so and boil it down to a syrup to garnish the finished dish. And sometimes, I brush the
poached pears with the syrup and then bake them to a lovely burnished sheen.

You can serve the pears like plain Janes or drizzle them with the reduced poaching
liquid, dress them up with sauces (crème anglaise works beautifully) or cream cheeses,
such as mascarpone or a rich, runny brie, or whatever works for you. If you have poached
them in white wine and they remain pale
in color, they look wonderful floating on
a circle of bittersweet chocolate sauce.

No matter what I choose, I usually add some cookies—ginger, if I have
them. If not, I cut homemade white
bread into little rectangles, butter it pro-
digiously, sprinkle with cinnamon-sugar
and bake until crisp. Who's to know that
I didn't spend a day in the kitchen baking away?

6 Bosc pears with stems

4 to 6 cups red or white wine

2 cups orange juice

1 cup light brown sugar (or more or less as desired)

A variety of preferred spices and seasonings (see previous page for suggestions)

Bittersweet Chocolate Sauce
(recipe follows)

1. Carefully peel the pears, keeping the stems intact. Place them in acidulated water (cold water with the juice of 1 lemon). This will keep them from discoloring as you finish up the whole batch. Carefully cut a small piece off of the blossom ends so that the pears will stand up straight.

2. Combine the wine, juice, sugar, and seasonings in a large nonreactive saucepan over medium heat. Bring

to a simmer; then, immediately add the pears, standing them upright, if possible. Cover and again bring to a simmer. Uncover and simmer, taking care that the fruit remains submerged, for about 30 minutes, or until pears are tender but not mushy.

3. Remove from the heat and allow pears to cool in the poaching liquid. If using within a couple of hours, let stand at room temperature. If not, store in the poaching liquid, covered and refrigerated.

4. When ready to serve, remove from the liquid and gently pat dry. I sometimes let the pears sit for about 30 minutes on a double layer of paper towels so they don't weep on the serving plate. Serve as is, or garnish the plate with bittersweet chocolate sauce and pass cookies on the side.

Bittersweet Chocolate Sauce

MAKES ABOUT 1 CUP

1 cup heavy cream

½ pound bittersweet chocolate, in small pieces

2 tablespoons unsalted butter, room temperature

1 teaspoon pure vanilla extract

1. Place the cream in a small, heavy-bottomed saucepan over medium heat. When bubbles begin to form around the edge of the pan, remove from the heat and

immediately stir in the chocolate. As the chocolate begins to melt, return the pan to very low heat, add the butter and vanilla and cook, stirring, for about 3 to 5 minutes, or until the sauce is very smooth.

2. Use warm or at room temperature. May be made in advance and stored, covered and refrigerated, for up to a week. Reheat, stirring constantly, in a double boiler over boiling water.

Choux Paste

Choux paste (*pâte à choux* in French) is made in the exact same way we make our Gougères (page 149), except there is no cheese added. Should you wish to make profiteroles, make the gougère dough without the addition of the cheese and use the ½-inch tip on the pastry bag to create large puffs. Bake as directed in the gougère recipe. Once baked, set aside to cool. When cool, slice each puff in half crosswise, fill the bottom with a scoop of vanilla ice cream, cover with the top half, and set on a dessert plate in a pool of chocolate sauce. You can make the puffs in advance of use, but make sure that you store them in a cool, very dry spot, or they will soften and be unusable.

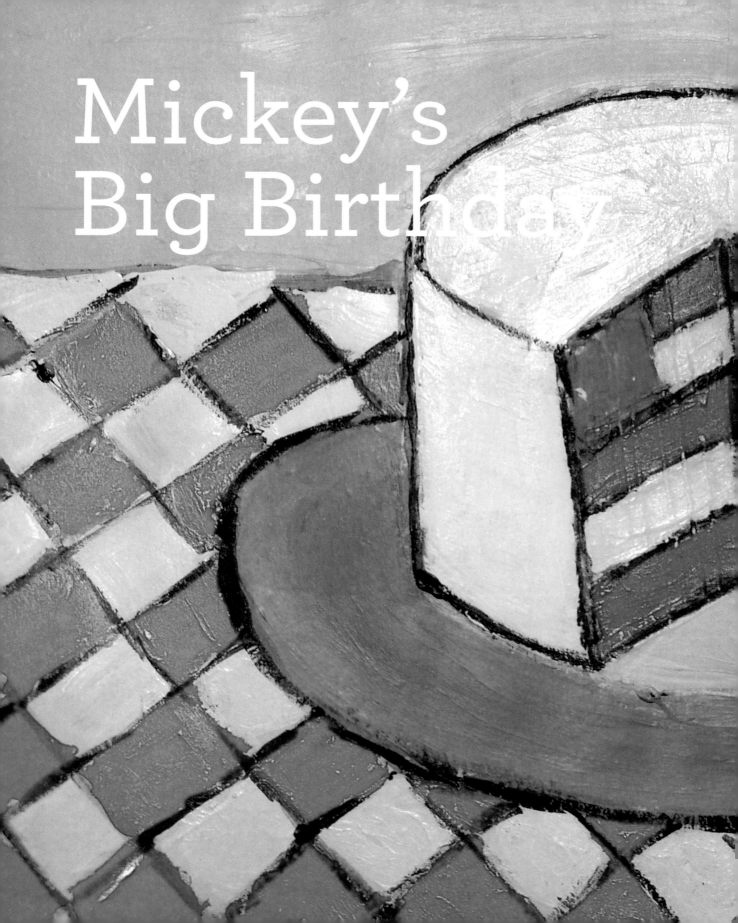

Mickey's
Big Birthday

A French Feast

Time does pass quickly, particularly when you are having fun. And, I can assure you I've had a lot of that! However, I woke up one day to realize that my firstborn was going to be as old as I thought I was and that wasn't such a riot. I couldn't believe how many years had elapsed since I held that baby boy in my arms for the first time. But so it was, and there was nothing to do but celebrate.

As we all now know, Mickey is the ultimate foodie, so his 50th birthday celebration was based on all the foods and people he loves. The West Coast Choates (Chris, Heather, and Canada) flew in to New York for the weekend and we all spent three days together. The first day we shopped at Manhattan's Union Square Greenmarket in the morning (for Saturday's feast), followed by lunch at Gramercy Tavern, one of Mickey's favorite restaurants in the city. We then all reconvened in Mickey's kitchen on Saturday to cook and cook and cook and eat and eat and eat and drink and drink and drink. The late morning started the festivities with Champagne (Mickey's favorite, Billecart-Salmon, and Chris's favorite, Henriot) and oysters, and went on throughout the day to complete eleven French-inspired courses.

Each of us had specific assignments, which Mickey doled out in a trail of e-mails.

From: Mickey
To: All
Date: April 24th, 2012

Here are my thoughts on my 50th birthday celebration. On Friday, June 22nd we will all meet in the morning at the Greenmarket to shop for Saturday's cooking event. After shopping, I think we should have lunch at Gramercy Tavern—perhaps in the private dining room. Initially I had thought I might just do a men's lunch, but I want to include everyone.

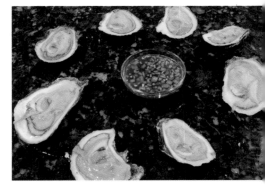

On Saturday, June 23rd, we will spend all day at home cooking, using some of my favorite ingredients. I think it might be fun if everyone picks a couple of dishes to do. Laurel will do the birthday cake. Let's begin a dialogue about who will do what so we can purchase some of the ingredients in advance. Of course, the idea is also to get inspired by the fruits and vegetables at the market on Friday morning. On Saturday morning, I will run up to the fish market in Greenwich or I might just shop at Wild Edibles (**Judie:** "an excellent seafood market") in Grand Central on the way home Friday. I will get cheeses at Murray's (**Judie:** "an excellent cheese shop") there also. Ideally, I'd like to purchase as much as we can in advance so we don't have to spend much time shopping on Saturday.

We can drink some wine from my cellar, but I'd also like to get some special Champagne and seek out a few interesting bottles of other wines. Chris, can you help here? Of course, the theme should be French, but I'm open to other wines as well.

Here's my list of ingredients:

Oysters
Raw tuna
Foie gras
Scallops
Lobster
Halibut, sea bass, sole, or salmon
Squab
Veal
Lamb
Wild mushrooms—chanterelles, porcini, morels
Summer fruits—apricots, cherries, berries

Then he got specific:

From: Mickey
To: All
Date: May 7th, 2012
Okay, here's what I'm thinking for Saturday. Please give me your comments and tell me who wants to prepare what dish where I don't have someone listed.
We'll kick things off around noon and here's my suggested order:

1. Oysters, tuna tartare (Uncle Kol), other raw seafood?
   Champagne (Chris), but of course: Billecart-Salmon Rosé for sure
2. Pizza on the grill (Grammy, Laurel, Heather)—we'll pick up prosciutto and other fixings (page 126)
   Rosé wine—maybe Bandol Domaine Tempier?
3. Grammy's Gargouillou—Homage à Bras (Grammy)

So, I had my main dish—Grammy's Gargouillou—*Homage à Bras*, an elevated arrangement of vegetables and fruit from the Greenmarket. This was a tribute to Chef

Michel Bras (in case you don't know him—a much-esteemed French chef who owns Restaurant Bras in Laguiole, France), which we called "homage à Bras," as it was based on his famous vegetable dish "la gargouillou." On the actual shopping day, I went to the greenmarket with $200 in my pocket and had nothing left after buying all of the pristine veggies and flowers I needed for my composition. There is no recipe—you can, if you like, poach or steam some of the vegetables. Chef Bras gathers his from his garden and the surrounding countryside and lets their freshness shine. I left all of mine raw, as they seemed to be able to stand as Mother Nature made them. I toasted a brioche to an almost inedible darkness to create some "dirt" for the plate. I then made a little sauce of pureed parsley, orange zest, a bit of orange juice, and extra virgin olive oil to add just a streak or two to the tray and to dip the delicate veggies in. It was almost too beautiful to eat.

Back to the rest of Mickey's e-mail:

4. Foie gras terrine—(me) I'll make with some kind of fruit
    compote
    Vendage Tardive?
5. Scallops—a dish with beurre blanc (Chris); include some veg
    from the market
    White Burgundy
6. Lobster (?)
7. Fish dish (?)
8. Veal with wild mushrooms (me)—also I'll do a pork tenderloin for those who don't
    like veal. Some sort of potato dish should accompany.
    Red Burgundy or Kistler Pinot Noir
9. Squab (me) I'm thinking apricots, almonds, spinach, and baby turnips
    Red Burgundy or Kistler Pinot
10. Lamb (Uncle Kol)—I'm thinking Duo of Lamb—grilled loin along with braised meat
    from the shank or shoulder chops that could be put into
    some type of roulade—you know how I love those roulades!
    Bordeaux or Rhone wine—I have a Chave Hermitage and
    Chris has a great Côte-Rôtie

11. Cheese (we can all pick up from Murray's)
    I have a '77 port in the cellar
12. Cake (Laurel) along with an apricot tart (Grammy) and we
    can drink the half bottle of Y'Quem that the old folks
    (**Judie:** "that being Steve and me") gave me for my 40th.

Well, looking at this, I'm thinking that maybe we shouldn't attempt both lobster and fish—let's just do one. Thoughts everyone?

And yet further ideas from Mickey a few days later:

From: Mickey
To: All
Date: May 10th, 2012
Since we want to grill as much as possible, maybe instead of tuna tartare we should grill tuna

for some sort of small plate to go along with the oysters (Kol). Maybe the other seafood hors d'oeuvres should be shrimp.

We will need tomato sauce for the pizza (Grammy). Other toppings might be roasted peppers, arugula, red onion. We can pick up cured meat at Murray's, or Grammy, you can pick up meats from Cesare's (**Judie:** "that being Chef Cesare Casella of the restaurant Salumeria Rosi in New York City").

I am beginning to grasp the cost of this—we will need 4 lobsters (Clara and Alexander won't eat), giving half a tail and claw each. I'd like to do a fancier preparation rather than just throwing them on the grill or steaming. I'll think about it.

Here's what we need to buy:

Tuna, shrimp, dozen oysters, 2 lobsters—Mickey and Uncle Kol

Fish, dozen oysters, 2 lobsters—Mom and Chris

Mom, do you want to pick up the Billecart-Salmon from Whole Foods?

I hope this gives you a sense of the meticulous planning and ruminating that went into Mickey's birthday celebration. Most of the dishes were very complex and difficult to prepare and I don't know of many other home cooks that would attempt them, particularly on their own birthday. But it was a wonderful, wonderful way for Mickey to begin the second half of his life, surrounded by those he loves the most, eating the foods and drinking the wines that signify the quality he seeks in life and at the table. It made me extremely proud to be his mom.

For those of you with a bit of ambition, here are a couple of the simpler dishes.

Grilled Lemon Shrimp with Fennel Slaw

SERVES 6 AS AN APPETIZER

One pound of extra-large shrimp, clean and deveined with the tails intact

Extra virgin olive oil

Juice of one lemon, plus a bit more

2 cloves garlic, minced

2 fennel bulbs, with fronds reserved

Lemon-flavored olive oil

Salt and pepper

1. Marinate the shrimp in extra virgin olive oil, the juice of one lemon, and minced garlic for about 30 minutes.

2. While the shrimp are marinating, to make the slaw, slice fennel bulbs on a mandoline—you want thin shreds. Be sure to reserve some of the fronds when you trim the fennel. Toss the shredded fennel with a touch of lemon-flavored olive oil and a hint of fresh lemon juice. Chop some of the reserved fronds—you'll want about a tablespoon or so—and add them to the mix. Season with salt and pepper.

3. Then, season the marinated shrimp with salt and pepper and toss them on a hot grill for a couple of minutes (you can skewer them to make them easier to handle while grilling).

4. Place a nice mound of fennel slaw in the center of a luncheon plate, top with 4 grilled shrimp, and garnish with a fennel frond. See how easy that was....

Halibut with Succotash, Spinach, and Mushrooms

SERVES 6 AS A MAIN

4 ears fresh corn, shucked and cleaned

1 pound fava beans

1 red bell pepper

A handful of chanterelle mushrooms (if you can't find them, forget 'em)

2 tablespoons butter, plus a bit more

¼ cup chicken stock

Salt and pepper

1 pound fresh large crinkly-leaf spinach (not the baby variety), washed and dried

Olive oil

6 (6-ounce) pieces halibut

Canola oil

1. Make the succotash first: Using a sharp knife or corn-kernel remover, remove all of the kernels from 4 ears of fresh corn. Shell and skin a pound of fava beans (see page 36 for a word about this). Dice 1 red bell pepper. Clean chanterelle mushrooms.

2. Melt about 2 tablespoons of butter in a heavy-bottomed saucepan. Add the vegetables, along with about ¼ cup of chicken stock. Season with salt and pepper and cook, stirring frequently, for about 5 minutes, or until just barely tender. Remove from the heat and keep warm.

3. Sauté spinach in a light mix of olive oil and butter. This won't take but a couple of minutes as you just need it to wilt. Season with salt and pepper and set aside.

4. Season halibut with salt and pepper. Place in a very hot pan slicked with a bit of canola oil. Sear for about 4 minutes or until golden brown. Turn and sear the remaining side until golden and the fish is just barely cooked, about another 3 minutes.

5. Place equal portions of the spinach in the centers of six dinner plates. Place a piece of halibut in the center and spoon the succotash around the plate. Serve hot and tasty.

Easter

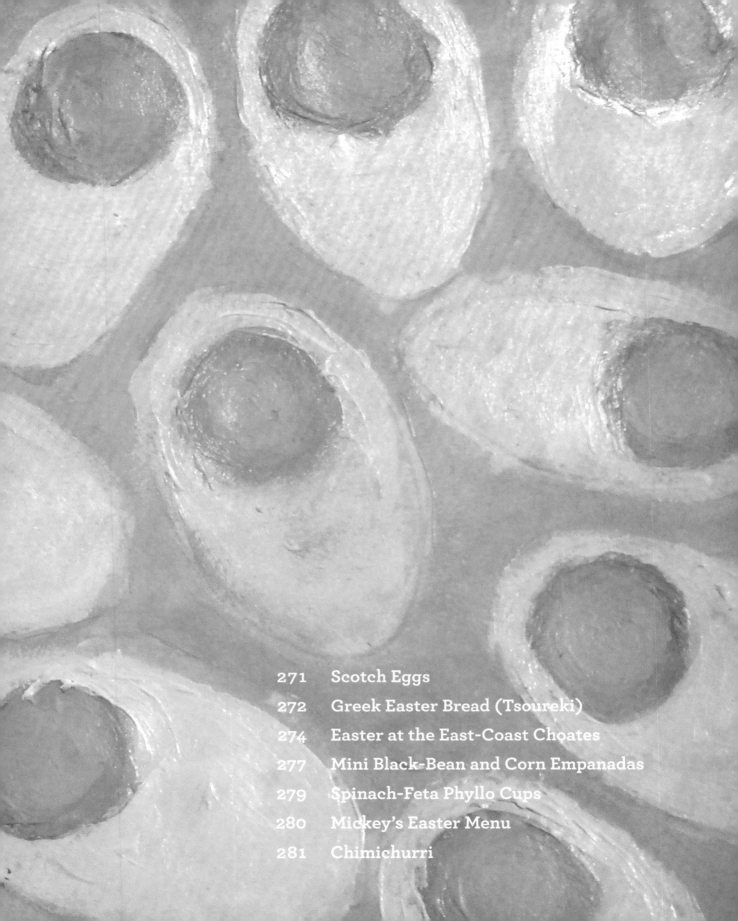

Scotch Eggs

Although I am more than aware that Easter is an important religious holiday, I have always associated it with dying eggs. For as long as I can remember I have loved to color eggs and then have an Easter-egg hunt after the bunny's arrival. Well into my teens, Easter was a big deal in my family—I always got a new outfit (including shoes—either white or patent leather) to wear to church (to which there might have been two trips —one for the sunrise service and one later in the morning); the Easter bunny hid the eggs I had colored and generously left a beautiful basket filled with chocolate and marzipan; and my mom cooked up a feast to welcome spring—usually with a ham at the center of the table.

All these years later I still color eggs just for my own pleasure and to have on hand to make Greek Easter bread. But I'm always left with the problem of what to do with all of the eggs that remain, particularly because doctor's orders say I'm not supposed to eat them.

One of my mom's favorite ways to use up an Easter basket of hard-cooked eggs was to make Scotch eggs. I don't know if this was because she was Scots, herself, or if it just gave her a reason to make a fancy dish out of everyday food. Hers is less of a recipe and more of a simple guideline depending on how many left-over Easter eggs you have, but if you'd like to try them, here is what you do: peel hard-cooked eggs. Make sure that the outside is a bit damp and lightly dust them with flour. Carefully enclose each whole egg with uncooked, loose, breakfast sausage meat, making a thin, even layer. Then (as if that isn't enough!) dip the eggs in beaten egg seasoned with pepper, and generously coat with bread crumbs (Panko would be good to add that extra crunch). Now comes the good part—this cardiologist's nightmare gets deep-fried in a pot of vegetable oil. Elegant ladies often served these with Mornay sauce (a simple béchamel sauce with a bit of shredded or grated cheese added, usually Gruyère or Parmesan).

Greek Easter Bread (Tsoureki)

MAKES 2 LOAVES

This bread has enormous significance to the celebration of Greek Easter. The yeast dough's final rise represents the resurrection of Christ and the red eggs his blood, while its sweetness announces the bursting of spring from the cold winter months. A Greek friend has told me that everyone in his village made this bread, and once the fragrant loaves were presented on Easter they were banged together in a game to try to crack the eggs. Whoever was left with the last unbroken egg was the winner of a simple prize.

Greek Easter bread can be shaped in one of two ways: braided with four red colored eggs nestled in the braid or formed into a round loaf with one red egg in the center and two strips of dough laid over the egg to form a cross. I always do the braid. This bread has historically been made to mark the end of Lent and to celebrate spring.

The dough is traditionally flavored with mahlepi (or mahlab) which is a Middle Eastern seasoning made from ground cherry pits. In Greek cooking, it is generally used in pastries to add an almond-like flavor. I have left it out, as it is not easy to track down; however, should you have it on hand, 1 tablespoon can be added.

6 cups unbleached flour, plus more if necessary

½ cup sugar

1 tablespoon freshly grated orange zest

2 teaspoons salt

1½ teaspoons anise seed

2 tablespoons instant yeast

1 cup warm (no more than 120°F) milk

½ cup warm (no more than 120°F) water

3 large eggs, room temperature, beaten

½ cup melted unsalted butter, cooled slightly

8 to 12 hard-cooked eggs, dyed red

Egg glaze—1 egg beaten with 1 tablespoon each water and sugar

1. Combine the flour, sugar, orange zest, salt, and anise seed in a large mixing bowl. Stir in the yeast.

2. Combine the warm milk and water with the eggs and melted butter, whisking to blend well. Add the liquid mixture to the flour, stirring as vigorously as possible to blend. When blended and stiff, scrape the mixture onto a lightly floured board and knead for about 10 minutes, or until smooth and elastic. (This process may also be done in a heavy-duty standing electric mixer fitted with the dough hook. I just prefer the intimacy of working my hands into the dough as I knead.) If the dough seems very sticky, add additional flour, no more than ¼ cup at a time.

3. Lightly butter a large bowl and scrape the dough into it. Cover and set aside in a warm spot to rise for about an hour or two or until doubled in size.

4. Line two baking sheets with parchment paper or silicone liners. Set aside.

5. Gently deflate the dough and divide it into two equal pieces. Cover one piece while you form the other one.

6. Divide each piece of dough into 3 equal pieces and, using your hands, roll each piece out into a rope about 2 feet long. You might need to flour the surface lightly—I use Wondra flour when I roll. Lay 3 ropes down, the length facing you. Lightly pinch the top ends together and begin braiding the ropes. When you get to the end, gently form the braid into a circle and pinch the ends together. Carefully transfer the circle to one of the parchment-lined pans and nestle 4 to 6 eggs equidistantly into the braid. Form the remaining 3 ropes of dough into a braided loaf as above. Cover the two breads with a clean kitchen towel and set aside in a warm spot to rise for 1 hour.

7. Fifteen minutes before baking, preheat the oven to 350°F.

8. Uncover the breads and, using a pastry brush, lightly coat the dough with the egg glaze. Place in the preheated oven and bake for about 30 minutes or until golden brown and perfectly risen. Remove from the oven and set on wire racks to cool before cutting.

Easter at the East-Coast Choates

Easter at Mickey and Laurel's is more informal than their typical culinary extrava-ganzas. However, Mickey's version of casual still includes his little copper pot of "sauce" (the most luscious reduced veal/lamb/beef demi-glace) on the back burner and a large potato gratin in the oven. The vegetables and the meat are always simply done, often on the grill. Perhaps this is because it's around this time of year that we begin to feel the warmth of the coming summer on the East Coast. We are usually joined by our chef-artist in residence, Steve Kolyer (aka Uncle Kol), who takes care of all the hors d'oeuvres.

Laurel is in charge of what has now become an Easter tradition: a cake to celebrate the bunny that is nothing more than the traditional 1-2-3-4 cake pieced together in the shape of a rabbit head and covered in a lovely pink frosting.

Uncle Kol's hors d'oeuvres are always a hit at holiday gatherings. From year to year, guests remember and request their favorites from previous celebrations, but Kol always comes up with something new. Some of the bites that he has served up over the years: Spinach-and-feta phyllo cups, melon balls wrapped with prosciutto, mini black-bean and corn empanadas, Cheddar-cheese-and-smoked-paprika madeleines, nacho corn cups, warm green curry shrimp with dipping sauce, apple-chutney-topped parsnip pancakes, orange-beef skewers, Manila clams with chorizo, and lotus-root chips with seared sesame tuna. And there is always pizza for the kids. Here are a couple of our favorite Kol recipes, which will add pizzazz to any gathering, holiday or not.

Mickey's Easter Menu

A typical Easter menu directly from Mickey's hand:

Grilled Leg of Lamb

I buy a whole lamb leg (about 7 to 8 pounds) and bone it out into 4 separate roasts. Boning the lamb is pretty involved and time-consuming. You sort of follow the seams in the muscles and cut out all the fat and silverskin. (**Judie:** "I suggest finding a good butcher who will do this for you!") Then, I rub the inside with roasted garlic, parsley, thyme, and rosemary, and tie each roast up. The smallest roast is usually too small to tie up, so it goes on the grill as is.

I grill the roasts first to give a little grill smoke and markings and then finish them in the oven. A little extra note—I brine lamb in a recipe culled from *Cook's Illustrated* magazine, but I don't think it's necessary. And oh, to complete my lamb presentation, I roast a whole rack of lamb as well, after searing it on the stovetop. (**Judie:** "Just in case we don't already have enough lamb on the table.") Lamb should be roasted to about 130°F.

Potato Gratin

Cook 5 pounds of sliced russet potatoes in a quart of half-and-half with some garlic cloves, nutmeg, salt, and pepper on the stovetop just until the liquid is simmering. I pour the mixture into a gratin dish that I butter heavily and rub with a garlic clove. Place it in a 350°F oven for an hour, or until the potatoes are tender and the liquid is thick. I often have to add some more half-and-half as the quart doesn't seem to be quite enough, but if you scale down the amount of potatoes (5 pounds is a lot), the quart would probably be adequate. I cover the top with grated Gruyère cheese and bake the gratin for another 15 minutes. The top should be bubbling and golden brown.

Orange-Cumin Carrots

This is just a simple (**Judie:** "Yeah, right!"), classic French recipe from Joël Robuchon. Slice carrots and cook them with a bit of water and butter seasoned with toasted cumin seeds, just until they start to soften. Add some fresh orange juice and finish cooking them until glazed and tender.

Grilled Asparagus

Just peel a bunch of asparagus stalks, season with a little olive oil and salt and pepper, and throw them on the grill until just barely tender and nicely colored.

Roasted Baby Artichokes

Trim and cut baby artichokes in half. Season with olive oil and salt and pepper and roast in a 400°F oven until tender and crisp.

Pearl Onions and Cremini Mushrooms

Cook fresh (or frozen) pearl onions in butter, sugar, salt, and pepper in a covered sauteuse (**Judie:** "Of course we all have a sauteuse or two sitting on the shelf.") with a bit of water, just until tender. Add some cut-up cremini mushrooms and fresh thyme sprigs and sauté, uncovered, until nicely browned.

Oh, I almost forgot to say that I use the bone from the lamb leg with some lamb stew meat and left-over lamb bones to make lamb *jus*. I roast the bones, put them in a pot, cover with water, add tomato paste, onions, carrots, leeks, garlic, thyme, bay leaf, and parsley stems; then, cook it all for about 5 or 6 hours. You need to skim the stock a lot to remove all the lamb fat and scum. Then, I strain the stock and cook it down to a saucelike consistency. And if I have it on hand, I add some fresh rosemary along the way. I always serve grilled lamb with a little drizzle of *jus*, but Mom scoffs at my French style and always brings along her chimichurri.

Chimichurri

MAKES ABOUT 2 CUPS

1 cup flat-leaf parsley
¼ cup chopped scallions, including some green part
1 tablespoon fresh oregano
1 tablespoon fresh cilantro
1 tablespoon chopped garlic
Juice and zest of 1 lemon
½ cup olive oil
2½ tablespoons white wine vinegar
Coarse salt

1. Combine the parsley, scallions, oregano, cilantro, garlic, lemon juice, and zest in the bowl of a food processor fitted with the metal blade. Pulse until just minced.

2. Scrape the mixture into a bowl and stir in the oil and vinegar.

3. Season with salt and serve. Can be stored, covered and refrigerated, for up to 3 days.

Thanksgiving

Chris's San Francisco Thanksgiving

In the years that we don't have the West-Coast Choates home for Christmas, we usually go to San Francisco to celebrate Thanksgiving with them. And even some years when we do expect them back East, we pack up and head west in November anyway.

As over the top as Mickey's celebrations and dinners are, Chris's traditional Thanksgivings can give them a run for the money.

Unlike anyone I know, Chris makes three turkeys: the first for a friend who does wine pairings for his customers, the second for a complete Thanksgiving dinner on the Sunday before the holiday so he will have leftovers to nosh on all week, and then the final bird for the big day. Can you imagine?

When Chris moved to California, I think he got quite homesick when the holidays rolled around, so he, just as I once did, began to make traditions of his own. What started as a small group of mostly single (I think Chris was the only married guy) young folks gathering to make a home-style Thanksgiving feast has grown into a much-anticipated all-day affair. When the event ballooned to almost a hundred, as wives, husbands, children, and in-laws slowly joined the group, the hosting house (of Doug Collister and Babs Yamanaka, Chris's best friends) decided that it had expanded a bit too much for comfort. It has since decreased to a much more manageable head count with just a few families participating, but it is no less of a culinary adventure, which begins in the morning and continues through the evening hours.

And here's how it goes:

10 A.M. Chris's Famous Fried Egg with Shaved White Truffle: just like it sounds— an oozy fried egg with white truffle shaved over the top. It is served with a slice of toasted baguette—buttered with a drizzle of honey—to dip into the yolk. Chris usually fries somewhere around 4 dozen eggs. The truffle is the luxe ingredient of the day—usually hitting the $500 mark. (**Chris's suggested pairing:** Moscato d'Asti—low alcohol, fresh, often tasting of white peaches with acidity to awaken the palate. It is terrific with this dish and a great way to start the day.)

12 P.M. Complete caviar service: caviar in hard-boiled quail egg-white halves with chopped quail egg yolk and minced red onion, and tiny toasts. (**Chris's suggested pairing:** iced vodka, always the latest brand[s] to hit the market.)

2 P.M. Herm's (Chris's friend Dave Herman) Cheese Selection: a variety of expertly chosen cheeses served with baguettes, crackers, and fruit, always with some type of gag—a little plastic animal representing the type of milk used was one year's. He has even been known to order unpasteurized cheese directly from France. He is a cheese maniac! (**Chris's suggested pairing:** red Burgundy, when we can afford it!)

5 P.M. Traditional Turkey Dinner: the whole kit and caboodle—turkey with stuffing and gravy; mashed potatoes; brussels sprouts or some type of green; carrot-parsnip puree; cranberry sauce and relish; rolls or biscuits; and whatever desserts the guests bring to the table. (**Chris's suggested pairing:** Gamay, the red grape that Beaujolais is made from, and Gewürztraminer, the best of which comes from Alsace, are hands down the two best turkey wines. However, I think that pinot noir and a really zippy sauvignon blanc also work well. If you want to try an absolutely fantastic domestic Gewürztraminer, I suggest that you search out a California from Navarro Vineyards in the Anderson Valley. In my opinion, it is the best!)

Talking Turkey

In recent years the proliferation of all manner of turkey pieces and parts, whole or ground, has not dampened my love for the traditional holiday bird. I very clearly remember the days when turkey was "special" and how I so looked forward to seeing a huge bird sitting quite majestically, burnished and golden, at the center of our Thanksgiving table. It wasn't found in the market any other time of the year, except around Christmas, and the flavor was so deep and rich. I also remember what a chore it was to cook.

First came the stuffing. My mom saved all manner of stale bread (we didn't then have much more than white or whole wheat—and once in San Francisco a sourdough loaf, which Mom didn't like to add to the mix) in a big brown bag in the garage all year long—why critters didn't get at it I don't know—to make holiday stuffing. (It's hard not think of how wasteful we have become; I can't even imagine taking months of saving nowadays to get enough bread to make a batch of stuffing). I hated the job of cubing it all; the bread was dry and scratchy and my fingers would get nicked and sore.

Then the giblets and neck would have to be cooked to yield the necessary broth. Mom added some onion, celery, and a few peppercorns to the cooking water to add a little flavor to the pot. She made enough broth (we now call it stock) to moisten the stuffing and make the gravy. This was often done the night before the bird was to be roasted. Once she had the savory broth, she would strain it through a sieve, reserving the clear broth. She would strip the neck of its meat and chop it up, along with the heart, gizzard, and liver. These nuggets would enrich the gravy. This is something we all still do. Chris takes his a step further and uses an immersion blender to create a thick sauce with no sign of the little unidentifiable meat pieces that might cause some diners to balk.

This was the preliminary activity before the stuffing was made early on Thanksgiving (or Christmas) morning. Mom would be up at the crack of dawn and you would almost immediately smell the sautéing onions and celery with the added dried sage and thyme. The cubed bread would be in a huge bowl ready to receive the softened aromatics being scraped hot from the pan right into it. Our family still begins this way, except we generally use fresh herbs; I add walnuts and dried fruit, Chris adds sausage, and Mickey adds dried apricots for himself and no embellishment for the rest of his family.

The roasting pan would come out of the cupboard—no disposable aluminum pans then—and the rack would go in, ready to receive the bird. Mom would wash the turkey clean and pat it dry. Then, she would season it with salt and pepper, inside and out. In went the stuffing next, and stuff it she did, pushing and packing the cavity and under the flap of skin at the head until the bird was ready to burst. If she was feeling rich, she would rub a little butter on the skin and then pop it into the oven. No foil covering, no lid, no turning halfway through—it just roasted until she decided it was ready. And when I was a child, it seemed

as though this took practically all day and I guess it did, though nowadays I can roast a turkey in just three hours or so. (I do, however, like to give the bird a good long brine—overnight does it for me. Just before cooking, I rub the skin with salt and lemon juice, stuff it to the nths, add some white wine to the pan, cover, and let it almost steam for the first 45 minutes at 450°F; then, I lower the heat and cook for another 45 minutes or so. Finally I uncover and baste, and continue roasting until the skin is crispy and golden.)

Once the turkey was out of the oven and resting on its platter, Mom would use the pan drippings as the base for gravy. She simply stirred some flour into the hot pan and when a nice dark roux was formed, she would pour in whatever broth remained. Sometimes she added a little milk, as she preferred a creamier gravy. My gravy routine today is no different from Mom's back then.

I guess turkey, stuffing, and gravy at the center of the Thanksgiving table has, for generations now, stayed pretty much the same in our kitchens. Even the sides are fairly standard: brussels sprouts (Mickey's—roasted with slab bacon and chestnuts; Chris's—sautéed with guanciale; mine—roasted with pancetta and orange), carrot-parsnip puree, mashed potatoes (Mickey follows Joël Robuchon with tons of cream and butter so that they are a silky blend; Chris and I stick to the denser, traditional American kind), and homemade cranberry sauce and/or relish (and canned jellied cranberry sauce for Steve, who cuts it into exceedingly neat slices demarked by the ridges and gets very annoyed when anyone does otherwise). The rolls are either biscuits (page 219) or my easy ones (page 290). Desserts vary: I love pumpkin pie but nobody else does; Steve loves sweet-potato pie but nobody else does. When a crowd has gathered I always add something chocolate (Chocolate Chess, page 232), and we usually have an apple tart (page 252). In recent years, I've stuck in a cranberry cake (Clafoutis, page 158) of some sort.

My Stuffing

MAKES ABOUT 12 CUPS

12 cups dried white and whole-wheat bread cubes

½ cup unsalted butter

1 cup diced onion

¼ cup finely diced celery

1 tablespoon minced flat-leaf parsley

1½ cups diced dried apricots

2 to 3 cups warm turkey stock or water

1 tablespoon poultry seasoning

1 teaspoon chopped fresh sage

1 teaspoon chopped fresh thyme

1 teaspoon chopped fresh marjoram

Salt and pepper

1 cup (or more) toasted walnut pieces

1. Place the bread cubes in a large mixing bowl. Set aside.

2. Place the butter in a large frying pan over medium heat. When melted, add the onion, celery, and parsley and cook, stirring frequently, for about 7 minutes, or until softened. Add the apricots along with 1 cup of the stock and the poultry seasoning, sage, thyme, and marjoram. Cook, stirring occasionally, for 5 minutes.

3. Remove from the heat and scrape the mixture into the bowl of bread cubes. Add another cup of the stock and, using your hands, toss to combine. Season with salt and pepper and, if necessary, add just enough stock to make the mixture very moist but not wet. Toss in the walnuts.

4. Use as a poultry or other meat (such as a pork loin) stuffing, or bake in a well-greased casserole for a side dish. Do remember that you should not stuff poultry in advance of roasting, even if refrigerated, as bacteria can form quickly and cause devastating illness.

Brussels Sprouts

It used to be that you only saw brussels sprouts for a very short period in the fall—
just through Thanksgiving. I loved them then and I love them now. The difference being
that then they were usually boiled or steamed to near sogginess, and now we eat them
raw, roasted, grilled, steamed, pulled apart, sliced, halved, or whole. It's a whole new
brussels-sprouts ball game!

I have lots of ways to cook them. One of my favorites is a little tedious to prepare but quick to finish. First, pull the leaves from a couple of big handfuls of brussels
sprouts. This will take a little time, but you can do it while having an aperitif. Then fry up
about a third of a pound of diced slab bacon, pancetta, or guanciale. When crispy, toss in
the leaves and, using tongs, toss and turn until just slightly wilted. Add a good dose of
cracked black pepper and the zest of one orange. Sprinkle with a bit of moscato vinegar
and serve as a side dish with grilled
chops, or toss the whole mess with
some pasta.

For a less time-consuming
dish, cut or quarter the brussels
sprouts (depending on how large
they are) and roast them in olive
oil, seasoned with a good handful of
diced pancetta (or whatever smoky
meat you have on hand), orange
zest, and salt and pepper. People
who say they hate brussels sprouts
invariably ask for seconds!

Carrot-Parsnip Puree

Carrot-parsnip puree is another Choate Thanksgiving constant. It is this dish that
made Chris say: "I know why we love your cooking so much, it's all that butter and cream."
And, for this puree he is right. Here's what you do: The amount depends upon how many
you have to feed. I usually do equal parts carrots and parsnips—two pounds each for a
gathering of 8 or so. I steam them until very soft, then into the food processor fitted with
the metal blade they go, and I start the pureeing process by adding softened butter and
warm heavy cream to batches of the soft vegetables. I season with salt and white pepper
throughout. By the time all of the veggies have been pureed, I've added quite a bit of butter and cream, and that's why we enjoy this unctuous dish only once a year.

Easy Rolls, At Least I Think They Are

MAKES ABOUT 20

I often wonder how my mother had the time to do all she did and I particularly wonder about it around the holidays. Looking back, I can only imagine how tired she must have been (she worked six days a week from 8 A.M. to 6 P.M.) and yet, once the fall and winter holidays were in the air, she cleaned and cooked as though she had a household staff.

Among the homemade treats that we always had on our Thanksgiving and Christmas tables when I was growing up were hot-from-the-oven rolls, usually shaped like clover leaves. When I started cooking for my own family I always felt I ought to make those rolls myself, but usually they came as an afterthought, and often I ended up serving some rather ordinary store-bought variety. Then, a number of years ago, I decided to make a dough that I could refrigerate overnight, to see if I couldn't produce that homemade-and-hot memory without the early-morning task of preparing the dough and then letting it rise. (I learned the cutting method used in this recipe from Steve's Auntie, who said it's the way Southern cooks made their rolls.)

Although the rolls do take some "morning-of" preparation, they can also be baked ahead and stored frozen. They can then be placed in the hot oven to reheat while the turkey is resting before being carved—twenty minutes or so should bring them right back to perfection. These slightly sweet dinner rolls are now a family favorite—with the exception of Mickey, who still prefers the rolls he found in a Joël Robuchon cookbook and insists I try to duplicate whenever we have Thanksgiving together.

2 packages instant dry yeast

⅓ cup unsalted butter, room temperature, plus more for greasing the bowl

½ cup sugar

2 teaspoons salt

1 large egg, room temperature, beaten

1 cup cool water

4 to 5 cups all-purpose flour, sifted

¼ cup melted unsalted butter

1. Place ½ cup warm water in the bowl of a standing electric mixer fitted with the dough hook. Add the yeast, stirring to dissolve. Add the butter and stir until almost melted. Then, stir in the sugar and salt. When blended, stir in the beaten egg, followed by 1 cup cool water.

2. Place the bowl into the mixer stand, add 4 cups of the flour and begin mixing with the dough hook. When blended completely, begin adding the remaining 1 cup of flour as needed until the dough is soft and pliable.

3. Coat the interior of a large bowl with butter. Scrape the dough into the bowl and, using your fingertips, poke to gently deflate a bit.

4. Cover with a clean kitchen towel and set aside in a warm, draft-free spot for about 1 hour, or until the dough has doubled in volume.

5. Uncover and gently poke to deflate. Cover with plastic film and refrigerate for at least 4 hours but no more than 12 hours.

6. Generously butter two 8- or 9-inch round cake pans. Set aside.

7. Lightly flour a clean, flat work surface.

8. Remove the dough from the refrigerator, uncover, and scrape it out onto the floured surface. Using your hands, gently flatten the dough; then, using a rolling pin, roll it out to a circle about ½ inch thick.

9. Using a 3-inch round biscuit cutter, cut the dough into circles.

10. Working with one piece at a time and using a pastry brush, lightly coat the tops with the melted butter. Using a kitchen knife, make a crease that goes through the center of each circle; then, fold the circle into itself, making a half-moon shape. Fit the rolls, sides touching, into the buttered cake pans.

11. When all of the rolls have been formed, cover and set aside in a warm, draft-free spot to rise for 1 hour.

12. Thirty minutes before you are ready to bake, preheat the oven to 425°F.

13. Place the rolls in the preheated oven and bake for about 25 minutes, until golden brown. Remove from the oven and serve hot.

Cranberry Relish

MAKES ABOUT 3 CUPS

This is about the simplest cranberry relish you can make. It can also be the base for many other cranberry mixes. You can add spices, chilies, other fruits, herbs—just about anything you like—to turn it into a year-round treat. I love cranberries and can eat this relish just like it was dessert.

1 large orange, preferably organic, washed well and dried

1 pound fresh cranberries

About 1 tablespoon grated fresh ginger

1½ to 2 cups sugar

1. Chop the orange and discard any seeds. Place in a food processor fitted with the metal blade and process until very finely chopped.

2. Place the cranberries in a heavy-bottomed saucepan. Add the orange, ginger, and sugar and place over medium heat. Bring to a simmer, lower the heat, and cook, stirring frequently, for about 20 minutes, or until the cranberries have popped open and the flavors have blended. Remove from the heat and set aside to cool.

3. When cool, transfer to a container, cover, and refrigerate until ready to use. This relish will keep, covered and refrigerated, for a couple of weeks.

Cranberry Ice

SERVES 8 TO 10

My mom always served cranberry ice as an accompaniment to our turkey. It never appeared on the table at any other time of year—a reasonable guess would be because you couldn't get cranberries except around Thanksgiving-time. As a child, the most amazing thing was that she served it at the middle of the meal in her mother's coupe glasses. Only when I was very much an adult did I learn that this course is called an intermezzo, a term I'm sure my mom had never heard of. In case it's new to you, too, it simply translates to a "palate cleanser" between courses—often a refreshing, not-at-all- sweet sorbet—and it is rarely served anymore, even in the fanciest of restaurants. How she came to this tradition I, regretfully, never asked. (As for the coupes, they were slightly iridescent; the lumines- cent colors fascinated me, but not enough as an adult to keep the glasses after my mom passed away. Of course, this is a decision I now rue.) The ice is refreshingly delicious and works just as well as a dessert, particularly with a bit of dark chocolate on the side. My mom's recipe calls for one bag of cranberries, which in her day, I'd bet, weighed one pound. However, the current 12-ounce bag seems to work just fine. Since you can now buy pure, unsweetened cranberry juice, you could probably use that also.

1 package fresh cranberries

3 to 4 cups sugar, depending on how sweet you want the ice to be

Juice of 6 lemons, strained

1. Place the cranberries in a large saucepan with cold water to cover over medium-high heat. Bring to a boil; then, lower the heat and simmer, stirring frequently, for about 20 minutes, until all of the cranberries have popped and are soft.

2. Remove from the heat and pour through a fine mesh sieve into a large heatproof mixing bowl, press- ing lightly on the pulp. You do not want to push any seeds through; the liquid should be clear. Discard the solids.

3. Add the sugar to the hot juice, stirring until dis- solved. Add the strained lemon juice (the straining is important as you want the juice to be completely clear). Measure the juice and add enough water to make 1 gallon of liquid.

4. Pour the liquid into shallow 1-quart containers or into ice-cube trays. Place them in the freezer and leave them for about 2 hours, or until almost com- pletely frozen.

5. Remove from the freezer and place in the bowl of a heavy-duty standing electric mixer fitted with the paddle (or a food processor fitted with the metal blade). Chop into chunks to facilitate beating. Beat or process until the consistency of sherbet.

6. Use immediately or return to the freezer for no more than an hour, or it will get too hard to serve easily. If it does get too hard, beat or process again. You can also freeze the mixture in an ice-cream maker, following the manufacturer's directions for freezing sorbets.

Christmas

Mickey's Christmas Dinner

I was, and I guess in some ways still am, the original Christmas nut. In my younger days, Christmas preparations began in the fall with fruitcake-making and continued right up to the very last minute. We had a huge party on Christmas Eve followed by presents and a mammoth meal on Christmas Day. The Christmas-Eve party was always a buffet with people coming and going from the late afternoon through the early-morning hours. I usually had a ham, a turkey, and some other meat, as well as a selection of sides and vegetarian dishes. Desserts and candies—all made by my mom and me—were spread throughout the house. Everyone got a take-home goodie bag and all of the children got presents. Sometimes I made an exotic punch and sometimes we had a bar. I remember one year I researched *glögg* (mulled red wine with various spices and fruits) and made vats of it. The sweet-spicy aroma filled the house and caused everyone to enthusiastically down the brew. I don't have to tell you how that evening ended.

As a family we are now only all together every other Christmas, on those years when Canada is with her dad. I am in charge of Christmas Eve and Mickey is the Christmas-Day chef. Chris doesn't cook at all when he's with us, but loves to give the rundown on what he *would* be cooking if in San Francisco: mushrooms on grilled bread with crescenza cheese; crab and avocado salad followed by pork loin with apple pan sauce, spinach, and rosemary roast potatoes; or maybe crab with beer and sourdough bread, or Barolo risotto; or cioppino or other fish stew. An unfussy yet certainly tasty California Christmas that pales in complexity next to Mickey's lavish meal.

For a long time I just made an easy dinner on Christmas Eve. It used to be a shellfish stew (which Mickey, Steve, and I loved) until the girls decided they didn't like it. As everyone's tastes kept changing, I'd try something different each year. They all finally wore me down and now I let everyone order their favorite dish from our local Chinese restaurant. The table ends up being as bountiful as it was in the old days, but now it is overflowing with take-out containers. I find it quite amusing, and almost everyone is quite happy selecting their own dish. Needless to say, Mickey hates it. No matter. I've traveled the world featuring Christmas dinners from countries that I think might make the cut for everyone, but I intend to stick with the take-out Chinese idea from here on out!

Mickey is completely and totally in charge of Christmas-Day dinner (including telling Chris and I what we are allowed to do under his supervision) and an elaborate one it is—far more French than traditional American. It never changes and, to quote him,

"I am aiming for perfection." It is unbelievably extravagant, and although I think we would all be happy enough with a simpler spread that entailed much less work for him, I believe that the meal is his Christmas gift to himself. And as such, we celebrate his genius in the kitchen as our Christmas gift to him.

The recipes are diverse and come from many places, which Mickey always generously acknowledges. The oysters come from Thomas Keller (found in his seminal *The French Laundry Cookbook*) as do the general instructions for the foie gras torchon. Mickey makes his own quince paste, which doesn't resemble the classic Spanish *membrillo*, but is more a chunky jamlike mixture: just quince cooked down with a little sugar, cinnamon stick, star anise, allspice, and white wine. The bisque comes, in part, from Julia Child. The tournedos Rossini are more Mickey's than classic French—which would be a large crouton of buttered brioche topped with a filet mignon, a slice of foie gras, and a mound of shaved truffles, all in a pool of Madeira sauce. Mickey, due to the fact that foie gras has appeared once on the menu already, simplifies the dish somewhat. His is a slice of slow-roasted strip steak on a potato galette with shaved truffles and the Madeira sauce. (**Mickey:** "I use a strip loin roast cut from a whole loin from Costco. I slow roast it in a low oven [275°F] for about 25 minutes until 120°F and then sear it quickly on top of the oven. Then let it rest for 10 minutes or so.") The *buche* is a classic genoise filled with sweetened whipped cream and iced, loglike, with chocolate frosting. On good years, one of us ladies gets it together to make meringue mushrooms to trim the log.

And the complete Christmas Dinner menu is:

Pickled Oysters on Cucumber with Caviar
Gougères (page 149)
Foie Gras *Torchon* **with Quince Compote**
　　(**Judie:** "And Roasted Beet Salad for the ladies.")
Lobster Bisque
Tournedos Rossini on Potato Galette
Tournéed Vegetables
Cheese Board with Grapes and Pears
　　(**Judie:** "Always Epoisse.")
Bûche de Noël
Chocolates and *Pâte de Fruits*
　　(**Judie:** "Purchased, but Mickey says he will attempt them at some point.")

 CHRIS'S SUGGESTED WINE PAIRING
MICKEY TELLS ME EXACTLY WHAT HE WANTS AT CHRISTMAS AND IT USUALLY GOES LIKE THIS: BILLECART-SALMON BRUT ROSÉ, *VENDANGE TARDIVE* ("LATE HARVEST") GEWÜRZTRAMINER FROM ALSACE, WHITE BURGUNDY, RED BORDEAUX, VINTAGE PORT

Making Fruitcakes for Christmas Giving

Since childhood, all of my Christmas traditions have been, for the most part, centered on food. My mom baked and I baked with her. Later, when I grew up, I baked and she helped me. And, it wasn't just a batch of cookies and a couple of cakes, it was scads upon scads of goodies. Cookies were baked by the thousand or so and boxed for giving. Candies were pulled, twisted, and shaped for eating and decorating the tree. Cakes and breads were lined up in their little tins and wrapped in cellophane for last-minute hostess gifts. The gingerbread house was the centerpiece of our mantel and the tree was awash in decorated sugar cookies, popcorn, and candy garlands. Once my boys

left home, Mom and I continued with these traditions for a few years. But as time passed and Mom did too, and everybody seemed to be on a diet, I gave up most of my baking. *But*, recent years have found me back on track. Christmas just never seemed to be Christmas without baking.

I happen to love fruitcake of any type and although I know that I am in the minority, the aroma of the spice, brandy, and sugar that comes together in that sturdy little

cake (I always make it in small loaves) provokes such a sensory remembrance of Christmas that it was the first baking that I returned to. I have made fruitcake with the recipe passed down from my Scottish grandmother and, while putting all of the ingredients together, I can't help thinking about what an extravagance the cake would have been in Victorian households, particularly in those of working-class families as were my forebears. The sugar, butter, and exotic candied fruits and peels were extraordinary luxuries. Not to mention the Scotch that my teetotaler grandmother used to soak the cake with. She probably made one cake and, since it was nicely inebriated and therefore kept for months, she likely also cut it into paper thin slices that were to be doled out in small measures. I now wantonly make ten little cakes and spend as much time looking for homes for them as I do making them!

Gramma's Dark Fruitcake

MAKES TEN 6-INCH LOAVES

1½ cups unsalted butter, room temperature

1½ cups sugar

8 large eggs, separated, room temperature

⅔ cup white corn syrup

1 cup buttermilk

1 teaspoon baking soda

½ cup brandy

1 tablespoon orange-juice concentrate, thawed

3 tablespoons ground cinnamon

1½ cups sifted all-purpose flour, plus enough unsifted flour to make a soft batter, about 7 cups

2 pounds chopped glazed fruit

1½ pounds pitted dates

1½ pounds dried currants

1 pound golden seedless raisins

1 pound dark seedless raisins

½ pound glazed red cherries

½ pound glazed green cherries

¼ pound glazed pineapple, chopped

1½ cups walnut pieces

½ teaspoon cream of tartar

Brandy, port, whiskey, or white wine for soaking

1. Preheat the oven to 300°F.

2. Lightly coat the interior of ten 6-inch loaf pans with nonstick baking spray. Set aside.

3. Place the butter in the bowl of a standing electric mixer fitted with the paddle and beat, on low, to soften completely. Add the sugar and beat until light yellow and creamy. Add the egg yolks and beat to incorporate; then, add the corn syrup and beat to blend thoroughly.

4. Place the buttermilk in a small bowl and stir in the baking soda. It will bubble up slightly. Add the mixture to the batter and beat to blend. With the motor running, add the brandy and orange-juice concentrate, followed by the cinnamon.

5. Place about ¾ cup of the sifted flour in a large bowl. Add the glazed fruits, dates, currants, raisins, cherries, pineapple, and walnuts. Sprinkle with another ¾ cup of the sifted flour and toss to coat. This will help separate all of the fruits and keep them from sticking together.

6. Pour the batter over the fruit/nut mixture and, using your hands, begin mixing, slowly adding the unsifted flour, using enough to make a soft batter. This generally takes about 7 cups.

7. Place the egg whites in the bowl of a standing electric mixer fitted with the whip. Add the cream of tartar and beat until stiff peaks form.

8. Using your hands, fold the beaten egg whites into the fruit batter, taking care to incorporate them without completely deflating them.

9. Scoop equal portions of the batter into the prepared loaf pans.

10. Place a container of cool water in the bottom of the preheated oven. Place the cakes in the oven, leaving room between each one. Bake for about 2 hours or until they are firm and dark golden brown, and the edges have begun to pull away from the pans.

Candy Everywhere

For almost as long as I have lived in New York City, my preparations for holiday baking have taken me to Economy Candy (see Sources) on the Lower East Side, where the bins are filled with the glazed, dried, and candied fruits and nuts that I will use in all manner of baked goods. And I have to admit, I'm also drawn by the stacks, bins, containers, and boxes of all measure of old-fashioned candies that were once the province of the now-extinct penny candy store.

Date-Nut Bread

MAKES THREE 6-INCH LOAVES

Every Christmas that I can remember, my mom baked this date-nut bread (along with many other sweets). I have absolutely no idea why she never made it at any other time of the year, since we all loved it, as did the many recipients of her largesse. It was a bit expensive, so that may be why she kept it as a special treat. Truth be told, it is still a bit pricey to make, but that doesn't stop me from keeping it on the holiday menu. It is so easy and makes a lovely gift, particularly when accompanied by orange-flavored cream cheese or cinnamon-scented mascarpone. I like to serve it slightly warm—and I always cut one "tester" to taste. Date-nut bread freezes very well.

1 pound whole pitted dates
1 teaspoon baking soda
1 tablespoon unsalted butter, room temperature
¾ cup sugar
1 large egg, slightly beaten, room temperature
1 teaspoon pure vanilla extract
¼ teaspoon salt
2 cups all-purpose flour
1½ cups walnut halves or large pieces

1. Preheat the oven to 325°F.

2. Lightly coat the interior of three 6-inch loaf pans with nonstick baking spray, such as Baker's Joy. Set aside.

3. Place the dates in a heatproof mixing bowl. Sprinkle with the baking soda. Pour 1¼ cups boiling water over the dates. Add the butter and, using a wooden spoon, mix just until the butter melts.

4. Stir in the sugar, mixing until it begins to dissolve. Stir in the beaten egg, vanilla, and salt. When blended, stir in the flour, a bit at a time. When all of the flour has been added, beat well to incorporate thoroughly. Stir in the walnuts.

5. Scrape an equal portion of the batter into each prepared pan.

6. Place in the preheated oven and bake for 10 minutes. Raise the temperature to 350°F and continue to bake for an additional 30 minutes, or until a cake tester inserted into the center comes out clean.

7. Remove from the oven and invert onto a wire rack. Drop the breads from the pans and turn them right side up to cool. When cool, wrap in plastic film or aluminum foil and store, refrigerated, for up to 1 week. Bring to room temperature or reheat slightly before cutting and serving.

My Never-Fail Chocolate Fudge

MAKES ABOUT 2 POUNDS

When I was in my full-blown homemade-Christmas-celebration years, I would make lots and lots of candy. The candy was always a hit simply because most people had never tasted homemade. Some of it came from my childhood—Mom's favorites were popcorn balls, bourbon balls, and divinity. Of these, I liked only popcorn balls, which I often used as tree decorations. Divinity was too sugary—even for me—and I have never liked any sweet that is flavored with alcohol. Most of the other candies I made were recipes I had gathered from old cookbooks or good home cooks. Peanut brittle and chocolate fudge were at the top of my list. Of all of these goodies, chocolate fudge is the only one that I continue to make every Christmas. Now with bittersweet chocolate and nuts for me, and no nuts for Laurel.

12 ounces bittersweet chocolate (bits or a block chopped into small pieces)

2 cups toasted walnuts or pecans (optional)

10 tablespoons unsalted butter, cut into pieces, room temperature

1 tablespoon pure vanilla extract

20 large marshmallows

4 cups sugar

Two 5-ounce cans evaporated milk

1. Lightly butter a 6-cup baking pan (square or rectangular) or a platter. Set aside.

2. Combine the chocolate with the nuts, butter, and vanilla in a large heatproof mixing bowl. Set aside.

3. Combine the marshmallows and sugar in a heavy-bottomed soup pot. Stir in the evaporated milk and place over medium heat. Stirring constantly, bring to a boil. Continuing to stir, boil for exactly 6 minutes.

4. Immediately remove from the heat and, beating constantly with a wooden spoon, pour the hot mixture into the chocolate mix. Beat vigorously for a few minutes, or until the fudge is creamy. Quickly scrape the fudge into the prepared pan or platter, pushing slightly with the back of the spoon (or a spatula) to spread the fudge evenly.

5. Cool for at least 1 hour before cutting the candy into small squares. Store, in layers separated by waxed paper, for up to 1 week or, refrigerated, for up to 3 weeks. Bring to room temperature before serving.

Cut-Out Sugar Cookies

MAKES ABOUT 4 DOZEN, DEPENDING UPON SIZE

What better way to welcome the holidays than with a tray of colorfully adorned cook-ies? For as long as I can remember decorated cutout sugar cookies have been part of my Christmas celebration. The boys helped when they were small, and then they hung their artistry on the tree. I often augmented our family ornaments with foods—popcorn and cranberry garlands, decorated cookies, candy canes, and stained-glass cookies (no more

than gingerbread formed into shapes with various openings into which you place Lifesavers before baking; as they bake the candies melt and form glasslike surfaces in colorful hues). Then one Christmas I woke up to find the entire tree covered with visiting ants, and that ended my "Crafty Kate" days.

Nowadays Laurel and Clara Grace, with intermittent help from Alexander and Uncle Kol, are in charge of Christmas cookie making. They have inherited all of my cookie cutters, some of which I used as a child. The cookies star at their annual tree-trimming party and the piled-high platter of them is always empty before the tree is ornamented. They are easy to make and fun to decorate. The more patient you are, the prettier the finished cookie, but no matter: it's the act of making them that is memorable, not how they look.

2 cups sifted all-purpose flour
Small piece of vanilla bean, ground
1½ teaspoons baking powder
¼ teaspoon salt
⅓ cup unsalted butter, room temperature
1 cup sugar
1 large egg, room temperature
2 teaspoons pure vanilla extract
¼ cup whole milk
Confectioners' sugar for dusting
Decorative Icing (recipe follows)

1. Combine the sifted flour with the vanilla bean, baking powder, and salt in the sifter. Set aside.

2. Combine the butter and sugar in the bowl of a standing electric mixer fitted with the paddle. Beat on low to combine; then raise the speed to medium and beat until light and creamy, occasionally scraping the inside of the bowl with a rubber spatula. Add the egg and vanilla and beat to blend. Add the milk alternating with the flour mixture, beating to make a soft dough.

3. Scrape the dough down and remove the bowl from the stand. Cover with plastic film and refrigerate for at least 1 hour or until the dough has firmed.

4. About 20 minutes before you are ready to bake, preheat the oven to 350°F.

5. Line 2 cookie sheets with silicone liners or parchment paper. Set aside.

6. Lightly dust a clean, flat, cool work surface with confectioners' sugar. (You can use flour, preferably Wondra, but the end result will be a drier cookie).

7. Working with about a quarter of the dough at a time and using a rolling pin, roll the dough out to a circle about ⅛ inch thick. Cut out into desired shapes using cookie cutters made for this purpose. If you wish to use the cookies as hanging decorations, use a skewer to make a small hole about ¼ inch from the top of each cookie.

8. Using a metal spatula, transfer the cookies to the prepared baking sheets, leaving about ½ inch between cookies. Transfer to the preheated oven and bake for about 12 minutes, or until just barely colored around the edges and set in the middle. Remove from the oven and transfer to wire racks to cool before icing.

9. Cover the tops and/or decorate with icing as you wish.

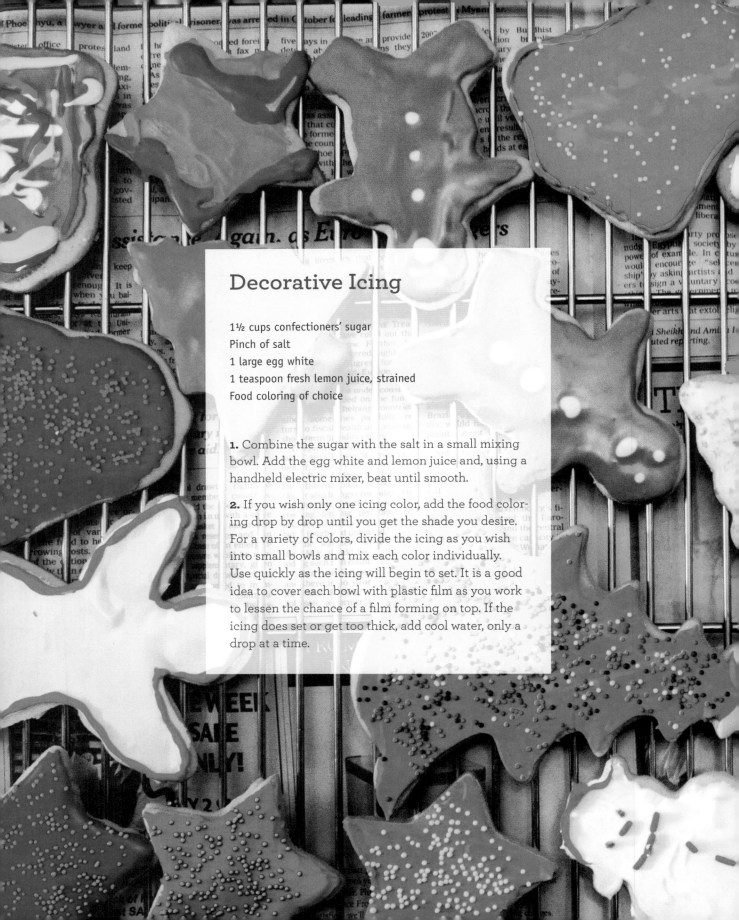

Decorative Icing

1½ cups confectioners' sugar
Pinch of salt
1 large egg white
1 teaspoon fresh lemon juice, strained
Food coloring of choice

1. Combine the sugar with the salt in a small mixing bowl. Add the egg white and lemon juice and, using a handheld electric mixer, beat until smooth.

2. If you wish only one icing color, add the food coloring drop by drop until you get the shade you desire. For a variety of colors, divide the icing as you wish into small bowls and mix each color individually. Use quickly as the icing will begin to set. It is a good idea to cover each bowl with plastic film as you work to lessen the chance of a film forming on top. If the icing does set or get too thick, add cool water, only a drop at a time.

Sources

Anson Mills (*heirloom grains*)
803-467-4122
www.ansonmills.com

Ball Canning Equipment
Available from many online sources as well as from
chain stores such as Walmart and Target

Citarella (*seafood, meat, produce, specialty foods*)
212-874-0383
www.citarella.com

D'Artagnan (*meat, game, and poultry*)
280 Wilson Avenue
Newark, New Jersey 07105
800-327-8246
www.dartagnan.com

Despaña (*Spanish products*)
www.despanabrandfoods.com

Economy Candy
108 Rivington Street
New York, New York 10002
212-254-1531
www.economycandy.com

Fairway (*specialty foods, produce, and meats*)
2127 Broadway
New York, New York 10023
212-595-1888
www.fairwaymarket.com

Gaia's Breath Farm (*artisanal meat products and
natural meats*)
219 Forrest Road
Jordanville, New York 13361
315-823-4299
mtoro@wildblue.net

The Gardener (*Weck jars, interesting tableware and
kitchenware*)
San Francisco Ferry Plaza (*among other locations*)
#26
San Francisco, California 94111
415-981-8181
www.thegardener.com

Heath Ceramics (*tableware, dishes, accessories*)
400 Gate Five Road
Sausalito, California 94965
415-332-3732
www.heathceramics.com

Kalustyan's (*kitchen supplies, specialty foods, spices,
herbs, rices, beans, etc.*)
123 Lexington Avenue
New York, New York 10016
212-685-3451
www.kalustyans.com

King Arthur Flour (*catalogue for flours, baking
ingredients, supplies, and cookware*)
800-827-6838
www.kingarthurflour.com

Murray's Cheese (*international and American cheeses*)
www.murrayscheese.com
888-MY-CHEEZ

Newsom's Country Hams
208 East Main Street
Princeton, Kentucky 42445
270-365-2482
www.newsomscountryham.com

Penzey's Spice House (*herbs and spices*)
12001 West Capitol Drive
Wauwatosa, Wisconsin 53222
800-741-7787
www.penzeys.com

Rancho Gordo (*heirloom beans, grains, and rices; herbs
and spices; dried corn; and chilies and chile powders*)
www.ranchogordo.com

Stone-Buhr Flour (*farm-to-product*)
www.stone-buhr.com

Sur La Table (*kitchen and cooking supplies*)
800-243-0852
www.surlatable.com

Wild Edibles (*sustainable seafood*)
www.wildedibles.com

Zabars (*specialty foods, cured fish and meats, breads,
kitchen supplies*)
2245 Broadway
New York, New York 10024
212-787-2000
www.zabars.com

Zingone (*family-owned neighborhood grocers*)
471 Columbus Avenue
New York, New York 10024
212-877-7525

Index

Acknowledgments

Judie

I wish I could thank absolutely every person who helped me understand the importance of eating and living well, but I'm afraid that the list would be miles long; there are just too many of you. If you don't see your name here, just know that I haven't forgotten. Here's but a few that I send loving thoughts to:

My late mother and brother, without whom. . .

My extraordinary family, you are all within these pages but I still have to say: "Whatever would I have done without all of you?"

Steve, more than you know. . .

Annie, can I count the ways?

Joel Avirom, who has held my hand through so many projects and taught me how to nurture a discerning eye.

Doug and Lynn, for good times past, present, and to come. What fun we have!

Aris, how you appreciate a beautiful table. Thank you.

Eddie and Richard, for sharing the bounty of the Cape and so many laughs.

Ellen and Greg and Alice and Richard. Who knew that coffee would lead to such a wonderful friendship?

Michael, Chris, Fai, and Laurel, at Loupe Digital. You make us feel like family.

Sarah Afana, the Boss. Gratitude unlimited.

Those I especially love to gather around the table, Arlene and Alain, Linda and Ken, Jane and Dan, Stuart and Dean, Mary and Tim, Valerie and Didier, Alex and Nick, Deena and Michael, Jessica and Kurt.

Jimmy "Shoes" Canora, no job is as much fun as when you are beside me.

Lena Tabori, Katrina Fried, and Gregory Wakabayashi, for making my dream book come true.

Allison Hunter and Kim Witherspoon at Inkwell Management, for believing in my dream.

All the chefs and food personalities who have shared their passion with me, particularly David Burke, Dean Fearing, Charlie Palmer, and Alain Sailhac.

All the people who care deeply about where, what, and how they eat. For some this is simply how it has always been, while others might not have begun knowing anything about foraging, gardening, agriculture and/or animal husbandry, but they have made it their business to find out. Thank you for making the world better for all of us.

Mickey

I'd like to thank my mom for awakening me to the pleasures of the table. I have to acknowledge the role that Charlie Palmer and his seminal restaurant Aureole on East

61st played in teaching me to cook the way I do. The other chefs from whose works I've drawn inspiration and deserve mention are Joël Robuchon, Thomas Keller, Daniel Boulud, Eric Ripert, Tom Colicchio, Alfred Portale, and Christian Delouvrier. To Chris, Pool, and Uncle Kol for taking the journey with me. And to Laurel, Alexander, and Clara for putting up with me.

Chris

I would like to thank my mom and dad and Pool for raising me at the kitchen table where we ate dinner together almost every night, and for teaching me the community of sharing the day's experiences over home-cooked meals. I would be remiss if I didn't acknowledge Giovanni Perticone, may he rest in peace, the chef at Splendido who taught me how to cook risotto, and showed such unbelievable passion and creativity that I am still trying to recreate some of his dishes fifteen years later. I also need to thank my incredible friends for allowing me to cook crazy multicoursed meals often in their kitchens while leaving a disaster zone in my wake. Finally, I'd like to thank my daughter, Canada, and my wife, Heather, for putting up with me, allowing me to spend entire weekend days in the kitchen and pushing me to cook interesting vegetarian dishes (for them, of course).

Steve Pool

To the "big kids," Chris and Mickey, who, while wrestling with their own trials of majority, took on the burden of a chronological adult struggling to become an actual grown-up. And to the "little kids," Canada, Alexander, and Clara Grace, who show me the way ahead as guides and teachers to the possibilities of all of the newness that is and will be their worlds. . .my deepest gratitude, but mostly my love. I would never have gotten here without all of you.

To Joel, who, after saying that he had neither time nor interest to waste on my photographic fantasies, continues to instill the most basic principle that the freedom in all creative pursuits requires the greatest discipline, with constant attention to the desired goals. I am sore from the beatings but honored to say that I remain in your "design studio seminar."

To Michael Tolani, how much you have taught me and how much I still have to learn. Truly, I wouldn't be behind the camera without you.

Stephen Kolyer

I would like to thank my Kolyer family and my 84th-Street family for all of their love and support.

AN AMERICAN FAMILY COOKS

Published in 2013 by Welcome Books®
An imprint of Welcome Enterprises, Inc.
6 West 18th Street, New York, NY, 10011
(212) 989-3200; fax (212) 989-3205
www.welcomebooks.com

Publisher: Lena Tabori
President: H. Clark Wakabayashi
Associate Publisher & Editor: Katrina Fried
Designer: Gregory Wakabayashi

Library of Congress Cataloging-in-Publication Data on file

ISBN: 978-1-59962-124-1

First Edition
10 9 8 7 6 5 4 3 2 1

PRINTED IN CHINA

If you notice an error, please check the book's website listed below where there may
already be a posted correction. If there is no correction posted, please alert us by emailing
info@welcomebooks.com and we will post the correction as soon as possible.

For further information about this book please visit online:
www.welcomebooks.com/americanfamilycooks

For further information about the author please visit online:
www.notesfromjudieskitchen.com

For full USDA guidelines on canning, relevant to pages 198 through 209, see
http://nchfp.uga.edu/how/can_home.html.